KU-517-680

Service Learning
Linking Library Education and Practice

Edited by Loriene Roy, Kelly Jensen,
and Alex Hershey Meyers

AMERICAN LIBRARY ASSOCIATION
CHICAGO 2009

Loriene Roy is professor in the School of Information of the University of Texas at Austin, where she teaches graduate classes on public libraries, reference, and library instruction/information literacy. She is founder and director of If I Can Read, I Can Do Anything, a national reading club for Native children. She is Anishinabe, enrolled on the White Earth Reservation, and is a member of the Minnesota Chippewa Tribe. She was elected 2007–2008 president of the American Library Association. **Kelly Jensen** finished her master's degree in information studies in December 2008 from the University of Texas at Austin. Jensen is involved in numerous service projects in the Austin area, and her professional interests include the use of web technology in the library and in serving specialized population groups. **Alex Hershey Meyers** earned her master's of science in information studies in December 2008 from the University of Texas at Austin. Meyers's professional interests include reference, library instruction, and digital collections.

While extensive effort has gone into ensuring the reliability of information appearing in this book, the publisher makes no warranty, express or implied, on the accuracy or reliability of the information, and does not assume and hereby disclaims any liability to any person for any loss or damage caused by errors or omissions in this publication.

The paper used in this publication meets the minimum requirements of American National Standard for Information Sciences—Permanence of Paper for Printed Library Materials, ANSI Z39.48-1992. ♾

Library of Congress Cataloging-in-Publication Data
Service learning : linking library education and practice / edited by Loriene Roy, Kelly Jensen, and Alex Hershey Meyers.
    p.   cm.
Includes bibliographical references and index.
ISBN 978-0-8389-0981-2 (alk. paper)
1. Library education—United States. 2. Service learning—United States. 3. Library schools—Curricula—United States. 4. Library science—Fieldwork. I. Roy, Loriene. II. Jensen, Kelly. III. Meyers, Alex Hershey.
Z668.S47 2009
020.710973—dc22   2008045377

Copyright © 2009 by the American Library Association. All rights reserved except those which may be granted by Sections 107 and 108 of the Copyright Revision Act of 1976.

ISBN-13: 978-0-8389-0981-2

Printed in the United States of America

13   12   11   10   09   5   4   3   2   1

Contents

Preface

Supporting LIS Education Through Practice
Highlights of an ALA Presidential Year

Loriene Roy

Each year the membership of the American Library Association (ALA) elects one of its own to serve a year as president-elect. The president-elect continues his or her service as president, immediate past president, and then past president for life. Presidents do not have themes; instead, they support the key action areas of the association.

The president will spend much of her service year responding to routine presidential duties and new duties as they arise. Standing responsibilities include responding to media requests, writing a monthly column for *American Libraries,* organizing president's programs for the ALA Midwinter Meeting and Annual Conference, and chairing the meetings of the ALA Council, ALA Executive Board, ALA Executive Committee, and the Council and Board of the ALA–Allied Professional Association. New duties often emerge from federal legislation alerts and the challenges that librarians face in their work.

In addition to these expected and new assignments, ALA presidents usually organize one or more demonstration efforts related to their backgrounds, campaign platforms, or in response to requests from the membership. Presidents come to their role with years of professional service and connections to the field of librarianship. The strongest connections are forged through workplace environments.

Throughout my term as ALA president I sought to support initiatives related to three task force areas, three demonstration projects, and several new collaborations. The three task force areas were drawn from my career as a librarian educator, my prior work as a medical imager in community hospitals, and the service work my students and I conduct with schools that enroll indigenous children. These were the task forces on the Circle of Literacy, Workplace Wellness, and Supporting Library and Information Science (LIS) Education Through Practice. The demonstration projects included producing podcasts on meeting effectiveness, participating in discussions on hosting national library camps for youth, and launching a national oral history project capturing the life histories of library workers who were exiting the field due to retirement. Collaborations were initiated with the Lance Armstrong

Foundation and WGBH-Boston and its production of "We Shall Remain," the largest *American Experience* television series. Each task force, demonstration project, and collaboration resulted in some tangibles—websites, discussions, events, podcasts, and publications.

Along with the ALA's Committee on Education, the presidential task force on Supporting LIS Education Through Practice hosted several education forums. One forum, held at the ALA's 2008 Midwinter Meeting, focused on the current research of LIS doctoral students. Students shared brief summaries of their work, with practitioners providing feedback on the research. The forum held at the 2008 ALA Annual Conference featured master's students involved in service learning.

The Contents of This Book

Service Learning: Linking Library Education and Practice is another product of the task force on Supporting LIS Education Through Practice. This book serves several purposes. First, it highlights the good news of what is taking place in the curricula of LIS programs. There has been tension between practice and theory since the inception of formalized LIS education. One only has to walk the halls of an ALA conference or observe the discussion on the floor of an ALA Council meeting to hear debate and disagreement over curricular offerings and ongoing complaints about the perceived deficiencies among first-day library employees. The reality is that preparing the next generation of librarians is a shared responsibility. Students enter their graduate studies with wide-ranging undergraduate preparation and sometimes without paraprofessional library employment. They usually complete twelve graduate courses over one to two years and graduate without personal credentials: they are graduates of master's-level programs accredited by the ALA and/or the National Council for Accreditation of Teacher Education. While graduates emerge with a palette of skills, knowledge, and personal attributes, they still need support in their work environment to continue to learn and become acquainted with practices at individual libraries. Through service learning, students address community needs through the application of course content. They work in cooperation with community members and reflect on the activity, gaining a deeper understanding of course content. Service learning serves as one bridge, connecting students with their need to learn, faculty members with their need to stay refreshed and connected to today's work environments, and librarians who need to help prepare new librarians. Service learning is good news.

The content in this book explains my personal teaching philosophy in creating communities of service. My graduate students and I have engaged in service learning experiences over the past twenty years. Students in the advanced humanities and social sciences reference classes have created pathfinders—textual documents leading the user to selected resources on narrowly defined topics—for clients around the world. Students in the library instruction and information literacy classes have provided face-to-face training on the use of electronic resources for police cadets, songwriters, and library staff employed at small rural libraries in central Texas. They created websites, including a virtual library of education resources for education majors at a tribal college, a bridge to resources on WebJunction, and an instruction site on the use of statewide databases for the Texas State Library and Archives. In 1998 my students and I also organized a national reading club for Native children, working with the librarians at tribal schools. Through the If I Can Read, I Can Do Anything program, we have delivered over $100,000 in new books to tribal school libraries and have assisted librarians in planning reading-promotion events such as family reading nights and storytelling open microphone celebrations. Over time, I have observed students gain experience in project management and acquire other skills and self-analysis through the reflective process we associate with service learning.

Service-based education has been a part of the LIS curriculum since its origin. When Melvil Dewey designed the curriculum for the first School of Library Economy at Columbia in 1896, he acknowledged that "lectures and reading alone will not achieve the best results in training for librarianship without the conference, problems, study of various libraries in successful operation, and actual work in a library."[1] Over time, many librarian educators withdrew from the service model.[2] As a result, LIS programs find themselves today on the fringes of the service learning movement, although there is evidence that this is changing. Authors of recent journal articles describe student involvement in community engagement: students in the Special Library Association student chapter at the School of Information and Library Science of the University of North Carolina at Chapel Hill received a grant to build and organize a library at a homeless shelter for women and their children.[3] Highly ranked LIS programs, including those at the University of Illinois, University of Michigan, and University of Texas at Austin, provide students with opportunities to incorporate service learning in their courses of study; in some cases, community engagement is a requirement for graduation. Students involved in such experiences may acquire socialization in their field, useful professional connections, and a competitive edge in their job searches. Oberg and Samek observed that a practice experience "strengthens students' appreciation of their LIS education and of how it prepares them for professional work."[4]

Some chapters in this text describe components of service learning. Others describe the role of students, faculty, and field supervisors. A number of contributions highlight the opportunities within specific LIS programs, settings, or courses and discuss the role of service in engaging with specific communities.

Lorna Peterson offers some highlights in the history of service learning within LIS, noting specifically the impact of the Library Services and Construction Act on the construction of new library facilities that served as laboratories for student engagement.

Service learning has a number of components: it is site-situated, user-centered, and employs reflection as a tool for personal understanding and growth. Kathleen de la Peña McCook frames reflection, the hallmark of service learning, in the context of human rights. All partners in the educational experience must incorporate a reflective position—including the faculty member, field supervisor, and students in their beginning and summative thoughts and assessment of their own work. She observes the increasingly repressive milieu of higher education and calls on faculty to be more vocal supporters of free speech. She identifies several indicators that librarians are promoting an orientation toward engagement. These include the actions of librarians from five ethnic library associations affiliated with the ALA to organize the first Joint Conference of Librarians of Color, held in October 2006 in Dallas, Texas; librarian attendance at the United States Social Forum; and the writing and research of faculty, notably Toni Samek in the School of Library and Information Studies at the University of Alberta.

Ann Bishop, Bertram C. Bruce, and Sunny Jeong begin with the concepts underlying service learning and its place in participatory action research. They introduce the role of the social entrepreneur and describe the Community Informatics Initiative in the Graduate School of Library and Information Science at the University of Illinois at Urbana-Champaign.

The roles of students, faculty, and site supervisors are centered in four chapters. Although Rae-Anne Montague, Martin Wolske, and Beth Larkee argue that service learning is tied to both institutional and LIS professional goals, they are also aware of the need for flexibility, leadership, and dedication to ensure success. They describe the process of incorporating a service component involving students in an Introduction to Networked Systems class in community technology centers in East St. Louis. Larkee, a student in this class, describes the class activities and what led her to take what she learned in Illinois to a service opportunity in Africa. Sara Albert and A. Arro Smith provide advice for students on preparing for their service learning experiences. They close by contributing three scenarios that illustrate the benefits of engaging in service learning. Practica have long been incorporated into the professional preparation of school librarians. Johan Koren gives examples of how coursework in this area can build on a framework of theory, service, practical professional experience, and reflection. Gilok Choi writes about the benefits and challenges facing international students who are involved in service engagement during their U.S.-based studies.

Although engagement with underserved populations is a recurrent theme in much service learning work, two chapters highlight activities with communities of color. I provide background on issues of motivation for civic engagement. I discuss the insider/outsider dichotomy when conducting work in communities unlike one's own, introduce the concepts of protocol and etiquette, and present a draft protocol for working with tribal communities. Jamie Campbell Naidoo's chapter is placed within the demographic profile of the Latino population of South Carolina. He describes how he addresses the needs of preparing information professionals to serve this growing population in a course he has designed, Library Materials and Services for Latino Youth, and a resulting service engagement project, SPLASH!

The authors of several chapters cover the service learning options available in their programs of study and in individual courses. Sara Albert provides a summary of service learning curricular options at nine LIS programs. These range from required courses to electives, practica, fieldwork, capstones, internships, independent studies, directed readings, workshops, and research classes. In some cases, the coursework is taken for credit, while in other examples students are not evaluated or are assigned a pass/fail evaluation. A number of programs require students to produce culminating graduation products such as e-portfolios. Students in other programs summarize their service learning experiences through recorded logs or journals, written midterm and end-of-term reports, oral presentations, recordings of on-site performance, poster session presentations, and exit interviews with their faculty supervisor.

Clara M. Chu reports on the service learning aspects of the first LIS-required course on diversity, called Ethics, Diversity, and Change in the Information Professions, at UCLA's Department of Information Studies. C. Olivia Frost provides the history of the many service learning options available for students at the University of Michigan's School of Information, including a wide range of projects through the Cultural Heritage Initiative for Community Outreach (CHICO) as well as student efforts focused on building technological capacity in the United States and in Africa. Denise E. Agosto, Eileen G. Abels, Lorri Mon, and Lydia Eato Harris involve students in the Internet Public Library's Ask a Question Service. In the next chapter, by Bharat Mehra, we receive a road map or strategy for building service into a core or required graduate course. He and Robert J. Sandusky provide a supplemental chapter describing three approaches to incorporating community-based research in elective coursework. Joe Sanchez proposes placing service learning into virtual environments, such as Second Life, as a way to add another dimension to the service learning model, that of fun.

Two final chapters examine topics related to the evaluation of service learning. Gary Geisler and Elaine Yontz describe the difficulties in evaluating the impact of service learning on students. They suggest the use of blogs for monitoring individual and group reflective discussion. And they present an evaluation rubric useful in both self-evaluation by students and evaluation by professors.

Molly Krichten, Sarah Stohr, and Stefanie Warlick summarize the results of a survey they conducted of recent graduates of LIS programs to assess their involvement in service learning and their interest in the development of a national database of service opportunities. They found that while half (52 percent) of those responding to the survey were not required to complete a practicum or internship, over half did participate in one or more experiential activities during their graduate programs. Ninety-five percent of respondents agreed that a field experience should be required. Recent graduates helped conceptualize a possible national database but cautioned that such a product would require constant updating to include fieldwork opportunities and reflect curricular changes.

We are grateful to the contributors for helping us present not only parallel definitions for service learning but also for providing examples of application, in this world and in the world of the virtual.

NOTES

1. Melvil Dewey, "School of Library Economy at Columbia College," *Library Journal* 9, no. 7 (July 1894): 118.

2. Kathleen de la Peña McCook, "Reconnecting Library Education and the Mission of Community," *Library Journal* 125, no. 14 (September 1, 2000): 164–65.

3. Jennifer Burek Pierce, "Library Students Making a Difference," *American Libraries* 36, no. 7 (August 2005): 83.

4. Dianne Oberg and Toni Samek, "Humble Empowerment: The LIS Practicum," *PNLA Quarterly* 63, no. 3 (Spring 1999): 20–22.

Chapter 1

A Brief History of Service Learning in LIS

Lorna Peterson

This chapter identifies selected resources on the history of service learning and briefly highlights several noteworthy examples. The author suggests that library and information science programs that are starting to incorporate more service learning opportunities are likely to flourish under stronger support nationally and the development of evaluation tools.

History of Service Learning

A history and chronology of service learning in the United States is located at the National Service-Learning Clearinghouse.[1] The brief historical time line begins in 1903 with the Cooperative Education Movement founded at the University of Cincinnati.[2] The "Annotated History of Service Learning" provided at the clearinghouse begins with the 1862 Morrill or Land Grant Act. It is important to remember that the Land Grant Act had an impact on service learning under segregated conditions when it extended its support to founding universities for blacks in 1890.

Although American higher education has a long history with service learning, it is one where educators and policy makers have been unable to agree on whether or not it is a worthwhile academic endeavor.

Definition of Service Learning

Service learning takes theory and the academic rigor of the classroom, applies it to a community need, and works in cooperation with community agencies. Waterman defines service learning as "an experiential approach to education that involves students in a wide range of activities that are of benefit to others, and uses the experiences generated to advance the curricular goals."[3] Incorporating service into the curriculum has a long tradition in American higher education where service is one of its distinguishing hallmarks. The Wisconsin Idea that emphasizes that education should improve lives outside the university, land grant universities, and, more recently, legislation such as the National and Community Service Trust Act of 1993 all influenced our universities to not

1

behave as ivory towers but to be engaged in American democracy by taking research and knowledge into communities.[4]

Tension has existed in U.S. higher education about the role of service learning, and what we now call service learning has had its supporters and detractors over time. To some, service learning is an appropriate part of the higher education experience. To others, service learning is anti-intellectual work that detracts from knowledge for knowledge's sake. Early critics such as Robert Hutchins saw this involvement as tainting research and learning.[5] More recent scholars and pundits continue to debate service learning as either an appropriate part of the higher education teaching process or as misguided, anti-intellectual work.[6] It is not an exaggeration to state that service learning is marginalized and misunderstood in the university and sometimes dismissed as misplaced social work. But at the same time, national legislation has raised the profile of service learning, and this includes service learning in LIS education.

Service Learning Specific to LIS Education

Historically, LIS education has combined practical experiences with theoretical and formal study, classroom lectures, and readings. Established, systematized, programmatic service learning as action research can be identified from the mid-1960s through the present. An example worthy of exploration by library historians and policy analysts is the impact of the passage of the LSCA—the Library Services and Construction Act of 1964.[7] The LSCA and its resultant building of libraries in rural and urban areas combined with the 1960s social milieu's emphasis on relevancy and progressivism, and as a result LIS master's programs reached out to these communities being served by new libraries.

There are other examples of LIS service learning action from the 1960s and 1970s that would contribute to our understanding of the continuing importance of service in the field. For example:

- High John Project, University of Maryland, School of Library and Information Services, 1969–1972. An $88,000 U.S. Department of Education grant received by Mary Lee Bundy and Richard Moses sought to create a learning laboratory in the field using an urban public library branch. The name of the laboratory, High John, was drawn from the black folk hero who outwitted whites.[8]

- Alternative Week and Sight, Sound, Society course, University at Buffalo, State University of New York, School of Library and Information Studies, 1971–1972. Professors Don Roberts and John Ellison created opportunities for LIS students to engage in the public library community in ways that combined the theory of the classroom with action in the field.

- Seminar in creating a public library, Syracuse University, Roger Greer, 1970s. Students participated in survey research and needs assessment in a data-driven decision-making model in order to assist in creating public libraries.[9]

This period of service learning in LIS was not without its disappointments. The High John Project ended, much to the sorrow of its creators. John C. Colson, a University of Maryland SLIS faculty member, wrote of the experience in his article "The Agony of Outreach."[10] The University at Buffalo program ended due to faculty disagreement over its efficacy. Some faculty commented that students did not attend the sessions and instead saw opportunities to skip classes.

American Library Association Policies

Where does the ALA stand on this type of learning? The ALA's *Handbook of Organization* includes policy 60.5, "Library Education to Meet the Needs of a Diverse Society." The policy supports service learning in this way: "Collaboration between these programs [ALA-accredited master's programs] and local libraries and community-based organizations serving diverse populations is to be encouraged."[11]

Evaluating Service Learning

Our colleagues in the field of education have a better grasp on evaluation and research models for the study of service learning. It is recommended that practitioners and educators consult the Service Learning Research and Development Center at the University of California, Berkeley, where evaluation tools, release forms, and other research-based materials are deposited.[12]

Where Are We Now in Service Learning?

The publication of this book shows that service learning and outreach are concerns of both our practitioners and educators. From the ALA Office for Literacy and Outreach Services' publication, *From Outreach to Equity: Innovative Models of Library Policy and Practice*, to the chapters in this volume, we see that LIS education has merged theory and practice, advancing our discipline and profession in a service learning way.[13] As our research on service learning and our recognition of it in the history and tradition of our profession advances, there are sure to be many successes to continue to celebrate in the LIS profession.

NOTES

1. Learn and Serve, America's National Service-Learning Clearinghouse, "What Is Service-Learning? History," www.servicelearning.org/what_is_service-learning/history/index.php.

2. Peter Titlebaum and others, "Brief Historical Time Line" and "Annotated History of Service-Learning: 1862–2002," www.servicelearning.org/filemanager/download/142/SL%20Comp%20Timeline%203-15-04_rev.pdf.

3. Alan S. Waterman, ed., *Service-Learning: Applications from the Research* (Mahwah, NJ: Lawrence Erlbaum Associates, 1997), xi.

4. For more information about the Wisconsin Idea, see www.wisconsinidea.wisc.edu; and Learn and Serve, America's National Service-Learning Clearinghouse, www.servicelearning.org.

5. Robert Maynard Hutchins, *The Higher Learning in America* (New Haven, CT: Yale University Press, 1936); Donald R. Godwin, "Will They Heed the Call to Service? A Different Look at the Service-Learning Question," *Educational Horizons* 81 (Fall 2002): 16–17; and Joseph P. Shapiro, "Do-Gooding: When It Gets Complicated," *U.S. News and World Report* 114, no. 3 (January 25, 1993): 66.

6. Dan W. Butin, "Focusing Our Aim: Strengthening Faculty Commitment to Community Engagement," *Change* 39, no. 6 (November/December 2007): 34–37.

7. James W. Fry, "LSA and LSCA, 1956–1973: A Legislative History," www.ideals.uiuc.edu/bitstream/2142/6824/1/librarytrendsv24i1c_opt.pdf.

8. Anand Prahlad, ed., *The Greenwood Encyclopedia of African American Folklore* (Westport, CT: Greenwood, 2006).

9. Relevant readings include the following: Mary Lee Bundy and Richard Moses, *A New Approach to Educational Preparation for Public Library Service: An Experimental Program in Library Education to Work with a Specialized Clientele; Interim Report, Project no. 7-1139,* U.S. Department of Health, Education, and Welfare, Office of Education, Bureau of Research (March 1969); Mary Lee Bundy and Paul Wasserman, "A Departure in Library Education," *Journal of Education for Librarianship* 8, no. 2 (Fall 1967): 124–32; Mary Lee Bundy, *The Devil Has a Ph.D.* (College Park, MD: Urban Information Interpreters, [1974?]); Kathleen Weibel, "The Evolution of Library Outreach 1960–75 and Its Effect on Reader Services: Some Considerations," Occasional Papers, no. 156 (Champaign: University of Illinois, Graduate School of Library and Information Science, 1982); "Don Roberts" file, University at Buffalo, University Archives; Roger Greer, *Anatomy of a Small Public Library*, ERIC document ED115286 (Syracuse, NY: School of Information Studies, 1974).

10. John C. Colson, "The Agony of Outreach: Some Reconsiderations Based on the High John Project," *Library Journal* 98, no. 17 (October 1, 1973): 2817–20.

11. American Library Association, *ALA Handbook of Organization 2007–2008* (Chicago: American Library Association, 2007), 54.

12. University of California at Berkeley, Service Learning Research and Development Center, http://gse.berkeley.edu/research/slc/.

13. Robin Osborne, ed., *From Outreach to Equity: Innovative Models of Library Policy and Practice* (Chicago: American Library Association, Office for Literacy and Outreach Services, 2004).

Chapter 2

Human Rights as a Framework for Reflection in Service Learning
"Para que Otro Mundo es Posible"

Kathleen de la Peña McCook

> *Whereas recognition of the inherent dignity and of the equal and inalienable rights of all members of the human family is the foundation of freedom, justice and peace in the world . . .*
>
> —Universal Declaration of Human Rights

"Reflection" is the most important aspect of the student service learning experience in library settings. Through reflection, service learning abides in a larger context as part of librarianship's broader connection to the public sphere. Reflection allows students to realize "para que otro mundo es posible" (another world is possible) and that through their commitment to the work of librarianship they will have a role in bringing another world into existence. As a framework for reflection, a model of library service based on human rights provides the pathway to change the world by helping people develop their full capabilities. What could be a better guide for reflection than the Universal Declaration of Human Rights? Article 26 echoes the raison d'être for the foundation of the public library in the United States and is a wise rationale for the work of librarians: "Education shall be directed to the full development of the human personality and to the strengthening of respect for human rights and fundamental freedoms."[1]

The reflective aspect of service learning placements in librarianship requires three components:

1. A faculty supervisor/mentor who is a reflective being
2. A placement that is an opportunity for reflection through the work being done and interaction with other workers
3. The student's preparation to encounter the service opportunity in a reflective manner and the student's post-experience assessment of the placement

Faculty as Reflective Beings

Before faculty can incorporate reflection as an aspect of service learning for students, professors must be reflective beings themselves. In *Oneself as Another* the hermeneutic philosopher Paul Ricoeur has explained that "the autonomy of the self . . . [appears] to be tightly bound up with the solicitude for one's neighbor and with justice for each individual."[2] Or, as Saul Alinsky stated in *Reveille for Radicals*, "In order to work with people we must first approach them on a basis of common understanding."[3] Faculty who supervise service learning placements will provide successful oversight characterized by a reflective and integrated worldview that values social justice and human rights. These first years of the twenty-first century have been a difficult period for members of the academy who hold concerns for human rights, intellectual freedom, and social justice. Political considerations and conservative forces have discouraged speaking out and dissent. After the tragic events of September 11, 2001, Lynne Cheney, the vice president's wife, and the organization she founded, the American Council of Trustees and Alumni, took swift action to condemn academics who questioned the government.[4] There was little resistance, as noted by Emilios Christodoulidis in his presentation of Ronald Dworkin for the 2007 Holberg International Memorial Prize, in which he observed that Dworkin

> has raised his voice eloquently and clearly against the American Academy's dubious complicity with its Administration's harsh and illiberal anti-terrorist "Patriot Act" and executive measures and practices. In articles and speeches, and most recently in *Is Democracy Possible Here?* he warns that such measures constitute a dangerous compromise of the values that underpin US legality.[5]

Library and information science educators must stand up on the side of human rights as political participants if service learning is to have validity in the context of intellectual freedom and civil liberties.

Today, the very essence of librarianship is threatened as the academy becomes more and more compromised. As teachers in universities, LIS faculty must understand and debate efforts by authoritarian forces to neutralize free speech within academe. There has been a post-9-11 McCarthyism to remove from the university "all vestiges of dissent and to reconstruct it as an increasingly privatized sphere for reproducing the interests of corporations and the national security state."[6] At my own place of work—the University of South Florida, School of Library and Information Science—our free and open student discussion list was shut down by administrators with no explanation in March 2003 during a rigorous debate about the then upcoming U.S. invasion of Iraq. The United Faculty of Florida's union contract guarantees academic freedom, but the issue had to be formally grieved for intellectual freedom to be restored to the LIS commons.

Recognition of the increasingly repressive twenty-first-century academic environment is the most important aspect of faculty reflection that can be brought to our work with service learning. Library educators in the United

States have one central discussion list called JESSE.[7] JESSE is moderated and censored. As I was preparing this essay, I was writing about the Vancouver Public Library strike at the blog *Union Librarian*. Over 800 library workers were on strike for pay equity in Vancouver. A simple post to the discussion list about the strike was ruled unacceptable by the moderator of JESSE. Discussion off the JESSE list found a number of professors who felt that the censored nature of the JESSE list went against the values that ought to inform the teaching of librarianship. A habit of reflection requires that educators have the opportunity to carry on discussions in an uncensored fashion about issues that affect the profession. To my way of thinking, any professor unwilling to stand for intellectual freedom should not be permitted to supervise service learning. How can students learn to stand up for their public when professors will not stand up for them? These examples of suppression in the public sphere, first at my own place of work where students were not allowed to discuss the war in Iraq, and second, the JESSE list wherein educators were not allowed to discuss a strike of library workers in Vancouver, indicate that threats to intellectual freedom are close at hand in the academy. LIS educators must reflect on the nature of discourse in our own discipline if we are to be effective advocates for service learning. Additionally, LIS educators should consider themselves as part of the university community at large and take into consideration the American Association of University Professors' 2007 report "Freedom in the Classroom," which concludes:

> We ought to learn from history that the vitality of institutions of higher learning has been damaged far more by efforts to correct abuses of freedom than by those alleged abuses. We ought to learn from history that education cannot possibly thrive in an atmosphere of state-encouraged suspicion and surveillance.[8]

Those supervising service learning must, above all, be reflective individuals. The definition of *reflection* in the glossary of the National Service-Learning Clearinghouse is at once applicable to those who supervise service learning experiences as well as those who enroll:

> Reflection describes the process of deriving meaning and knowledge from experience and occurs before, during and after a service-learning project. Effective reflection engages both teachers and students in a thoughtful and thought-provoking process that consciously connects learning with experience. It is the use of critical thinking skills to prepare for and learn from service experiences.[9]

Library workers reflected on their role in the twenty-first century at two historic events in 2006 and 2007: the Joint Conference of Librarians of Color (JCLC) and the United States Social Forum (USSF). Faculty who participated in these transformative events are prepared to work with students at a level of engagement that transcends traditional classroom experiences. Both events connected librarians to overarching societal issues and concerns such as war, economic injustice, environmental challenges, poverty, and racism.

The JCLC brought together library workers of all ethnicities to Dallas in October 2006. The event was a collaboration of the American Indian Library Association, the Asian/Pacific American Librarians Association, the Black Caucus of the American Library Association, the Chinese-American Librarians Association, and REFORMA (National Association to Promote Library and Information Services to Latinos and the Spanish Speaking). The participants shared experiences, best practices, research, and theory. They made new connections and built and strengthened coalitions.[10]

The USSF gathering, entitled "Another World Is Possible" ("Para que Otro Mundo es Posible"), took place in Atlanta, Georgia, in June–July 2007 under the auspices of the World Social Forum.[11] Library workers attending the USSF were participants and speakers on urgent issues of our time including poverty, environmental destruction, immigration, and human rights. They documented the USSF by collecting materials distributed by organizational and individual participants for the Labadie Collection, University of Michigan; surveying attendees about the services they need from libraries; volunteering skills as librarians at the Ida B. Wells Media Justice Center; and reflecting and learning about the social forum.[12]

Faculty involvement in conferences and forums like the JCLC or the USSF provide the opportunity to interact with thoughtful library workers who embrace values of equality and justice. Faculty who supervise service learning should be judicious and discerning. We hope they will answer affirmatively to the question asked by Lesley Rex of the Wingspread Access, Equity and Social Justice Committee: "*Are more faculty becoming engaged and increasing their efforts toward solving broad social problems?*"[13]

Placement as an Opportunity for Reflection

Service learning is collaboration between the community and the classroom that gives equal priority to student learning and community service. Unlike fieldwork, which focuses on skills, the student role is determined by the community's needs.[14] Students must be prepared to work with the community at hand. This can be achieved by an understanding of the principles of community organizing and involvement and by application of this understanding to the library context.[15] Librarians' involvement in community building has been long-standing but is not well articulated at the local level.

Reflection can happen in most contexts if the placement is done in a manner that fosters understanding of overarching socioeconomic and political considerations. Careful deliberation on the concept of library as "place," literacy as an adult education endeavor, homelessness as a product of economic injustice, incarceration as a result of a society that does not nurture people of all classes and colors, and lack of effort to develop cultural competence to serve people of different backgrounds are examples.

Twenty-first-century leaders in the ALA have endeavored to establish the librarian's role in building and transforming communities. During the presidency of Leslie Burger in 2006–2007, the ALA adopted an agenda for the twenty-first century: "Libraries Transform Communities; Communities Transform Libraries."[16] The 2007–2008 presidency of Loriene Roy included initiatives to operationalize the ideas of community transformation through the project Supporting LIS Education Through Practice. It should be noted for the purpose of expanding discussion that the use of *community* as synonymous with *place* can be problematic.[17] Libraries as culturally constructed places may succeed in supporting community or not.

To understand how communities can be transformed, we can look at *The Library as Place*, edited by Buschman and Leckie, and find different analyses of place that provide means of reflection—the Habermasian influence that allows us to make "normative and democratic claims about libraries as places."[18] The establishment of locations for service learning that provide an opportunity for reflection and community transformation has been discussed by Roy.[19] She provides a variety of examples with a diversity focus, including tribal community colleges and schools and cultural heritage institutions such as the National Museum of the American Indian.

Cuban and Hayes have reported on students placed in a community literacy agency and have described the need for literacy education curricula in LIS education.[20] The connection of the service learning experience to curriculum reform demonstrates a mechanism by which the classroom and the external site reinforce values. Reflective service learning placements require a setting where coworkers are intellectually knowledgeable about the philosophical and theoretical basis of service provided. Literacy for adults must be viewed as far more than a library challenge, and this can only be done through active engagement in the work of the American Association for Adult and Continuing Education (AAACE) and involvement with colleagues imbued with the AAACE vision "that lifelong learning contributes to human fulfillment and positive social change."[21]

At the University at Buffalo, Peterson has written how students engaged in a service learning seminar worked to turn a homeless shelter library into a satellite of the Buffalo and Erie County Public Library.[22] Peterson's use of the evaluation process as a mechanism for reflection provides a different way to carry out the reflective component of service learning. She has shown how engaged students can become change agents through the act of learning in places where they revitalize the idea of community. Through thoughtful placement, students can move the value of librarianship from the library to the homeless shelter or even to places where people are confined.

Ours is a prison nation with over 2,000,000 people incarcerated. Any of the hundreds of local, county, state, or federal jails and prisons are sites for service learning through libraries and the provision of literacy education. Clark and MacCreaigh demonstrate how a public library model can be used in correction facilities.[23] Mark discusses an internship at the Oshkosh Correctional Institution that she undertook after involvement with the student group at the University of Wisconsin that works with inmates at local jails.[24] Although she does not use the term *service learning,* her reflection on the experience through the article demonstrates an effort to move beyond tasks and skills. Mark describes books she read in preparation for the experience and comes to conclusions that transcend the work.

In *Still Struggling for Equality,* a thorough assessment of U.S. librarian initiatives to serve immigrants and minorities from 1876 to the present, Jones provides hundreds of examples of librarians who have looked to serve marginalized people and developed programs to provide basic information and literacy.[25] The use of Jones's book in concert with state and national policies and programs that were the framework for the JCLC helps students and their faculty supervisors to recognize the variety of opportunities for service learning that will contribute to a world without old structures and tired ideas.

So there are many opportunities for students to be placed in service learning situations where the work being done transcends a particular library or system and allows the student to address issues that are societal in scope, though perhaps individual in the here and now. By working with the homeless and reflecting on the factors that create homelessness, by working with people in jail and reflecting on the reasons they have been incarcerated, and by assuming a reflective mode of thinking about these issues, we will find that the opportunity to create change is amplified.

Student Preparation and Post-experience Assessment

Students prepare for service learning beyond the acquisition of the skills and theories of librarianship. They must learn about the placement and the conditions that surround the point of service. Reading is a reflective act. Writing is a reflective act. Those who choose to study to become librarians come in the main from that group of people for whom reading and writing are important. In spite of society's aggrandizement of technology and its concomitant undervaluing of traditional skills, these skills—reading, writing—form the essence of reflection. Before reflection on the service learning experience can take place, the larger philosophical questions must be addressed; there is a need to step back and have students read broadly to examine the context of service. This includes primary human rights sources such as the Vedas, the Bible, the Qur'an, the Analects of Confucius, and the Magna Carta on up to more recent documents like the 1992 UN Declaration on the Rights of Persons Belonging to National, or Ethnic, Religious and Linguistic Minorities or the 2006 Optional Protocol to the Convention against Torture and Other Cruel, Inhuman or Degrading Treatment or Punishment.[26]

See, for example, how one local effort connects to the universal. Irene Sweeney's family literacy project in rural Florida was conducted as a service learning placement, and her reflective article, "Learning by Doing: Engaged Service and the MLS," connected her to larger concerns through the ALA's Office for Literacy and Outreach Services.[27] This in turn required an understanding of the process that leads to established national policy: "The American Library Association reaffirms and supports the principle that lifelong literacy is a basic right for all individuals in our society and is essential to the welfare of the nation."[28] This in turn connects with Article 26 of the Universal Declaration of Human Rights: "Everyone has a right to an education."[29]

Students may also find that librarians who have struggled for social justice and human rights provide inspiration and encouragement. In the summer 2007 *Information for Social Change Journal*, Lowe and Samek highlight people who provide information and help to others who are caught up within conflict situations. They cover aspects of the work of peace libraries and of resources to aid those who are working within or upon various conflict situations throughout the world. Participation in service learning in college was shown to predict attitudes toward both personal and community responsibility for improving the welfare of others.[30]

These are deplorable times. Immigrants and refugees suffer, the poor have little access to health care or food security, and torture is condoned by the George W. Bush administration. The reflective student can review and examine these examples of human suffering and seek a close-up way in connection with an individual to enable change to make another world possible. In Moorehead's book *Human Cargo,* the chapter "Fence" is about migrants in San Diego and Tijuana. She ties together attacks launched against immigrant populations by George W. Bush that make use of the USA PATRIOT Act and shift policy from openness and tolerance to secrecy and obfuscation.[31] What can librarians do to assist people caught in the net of immigration? We can use the tools and policies of our profession to develop programs and services. The New Immigrants Center at the Austin Public Library provides tools to navigate different social norms, civic institutions, transportation systems, and different languages.[32]

Service learning can take place in all types of libraries. In "Learning by Serving," Sitter develops the argument that teacher librarians in school library media centers "have a unique opportunity to work with students, teachers, and community partners . . . to help our young citizens develop sensitivity to human need and a responsibility to serve."[33]

And sometimes service learning can be work within a system of services that librarians provide rather than direct service. Farmer has written of the new war on the poor in terms of structural social violence and lack of access to health care. His examination of social inequity relies upon the Universal Declaration of Human Rights as he pleads that everyone has the right "to share in scientific advancement and its benefits."[34] Farmer's emphasis on human rights finds voice in the work of the National Library of Medicine's Environmental Health Information Outreach Program, which includes representation from historically black colleges and universities, institutions serving Hispanic students, and tribal colleges. In addition to working with these institutions to promote the use of and access to electronic health information and related technology, this program brings attention to scientific research related to health issues that disproportionately affect minorities.[35] In the quietest ways, librarians can develop resources that will make a difference in people's lives.

Conclusion: The Meaning of Twenty-First-Century Librarianship— Service Learning for Human Rights

Students placed in service learning programs must reflect on the meaning of twenty-first-century librarianship. Samassékou asserts that "the development of the information society must be based on the framework of human rights, and should respect and uphold the United Nations Charter and the Universal Declaration of Human Rights."[36] Although a specific service learning experience might require certain technical skills (assisting with an information commons, digitizing archival materials), it is the core values of the profession that will illuminate the experience. And it is on these core values that reflection rests. As Katharine Phenix and I have argued, these core values should be based on a human rights model.[37]

For librarianship, Samek has gone the farthest of all scholar-philosophers in defining the manifestations of social action. The faculty member and student who plan a reflective service learning experience should review Samek's monograph *Librarianship and Human Rights* for models.[38] These provide tangible opportunities for service learning if the faculty supervisor is attuned to human rights and social justice considerations in librarianship. Samek gives many examples of specific forms of social action that would be the opportunity for reflective service learning. These include AIDS information and awareness, protests of library closures, serving the homeless, and digitization and development of memory programs.

Reflection requires quiet thought. And we librarians will find the topics and concerns not just in technical or professional literature but in the work of those men and women, those writers, who likely first brought us to this calling. We close with the words of José Saramago, Nobel laureate in literature whose speech was given on the fiftieth anniversary of the Universal Declaration of Human Rights:

> Let us think that no human rights will exist without symmetry of the duties that correspond to them. It is not to be expected that governments in the next 50 years will do it. Let us common citizens therefore speak up. With the same vehemence as when we demanded our rights, let us demand responsibility over our duties. Perhaps the world could turn a little better.[39]

NOTES

1. Universal Declaration of Human Rights, United Nations, Article 26, www .un.org/Overview/rights.html.

2. Paul Ricoeur, *Oneself as Another* (Chicago: University of Chicago Press, 1992), 18.

3. Saul Alinsky, *Reveille for Radicals* (New York: Vintage Books, 1946), 93.

4. Bill Berkowitz, "Mrs. Cheney's Campus Crusade," *Working for Change* (2001), www.workingforchange.com/printitem.cfm?itemid=12355.

5. Emilios Christodoulidis, "Presentation of Ronald Dworkin for the Holberg International Memorial Prize" (November 2007), www.holberg.uib.no/HP_ prisen/en_hp_2007_christodoulidis_dworkin.html; and Ronald Dworkin, *Is Democracy Possible Here?* (Princeton, NJ: Princeton University Press, 2008).

6. Henry A. Giroux, *The University in Chains: Confronting the Military-Industrial-Academic Complex* (Boulder, CO: Paradigm, 2007).

7. JESSE, http://web.utk.edu/~gwhitney/jesse.html.

8. American Association of University Professors, "Freedom in the Classroom" (September 11, 2007), www.aaup.org/AAUP/comm/rep/A/class.htm.

9. Learn and Serve, America's National Service-Learning Clearinghouse, "National Service-Learning Clearinghouse Glossary," www.servicelearning.org/welcome_ to_service-learning/glossary/index.php?search_term=glossary.

10. P. A. Goodes, "Historic Gathering Draws Hundreds to Dallas," *American Libraries* 37 (November 2006): 20–21.

11. José Corrêa Leite, *The World Social Forum: Strategies of Resistance*, trans. Traci Romine (Chicago: Haymarket Books, 2005).

12. Elaine Harger and Kathleen de la Peña McCook, "PLG—Presenté! Report from the United States Social Forum," *Progressive Librarian* (Winter 2007/08).

13. Leslie A. Rex, "Higher Education Has Done Well, We Can Do More: A Report from the Wingspread Access, Equity and Social Justice Committee," in *Taking Responsibility: A Call for Higher Education's Engagement in a Society of Complex Global Challenges*, ed. Penny A. Pasque, Lori A. Hendricks, and Nicholas A. Bowman (Ann Arbor, MI: National Forum on Higher Education for the Public Good, 2006), www.thenationalforum.org.

14. Catherine M. Lemieux and Priscilla D. Allen, "Service Learning in Social Work Education: The State of Knowledge, Pedagogical Practicalities, and Practice Conundrums," *Journal of Social Work Education* 43, no. 2 (Spring/Summer 2007): 309–25.

15. Frank Adams with Myles Horton, *Unearthing Seeds of Fire: The Idea of Highlander* (Winston-Salem, NC: John F. Blair, 1975), 203–16; Kathleen de la Peña McCook, *A Place at the Table: Participating in Community Building* (Chicago: American Library Association, 2000), 37–43.

16. Leslie Burger, "So Long, Farewell . . . ," *American Libraries* 38 (June/July 2007).

17. Gloria Leckie and John E. Buschman, "Space, Place, and Libraries," in *The Library as Place: History, Community, and Culture* (Westport, CT: Libraries Unlimited, 2007), 13.

18. Ibid., 15.

19. Loriene Roy, "Diversity in the Classroom: Incorporating Service-Learning Experiences in the Library and Information Science Curriculum," *Journal of Library Administration* 33, no. 3–4 (2001): 213–28.

20. Sondra Cuban and Elisabeth Hayes, "Perspectives of Five Library and Information Studies Students Involved in Service Learning at a Community-Based Literacy Program," *Journal of Education for Library and Information Science* 42, no. 2 (Spring 2001): 86–95.

21. American Association for Adult and Continuing Education, www.aaace.org/index.html.

22. Lorna Peterson, "Using a Homeless Shelter as a Library Education Learning Laboratory: Incorporating Service-Learning in a Graduate-Level Information Sources and Services in the Social Sciences Course," *Reference and User Services Quarterly* 42, no. 4 (Summer 2003): 307–10.

23. Sheila Clark and Erica MacCreaigh, *Library Services to the Incarcerated: Applying the Public Library Model in Correctional Facility Libraries* (Westport, CT: Libraries Unlimited, 2006).

24. Amy E. Mark, "Libraries without Walls: An Internship at Oshkosh Correctional Institution Library," *Behavioral and Social Science Librarian* 23, no. 2 (2005): 97–111.

25. Plummer Alston Jones Jr., *Still Struggling for Equality: American Public Library Services with Minorities* (Westport, CT: Libraries Unlimited, 2004).

26. The Vedas, the Bible, the Qur'an, Analects of Confucius, Magna Carta (1215), Milton's Areopagetica (1643), Locke's Letter Concerning Tolerance and Second Treatise of Civil Government (1690), Jean-Jacques Rousseau's Social Contract (1761), Thomas Paine's The Rights of Man (1791–92), the Declaration of Independence (1776), Abigail Adams's Remember the Ladies (1776), U.S. Bill of Rights (1791), French Declaration of the Rights of Man and of the Citizen (1789), Mary Wollstonecraft's A Vindication of the Rights of Women (1792), Kant's Perpetual Peace (1797), Britain outlaws slave trade (1807), Robert Owen's New View of Society (1817), Susan B. Anthony and Elizabeth Cady Stanton's Declaration of Sentiments at Seneca Falls (1848), Henry David Thoreau's Civil Disobedience (1849), John Stuart Mill's On Liberty (1859), Amsterdam Resolution against Colonialism (1904), Mahatma Gandhi's Passive Resistance (1909), Declaration of the Rights of Toiling and Exploited Peoples (1918), International Labor Organization Charter (1919), International Convention for the Suppression of the Traffic in Women and Children (1921), Declaration of the Rights of Children (1924), League of Nations Convention to Suppress the Slave Trade and Slavery (1926), Franklin Delano Roosevelt's Four Freedoms (1941), Universal Declaration of Human Rights (1948), Declaration of Rights of the Child (1959), Declaration of Rights of Disabled Persons (1975), Indigenous and Tribal Peoples Convention (1989), UN Declaration on the Rights of Persons Belonging to National, or Ethnic, Religious and Linguistic Minorities (1992), Optional Protocol to the Convention against Torture and Other Cruel, Inhuman or Degrading Treatment or Punishment (2006).

27. Irene Sweeney, "Learning by Doing: Engaged Service and the MLS," *American Libraries* 33, no. 2 (February 2002): 44–46.

28. American Library Association, "ALA Policy Manual," 50.6.2.

29. Universal Declaration of Human Rights, United Nations, Article 26.

30. Martyn Lowe and Toni Samek, "Editorial: Libraries and Information Workers in Conflict Situations," *Information for Social Change Journal* 25 (Summer 2007), http://libr.org/isc/index.html.

31. Caroline Moorehead, *Human Cargo: A Journey among Refugees* (New York: Henry Holt, 2005), 92.

32. Diana Miranda-Murillo, "New Immigrants Center at the Austin Public Library," *Texas Library Journal* 82, no. 4 (Winter 2006): 144–47.

33. Clara L. Sitter, "Learning by Serving," *Knowledge Quest* 34, no. 5 (May/June 2006): 23–26.

34. Universal Declaration of Human Rights, United Nations, Article 27.

35. Gale A. Dutcher, Melvin Spann, and Cynthia Gaines, "Addressing Health Disparities and Environmental Justice: The National Library of Medicine's Environmental Health Information Outreach Program," *Journal of the Medical Library Association* 95, no. 3 (July 2007): 330–36.

36. Adama Samassékou, foreword to *Human Rights in the Global Information Society*, by Rikke Frank Jorgensen (Cambridge, MA: MIT Press, 2006).

37. Katharine J. Phenix and Kathleen de la Peña McCook, "Human Rights and Librarians," *Reference and User Services Quarterly* 45, no. 1 (Fall 2005): 23–26.

38. Toni Samek, *Librarianship and Human Rights: A Twenty-first Century Guide* (Oxford, UK: Chandos, 2007), 47–180.

39. José Saramago, "Speech at the Nobel Banquet" (December 10, 1998), http://nobelprize.org/nobel_prizes/literature/laureates/1998/saramago-speech.html.

Chapter 3

Beyond Service Learning
Toward Community Schools and Reflective Community Learners

Ann Bishop, Bertram C. Bruce, and Sunny Jeong

Service learning addresses the progressive education goal of citizenship for a democratic society.[1] However, the current practices of service learning are limited in their capacity to fully engage students in community life. Too much emphasis is placed on student outcomes and not enough on the process of learning for all of the parties involved, including faculty, students, and community members. What actually happens to all as a result of community-based service learning? How does service learning affect community life and the student's understanding of the links between life, education, and community? How does it promote critical awareness of how to learn through service?

One reason for this limitation is that typical realizations emphasize one direction of learning—community and teachers working together for the benefit of student learning—as well as one direction of service—from the school or university to the community. Communities are typically viewed as passive partners of classes, teachers, or schools to receive services. Further, students have limited freedom to work beyond the structured teaching strategies imposed on both them and the community. Students' freedom to explore, discuss, and interact with the community are thus limited and less valued.

In this chapter we examine the educational principles and practices of service learning and suggest extending it via the conceptual framework of community inquiry. This framework allows us to focus on the community as a locus and source of learning. The first section below discusses current practices of service learning and some of its shortcomings. We view service learning as a pedagogy based in constructivism and experiential education. It holds within it the potential to promote deep learning for students, faculty, and community members, but it often falls short of this potential. The second section discusses participatory action research and social entrepreneurship, processes more familiar outside of library and information science and outside of the United States, which suggest the extension of service learning beyond narrowly defined, course-based models. The third section discusses community inquiry as just such an extension, one in which the school is seen as the social center of the community. The fourth section presents examples from the Community Informatics Initiative (CII).

Service Learning Today

Typically with service learning, students address community needs through the application of course content.[2] This intersects with teaching and research but also involves the investigation of real-life situations based on students' own experiences. This approach is a large and growing feature of K–12 and higher education in the United States.[3] In the 2006 survey of its member institutions, Campus Compact found that nearly 7,000,000 students at 1,000 college campuses participated in service learning activities for an average of 179 hours per year.[4] The participation rate had grown from 28 percent to 32 percent over the preceding five years. Other data show that the number of students participating for K–12 may be double the number in higher education, and there are service learning programs through community organizations outside of schools as well. The approach has clearly become a mainstream activity involving significant numbers of young people, educators, and organizations. Yontz and McCook have recognized the natural fit of LIS education into the growing national service learning movement.[5]

Although definitions and practices vary widely, most people see service learning as involving both service to the community and learning. It is not service learning without both of these ingredients. This is clear in the definition from the National Service-Learning Clearinghouse:

> Service-learning combines service objectives with learning objectives with the intent that the activity changes both the recipient and the provider of the service. This is accomplished by combining service tasks with structured opportunities that link the task to self-reflection, self-discovery, and the acquisition and comprehension of values, skills, and knowledge content.[6]

Eyler and Giles use a similar definition, but emphasize the experiential, community-based, and reflective aspects:

> Service-learning is a form of experiential education where learning occurs through a cycle of action and reflection as students work with others through a process of applying what they are learning to community problems and, at the same time, reflecting upon their experience as they seek to achieve real objectives for the community and deeper understanding and skills for themselves.[7]

Note that both of these definitions assume that the community has problems and will receive the benefit of service from the university. The community's provision of service to the university is undervalued, and the community's capacity for action and reflection is made invisible.

Experience is the foundation for learning, and community is the locus where learning takes place. Yet these definitions assert that among the parties involved in service learning, it is only the students who serve and learn. Reflection in service learning takes place as forms of thinking, discussing, and/ or writing about their service and learning experience among participants. As such, the main elements of service learning across various settings include (1) experiential learning, (2) contribution to community, and (3) reflection.

At its best, service learning promotes a variety of worthwhile goals, including social, emotional, and cognitive development in the context of more meaningful learning, teamwork, community involvement, citizenship, the ability to address complex problems in complex settings, and critical thinking. These attributes derive from the value inherent in promoting activities in which young people develop their capacity to serve others and to be more reflective learners.

Service learning advocates insist that service learning is neither an episodic volunteer program nor an add-on to existing curricula. Moreover, it should not be conceived as a requirement to fulfill a set number of community service hours or, worse yet, as a form of punishment. It should always benefit both the students involved and the community. Yet the fact that these cautions are deemed necessary is an indication that service learning as usually practiced may have shortcomings.

What could those shortcomings be? What could be wrong with an approach that meets both community and student needs, is rapidly growing in popularity, and fosters the attainment of laudable goals such as meaningful learning, teamwork, community involvement, citizenship, and critical thinking?

As the reader might infer from our critique of the definitions above, our position is not, as some critics have argued, that service learning is an unwelcome intrusion into the traditional classroom, but rather the opposite: service learning is a special, and somewhat limited, case of what education in general could be. A more comprehensive view of learning in relation to life leads us to conceive formal learning in a radically different way and leads to a reevaluation of service learning.

Let us first ask what might be missing from the usual definitions and practices of service learning. At the risk of overgeneralizing, we see the following as typical practices:

- Service and learning objectives are predefined, rather than growing organically out of lived experience in the community.

- Once class is done, engagement often halts and is neither encouraged nor supported, especially by the institution.

- The student is both the server and learner. Reciprocity means merely that the community receives a service, not that it learns or serves, thus limiting its active participation in the process.

- Similarly, it is the student who reflects, often in isolation from the community. A typical realization of the reflection is to write something about the experience, not to work that through with the community.

- The conception and implementation of service learning presuppose a separation of school and community. Indeed, it is the very separation that gives rise to the need for service learning, but that separation is never challenged, only mitigated.

- Although service learning invites critical reflection on social conditions, its maintenance of hierarchy—community as needy, school/university as the locus of knowledge and action—limits that reflection.

- Likewise, the course-based engagement of service learning constrains the kinds of community problems that can be addressed and the nature of the actions to address them. Service is connected to formalized learning, but neither to research nor to our everyday lives outside the classroom.

In conventional service learning, inquiry is defined as primarily individual; it is a component of the individual student's grade for the course. Sometimes there is a limited collective inquiry in the sense that students discuss their experiences in order to make sense of them. But reflection and learning are defined as activities of the student, not those of the community member. There is no third space for the construction of new knowledge through the collaboration of school and community members. This is not to say that it never occurs, just that the service learning model does not promote this as a vital component. Moreover, the student is positioned hierarchically above the community. The student is there to serve, not to be served, even though many students have health, emotional, financial, and other needs. Thus, despite the rhetoric about reciprocity, both the service and the learning are one-way.

Thoughtful practitioners of service learning have long recognized and struggled to work around these and similar problems. But the alternative is sometimes seen as no service learning. In that case, the limited engagement described above reduces to none at all. Are there other options? By proposing an extended service learning model, we emphasize experience as the context of education, community as the locus of education, learning as the goal for all parties involved, and service learning as one of the strategies to do that. Put differently, service learning should be conceived as part of the bigger picture of where and how education takes place in daily lives. Seeking the bigger picture, we turn to the theory of community inquiry, as developed by John Dewey and Jane Addams, and explore its contribution to the development of a new model of service learning.

Extending Service Learning

Although service learning often falls short of its ideals, there are aspects within current practices that point to useful ways to extend the model. Two aspects of service learning, participatory action research and social entrepreneurship, suggest extension of the concept beyond narrowly defined, course-based models.

Participatory Action Research

It is not surprising that the growth of service learning in higher education has been most prominent at the colleges and universities that emphasize teaching. Research institutions have been far less likely to support faculty involvement in service learning.[8] Given that faculty involvement is a strong predictor for institutionalizing service learning on college campuses, participatory action research provides a means by which faculty can use service learning experiences to engage in research related to important community issues.[9] Because participatory action research pursues the study of issues determined by the community and includes community members as researchers, it offers service learning a context for incorporating research with community empowerment.

A number of scholars, including Reardon, emphasize the value of participatory action research for faculty engaging in service learning. Because of its direct relevance to the needs and capacity of the community, participatory action research "increases the potential for implementation of recommendations emerging from these research efforts."[10] Combining participatory action research and service learning not only makes contributions to a body of disciplinary knowledge, but also culminates in a set of recommendations that are then implemented through action in the community. See, for example, the work of the Youth Action Research Institute in Hartford, Connecticut.[11]

Involving local leaders with research enhances the problem-solving capacity of community-based organizations. By sharing control over the research process with local residents, action researchers begin to overcome the distance established by previous campus-controlled community work. Finally, by promoting social learning processes that generate considerable payoffs for both campus and community participants, community-based participatory action research projects are likely to be more sustainable.

According to Greene, if students are introduced to reflective learning with and in the community, they will become aware of a dearth of understanding in their own domain, of the blocks to knowing and questioning.[12] Reflection in service learning can propel students toward a questioning of the social order and a desire to effect change. At the same time, by establishing relationships with people from all walks of life, learners can expand their worldview through a lens that is not limited to the colors and textures that inform their own narrow worlds. They can see people who are members of other groups as colleagues in a diverse world, breaking down the divisive relationship that often exists between the university and the community.

In sum, participatory action research encompasses rigorous inquiry and community action. This benefits all parties involved, and learning is multi-faceted: students, faculty, and community members are all learners who gain new understanding and skills, document and publish the results of their inquiry, and address local problems. Our critique of service learning lies not so much in educational practices but rather in how it is used to reinforce structures of power, and the rigidity of applying service learning for real-life engagement and collective learning in the community. Central to the reconstruction of service learning is the need to develop a discourse that accentuates the organic connections between learning and everyday life while reconstructing democratic public culture for action. Participatory action research helps in creating a new discourse for service learning; it emphasizes investigation leading to results that are felt in everyday life, with local community members in charge of the process. Social entrepreneurship also contributes to an expanded discourse. It moves service learning away from episodic activity in which the most substantive change often stays with the student to a sustained community venture that embodies important social change.

Social Entrepreneurship

According to Greg Dees, faculty director of Duke University's Center for the Advancement of Social Entrepreneurship, social entrepreneurs are change agents who recognize and pursue new opportunities to create and sustain social value while exhibiting a heightened accountability to the constituencies served. They engage in a process of continuous innovation and learning, acting boldly without being limited by the resources at hand.[13] Ashoka, an international organization devoted to social entrepreneurship, defines social entrepreneurs as individuals with innovative solutions to society's most pressing social problems. The Skoll Foundation, created by the founder of eBay, describes social entrepreneurs as people from all walks of life "whose approaches and solutions to social problems are helping to better the lives and circumstances of countless underserved or disadvantaged individuals" in communities around the world.[14]

Social entrepreneurship is gaining ground across universities in the United States as a learning process that unites students, faculty, and community members in systematic investigation and action that lead to positive social change. Unlike the traditional service learning model, it has a built-in bias toward disrupting the status quo, mandating that participants move beyond mere involvement in existing practices and programs that aim for single or small improvements. In social entrepreneurship we learn how to innovate, we learn a step-by-step methodology for institutional change that can transform lives.

To take an example from LIS, a service learning student might volunteer to assist with a public library's bookmobile that visits a poor neighborhood, gaining new skills and, hopefully, a deeper understanding of community outreach and her own goals and abilities. A social entrepreneurship student, on the other hand, might design and implement a new service in which libraries distribute weeded books to teachers, who give them to children at risk of losing school-year literacy gains over summer vacation. Thus, the most significant contribution of social entrepreneurship is to develop information professionals who are both innovative and pragmatic and who know how to design and resource creative community services that pinpoint critical needs and build the capacity of the community as a whole.

The Books to Prisoners program in Urbana, Illinois, is one example of social entrepreneurship combined with librarianship. An LIS graduate student in a service learning course, who himself had spent time in jail, began by exploring prisoners' access to books in our local community and across the state. He then researched possible program designs to improve the situation. He found partners in the community, as well as additional student volunteers. Currently, the Books to Prisoners program is a thriving community nonprofit venture, operated out of a local independent media center.[15] Volunteers collect and organize hundreds of donated books each week and mail them in response to requests sent by prisoners. Volunteers have also started two new local jail libraries, as well as held a national conference on prison library services.

Beyond Service Learning: Community Inquiry

Community inquiry recognizes the collective knowledge building implied by participatory action research and the broad-based social change implied by social entrepreneurship. It offers both a theoretical framework that extends service learning, as well as a practical model, the school as social center. We argue that if we reconceive service learning through these lenses, we can develop a much richer model for service learning that addresses many of the same goals while avoiding the shortcomings. Benson, Harkavy, and Puckett argue that this reconception is essential for universities today.[16]

Community inquiry is inquiry conducted of, for, and by communities as living social organisms. A community-based orientation emphasizes support for collaborative activity and for creating knowledge connected to people's values, history, and lived experiences. Inquiry points to support for open-ended, democratic, participatory engagement. Community inquiry is then a learning process that brings theory and action together in an experimental and critical manner.

Community inquiry frames service learning differently. Students and the school are seen as vital parts of the community. The community as a whole engages in inquiry to address its problems, which include those of the students.

Knowledge is found in the community as well as the school and is constructed anew by all participants. In this way, the borders between school and community are not accepted as fixed, only to be crossed under special circumstances, such as the service learning course. Instead, there is an explicit project to challenge those borders, to seek common purpose and common understanding.

A practical model for this is the school as social center proposed by John Dewey.[17] Inspired by the work of Jane Addams at Hull House, especially the Labor Museum, Dewey articulated a vision of education in relation to the social organism. He recognized the need for lifelong learning, and as a result the need to change the image of what constitutes citizenship as well as the image of the purpose of the school. Dewey saw the school as an integral part of the community, a place where the community becomes the curriculum.

These ideas have been developed in various forms. One notable avenue has been the community schools movement.[18] In her work in the rural South, Clapp drew from and extended Dewey's ideas. She argued for the "socially functioning school" and "socially functioning subject matter":

> A socially functioning school is a school which assumes as an intrinsic part of its undertaking cooperative working with the people of the community and all its educational agencies on community problems and needs with reference to their effect on the lives of the children and of the adults. Its special concern is with the process of growth and development.[19]

The key difference between conventional service learning and the community inquiry model we propose here is that in the former, the community and the school are seen, and are to some extent reified, as two distinct entities, with a strong, fixed boundary between them. This is illustrated in figure 3-1. In the community inquiry approach to service learning, the community becomes the unit. "Service" becomes action by community members, some of whom are students. "Learning" or "reflection" become activities engaged in by all community members, both individually and collectively, and across what had previously been the firm boundaries of town and gown, as shown in figure 3-2. Community inquiry is a more holistic approach where education is seen as an organism, not just an aggregation of unrelated segments of knowledge. Community inquiry emphasizes community capacity building, mutual learning, and reflection. As Dewey describes in his vision of the school as social center, classes are regarded as modes of bringing people together, of eliding the barriers that keep people from communion and work with common purpose.

The community inquiry model emphasizes the need to recognize education as part of life. Teaching, research, change, and learning are experienced by all community learners. Community learners document and reflect on their own experiences, becoming community teachers and researchers.

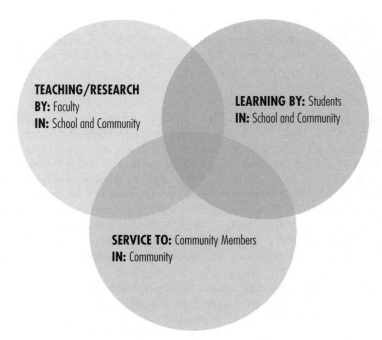

TEACHING/RESEARCH
BY: Faculty
IN: School and Community

LEARNING BY: Students
IN: School and Community

SERVICE TO: Community Members
IN: Community

Figure 3-1. Traditional approach to service learning

Community Informatics Initiative

At the University of Illinois, the Community Informatics Initiative provides a cross-campus home for research, learning, and action; a regional university/community base; a locus for building a critical mass of community informatics work in the United States; and an international hub for this growing field.[20] It creates new knowledge about community inquiry, including its processes, practices, and technologies; and it helps both individuals and organizations engage in more productive community inquiry through the development of, and action in, living laboratories that bring together people from all walks of life.

The CII is grounded in the philosophy of community inquiry. Its aim is to develop within community members and project participants a "critical, socially engaged intelligence, which enables individuals to understand and participate effectively in the affairs of their community in a collaborative effort to achieve a common good."[21] Thus, a cornerstone of community inquiry as practiced by the CII is that this inquiry aims to respond to human needs by democratic and equitable processes. Inherent in community informatics is the need to understand how knowledge is shaped and shared in communities, to investigate the underlying information phenomena and processes we find when we take an entire geographic community as our unit of analysis. Community informatics inquiry is conducted internationally in settings that range from

Figure 3-2. Community inquiry approach to service learning

inner-city neighborhoods to rural villages, exploring how individuals and institutions—for example, schools, libraries, grassroots groups, health agencies, and so on—come together to develop capacity and work on common problems. It addresses questions of community development, learning, empowerment, and sustainability in the context of efforts to promote a positive role for information and technology in society.

Some aspects of our CII present a challenge to the standard conception of service to communities in traditional service learning. Our work has increasingly focused on a model in which community members and those in universities or schools collaborate in setting goals, in the investigation of communities and community building, and in building new structures and processes together. Critical space around ideas such as service, expertise, or even community needs reframes the territory so that both service and learning are bidirectional.

Community inquiry adopts a pragmatic technology approach to community-based information communication technology (ICT) creation and use.[22] Pragmatic technology encompasses the common language notion of how to design tools to meet real human needs and to accommodate users in their lived situations. It also sees ICTs as developed within a community of inquiry and embodying both means of action and forms of understanding; ICTs are an end result of, as well as a means to accomplish, community work. Day and Schuler, in declaring the "subordination of ICTs to building healthy, empowered, active communities" and noting simply that "researchers are part of the world in which they live," resonate clearly with the ideas and practice of pragmatic technology.[23]

Several CII projects, described briefly below, illustrate the community inquiry approach to service learning. None of our projects are perfect. Each could be improved in areas such as its apparatus for reflection, its degree of participation by community members, its provision of adequate support to students, or the degree to which its results represent positive community change. We believe, however, that they represent useful illustrations that go beyond service learning and that each has benefited both the academy and the community. Our CII projects demonstrate how pragmatic, community-based informatics initiatives respond to human needs democratically and support participation and learning across institutional and social boundaries.

Paseo Boricua Community Library Project

The Paseo Boricua Community Library Project is a collaborative research, action, and learning initiative that partners with the Puerto Rican Cultural Center (PRCC) in Chicago's Paseo Boricua community, an inner-city neighborhood struggling to overcome poverty, racism, gang violence, AIDS/HIV, and a host of other problems that typically plague urban life. For thirty years, the PRCC has attracted international attention for its innovative, multi-generational approach to community-based learning and development. The Community Library Project in Paseo Boricua represents a long-term university investment in this community, begun about a decade ago, and ramped up this past year with about $1,000,000 in external and campus support to include a master's community informatics specialization taught on-site at the PRCC. The project's original goals were articulated jointly by LIS faculty and PRCC staff. These include generating new knowledge to address the "digital divide," figuring out how to create robust community inquiry that spans distance and cultural boundaries, and bringing more inner-city youth into LIS. Faculty and students in LIS and other disciplines benefit from the intellect, creativity, and vitality of Paseo Boricua, working together with hundreds of youth and community leaders to create learning activities, information resources, and digital media. Activities are documented so that each semester students and community members can pick up where others have left off. Assessment occurs through needs and evaluation studies, student reflections, course evaluations, symposium attendees' feedback forms, and frequent community meetings and workshops. Community informatics courses in Paseo Boricua include an introduction to participatory action research, social entrepreneurship, and community inquiry.

José López, director of the PRCC, summarized the project's community impact when he noted that "a new sort of university is being created in the community." On-site practical engagement courses, assistantships for underserved students including those from Paseo Boricua, the annual Community as Intellectual Space symposium, a Paseo Boricua high school student-curated exhibit at the famed Newberry Library, and participatory action research studies such as a recent project conducted with Paseo Boricua's youth-led Participatory Democracy program all demonstrate the cocreation of knowledge with local residents. Outcomes from the Paseo Boricua Community Library Project are also seen in new resources that support community projects. These include creating a library; providing instructors for the community journalism course that is part of the after-school Barrio Arts, Communication, and Culture Academy; producing a community health program manual; developing an urban agriculture high school curriculum and a computer curriculum for PRCC preschoolers; and conducting background research for local history plays produced by neighborhood youth. In 2008 the PRCC high school recognized the work of the Paseo Boricua Library Project by presenting it with the school's "Outstanding Community Partner" award.

Booker T. Washington After-School Library Program

The Booker T. Washington After-School Library Program (BTW) was founded by one of the authors three years ago in response to the urgent request of new Spanish-speaking immigrants in our local Champaign area who were worried about their children's future. In fact, it was developed from a discussion with parents that followed a service learning course in which several students participated in practical engagement projects in the immigrant community. Set in a local elementary school, the program's aims are to provide homework and literacy help, along with digital enrichment activities stressing family strengths; create stronger bridges between low-income families and schools; and develop an innovative service learning and research program for university students.

The BTW program has grown organically, with a small amount of funding provided by the campus and community partners for two graduate assistants and some supplies. It is primarily supported by the in-kind contributions of the program's partners, including the Don Moyer Boys and Girls Club and, in addition to LIS, the university's education, Spanish, and African American studies departments. Currently, the program offers free after-school activities for about 35 at-risk children each year. It operates three days per week, with about 90 university student volunteers each semester, providing a total of about 5,000 tutoring hours per year. BTW staff members have steadily increased their commitment to the program, as they see more evidence that the university intends to stick with the school in a long-term relationship.

BTW teachers report the following program outcomes: students are finishing more homework, students have improved reading and math skills and overall performance, and students gain social skills. Tutors report that the program is rewarding and fun and helps them contribute to the community while gaining knowledge and skills for their future. The BTW program was presented with the "Most Valuable Program" award by the Latino Partnership of Champaign County in 2007. Recent developments include the creation of new courses focused on the BTW program in several departments of the university. We are also pursuing a participatory action research project in which university and immigrant community members learn about each other's strengths through collaboratively creating digital media, such as YouTube videos of animated children's stories and family narratives captured on CDs, while exploring the theme of community funds of knowledge.

Prairienet

Prairienet, the community network of east-central Illinois, was founded as an LIS and community partnership in 1993. Currently operated as part of the CII, it is one of the longest-running and most successful community networks in the United States. In the 1990s Prairienet received federal funding to provide 700 low-income families in Champaign with computers, Internet accounts, and training. It has also helped hundreds of nonprofits create organizational websites and electronic discussion lists, as well as learn how to integrate technology with their mission. Prairienet also develops web-based applications for health and human services, such as a volunteer-matching database, a drop-in child-care system, and online health directories. Prairienet's real impact comes in integrating technology with community goals. Its work proceeds according to the needs and opportunities expressed by community orga-nizations and residents. For example, in response to a request from a county agency, it provided computers and training to a group of low-income women in a program that helped them set up a home day-care business.

For over ten years, Prairienet has collaborated with the East St. Louis Action Research Project. Using a service learning course taught by the CII's research scientist Martin Wolske and recycled computers, it has set up over seventy community technology centers in churches, day-care centers, homeless shelters, and other small nonprofits, mostly in East St. Louis, one of the poorest areas in Illinois. Recently, Wolske has reengineered his service learning course to partner with a local youth organization in creating a Teen Tech program. LIS students and East St. Louis teens learn how to create small community technology centers together. The teens also learn how to set up their own small businesses to provide ongoing community tech support. This past summer, several of those youth accompanied CII staff to help set up community tech centers in Africa, in partnership with local leaders in São Tomé e Príncipe.

Korean Cultural Center

Building a Korean Cultural Center (KCC) is an ongoing effort to form a new and innovative social enterprise to address current social problems related to the lack of needed resources and information for marginalized groups in the local community. This project was incubated and developed in spring 2006. For their project in an LIS service learning course, two Korean graduate students worked with community members to ascertain the local Korean community's needs and develop possible solutions.

The project team discovered that Korean families or families with adopted Korean children suffered from a lack of access to appropriate information and resources across a wide spectrum of service centers and institutions. They raised funds to rent space in the YMCA and launched the KCC, which functions as the social center where programs provide a vehicle to bring people together, to learn from each other, and to develop a critical social consciousness and the unity of a global family. The students created a library of children's books with hundreds of donated books from Korean publishers. With the help of local Korean churches and various Korean clubs on campus, they compiled a resource directory similar to the Yellow Pages and published 500 copies of it for Korean families. The KCC reached out to the Korean community by offering numerous cultural programs, including a summer camp attended by youth from both Champaign-Urbana and Korea. The Mobile Korean Cultural Center is a newly launched cultural program of the KCC where volunteers run a cultural program for Boy Scouts, Girl Scouts, public libraries, and schools. It is highly interactive in nature and fully engages children and youth with Korean cultural activities and games.

The LIS students were also driven by what they learned about the lives of their Korean peers at the university. They discovered that the Korean student suicide rate is the highest on campus and that Korean youth were sent alone at younger and younger ages to obtain an education in the United States. To study and create a positive response to the isolation felt by many Korean youth, one of the LIS students who cofounded the KCC taught an academic course in which youth learned how to create digital videos that documented their feelings and experiences.

The KCC is an example of dedicated students engaging in their own community; reflecting, collaborating, and making an effort to build a community guided by concepts of social justice and social action. The insights learned and shared among participants are various. Those who volunteered at the KCC came to be more aware of their social situation and said they became more engaged in campus and community affairs. Where previously they regarded others' social issues with indifference, now they are socially more aware and see the links between individual problems and structural community issues. Another value expressed by students involved in building the KCC is the discovery of creative, interesting, empowering, experimental, free, and enjoyable ways to learn and address social issues in, with, and by the community. The KCC is an example of promoting different modes of education through the intangible tools of art, science, and other modes of social intercourse, research, recreation, and daily lives. The participants in this project become community learners, researchers, and teachers by participating and working together.

Conclusion

The discourse of service learning sometimes limits its pedagogical implications by not considering bidirectional exchange in which both students and community members are learners. But learning cannot be an activity independent of learners' lives, experiences, and community. We suggest instead that students and community members work together to develop critical consciousness, democratic citizenship, and social justice.

We propose community inquiry as a framework for service learning that
- develops learning for all the participants; students, faculty, and community members all operate as community learners
- values ordinary experiences, which creates a public sphere for all learners
- centers on the community, with the historical, social, and cultural conditions that expand lived experiences for all; the school becomes a social center for the community and the community becomes the curriculum, the site where dialogue and interaction occur

Community inquiry provides the opportunity for educators and community workers to rethink and transform how people across campus and community institutions define themselves as an active community of learners capable of exhibiting critical sensibilities, civic courage, and forms of solidarity rooted in a strong commitment to democracy.

ACKNOWLEDGMENTS

The work of the CII is performed by countless dedicated faculty, students, and community members. While we cannot name them all individually, we nonetheless appreciate and acknowledge their contributions to the activities that inform this chapter. We are also grateful for the funding provided by our chancellor and a number of campus units, by the U.S. Institute of Museum and Library Services, and by our community partners. And we would like to thank the LIS schools in Michigan, Wisconsin, and Illinois for their intellectual and financial support.

NOTES

1. Edward B. Fiske, *Learning in Deed: The Power of Service-Learning for American Schools* (Battle Creek, MI: W. K. Kellogg Foundation, 2001), www.learningindeed.org.

2. Ernest L. Boyer, "The Scholarship of Engagement," *Journal of Public Service and Outreach* 1, no. 1 (Spring 1996): 11–20; Amy Driscoll and Ernest A. Lynton, *Making Outreach Visible: A Guide to Documenting Professional Service and Outreach* (Washington, DC: American Association for Higher Education, 1999); A. James Jr., "The Evolving Concept of Public Service and Implications for Rewarding Faculty," *Continuing Higher Education Review* 58, no. 3 (1994): 122–40.

3. Andrew Furco, "Advancing Service-Learning at Research Universities," in *Developing and Implementing Service-Learning Programs,* ed. Mark Canada and Bruce W. Speck (San Francisco: Jossey-Bass, 2001), 67–78.

4. Campus Compact, "Campus Compact Annual Membership Survey, 2006" (2007); www.compact.org/about/statistics/2006/.

5. Elaine Yontz and Kathleen de la Peña McCook, "Service-Learning in LIS Education," *Journal of Library and Information Science Education* 44, no. 1 (Winter 2003): 58–68.

6. Learn and Serve, America's National Service-Learning Clearinghouse, "Service-Learning Is . . . ," www.servicelearning.org/what_is_service-learning/service-learning_is/index.php.

7. Janet S. Eyler and Dwight E. Giles, *Where's the Learning in Service-Learning?* (San Francisco: Jossey-Bass, 1999).

8. Michael Rothman, Elisha Anderson, and Julia Schaffer, eds., *Service Matters: Engaging Higher Education in the Renewal of America's Communities and American Democracy* (Providence, RI: Campus Compact, 1998); Furco, "Advancing Service-Learning at Research Universities," 67–78.

9. Rebecca Bell and others, *Institutionalizing Service-Learning in Higher Education: Findings from a Study of the Western Region Campus Compact Consortium* (Bellingham, WA: Western Region Campus Compact Consortium, 2000).

10. Kenneth M. Reardon, "Participatory Action Research as Service Learning," *New Directions for Teaching and Learning* 73 (1998): 57–64.

11. Institute for Community Research, "Youth Action Research Institute," www.incommunityresearch.org/research/yari.htm.

12. Maxine Greene, "Teaching as Possibility: A Light in Dark Times," *Journal of Pedagogy, Pluralism and Practice* 1, no. 1 (Spring 1997), article 2, www.lesley.edu/journals/jppp/1/jp3ii1.html.

13. J. G. Dees, "The Meaning of 'Social Entrepreneurship'" (2001), http://fuqua.duke.edu/centers/case/documents/dees_sedef.pdf.

14. Skoll Foundation, www.skollfoundation.org/aboutskoll/.

15. UC Books to Prisoners, www.books2prisoners.org.

16. Lee Benson, Ira Harkavy, and John Puckett, *Dewey's Dream: Universities and Democracies in an Age of Education Reform* (Philadelphia: Temple University Press, 2007).

17. John Dewey, "The School as Social Center," *Elementary School Teacher* 3, no. 2 (October 1902): 73–86; J. Dewey, *The School and Society: Being Three Lectures by John Dewey Supplemented by a Statement of the University Elementary School* (Chicago: University of Chicago Press, 1907).

18. Elsie Ripley Clapp, *Community Schools in Action* (New York: Viking, 1939); Joy G. Dryfoos, Jane Quinn, and Carol Barkin, eds., *Community Schools in Action: Lessons from a Decade of Practice* (New York: Oxford University Press, 2005).

19. Clapp, *Community Schools in Action*.

20. http://ilabs.inquiry.uiuc.edu/ilab/cii/.

21. John Dewey Project on Progressive Education, "A Brief Overview of Progressive Education" (2002), www.uvm.edu/~dewey/articles/proged.html.

22. Larry Hickman, *John Dewey's Pragmatic Technology* (Bloomington: Indiana University Press, 1990).

23. Day and Schuler in declaring the "subordination of ICTs to building healthy, empowered, active communities" (15) and noting simply that "researchers are part of the world in which they live" (219) resonate clearly with the ideas and practice of pragmatic technology. Peter Day and Douglas Schuler, eds., *Community Practice in the Network Society: Local Action/Global Interaction* (London: Routledge, 2004).

Chapter 4

Service Learning from Three Perspectives
Administrative, Faculty, and Student

Rae-Anne Montague, Martin Wolske, and Beth Larkee

This chapter explores service learning from three perspectives within library and information science education—administrative, faculty, and student. It is based on experiences promoting and engaging in service learning opportunities through the Graduate School of Library and Information Science (GSLIS) at the University of Illinois at Urbana-Champaign.

In the first section, issues of service learning are considered in the context of the administration of LIS education—in particular, why and how this is a core component of professional growth. Special note is made of the role of service learning in online coursework and the administrative offering of such learning opportunities as practical engagement. In the second section, an experienced faculty member discusses his approach to developing a service learning course. In the final section, a GSLIS alumna shares details of her engagement as a student with two major service learning initiatives, including the implementation of a project in São Tomé e Príncipe, West Africa.

Service Learning: An Administrative Perspective

As the University of Illinois chancellor describes in his welcome, service is embedded in our learning culture. "We who work and study here strive to keep faith with our predecessors by constantly reaching for higher horizons of excellence, achievement, and service."[1] This sentiment reflects the widely recognized tripartite mission of higher education—teaching, research, and service. Recently, this mission has been reconceptualized as a dedication to learning, discovery, and engagement, illustrating the university's commitment to action in learner-centered terms.[2]

Within this action-focused higher education context, some schools of LIS, including GSLIS, seek to foster engagement by building on a dually reinforced commitment. As Estabrook describes, as part of a land grant institution, "outreach and extension have, from their early days, been essential to the mission [of the school]."[3] Additionally, within the field of LIS, we aim to promote access to information based on a user perspective and often seek to build collaborations to serve the underserved.

From a pedagogical perspective, service learning may be understood as "a teaching and learning strategy that integrates meaningful community service with instruction and reflection to enrich the learning experience, teach civic responsibility, and strengthen communities."[4] Yontz and McCook describe how schools of LIS often engage in service learning unsystematically or, at least, without much attention. Is this because service learning is so embedded in our culture? Or perhaps it is difficult to observe and measure? In reviewing several definitions, these authors note the significant potential of service learning based on fostering both reciprocity and reflection.[5] Reciprocity ensures that all involved are giving and gaining. Reflection facilitates deeper and more critical understanding.

Service learning may be incorporated into a variety of practice-based activities. The essence of this sort of engagement is integrating learning with community goals and objectives, enabling opportunities to consider and act on real-world issues. Ball and Schilling identify several competencies that may emerge and develop during service learning, including synthesizing information, problem solving, participating in teams, communicating effectively, decision making, critical thinking, and negotiating.[6] These sorts of competencies often form the basis of LIS program goals and learning objectives. Thus, there seems to be a direct and deep connection between our raison d'être and service learning engagement.

Additionally, service learning is considered a form of experiential learning, which is seen as a critical component of professional education by the ALA.[7] In seeking to hire LIS graduates, employers, too, place significant emphasis on service-based competencies. For example, Bajjaly reports that in a survey of eighty-seven LIS recruiters, 67 percent of respondents deemed service orientation "critical" to the overall assessment of candidates, while 26 percent indicated it was "very important."[8]

From an administrative perspective, planning to incorporate service learning in a school's strategic plan is a logical step. That said, it is not always possible to know in advance how to predict service learning project life cycles, or even what projects to pursue or which communities to partner with. This lack of predictability may be a cause for concern in terms of curricular planning and/or resource allocation. Engaging in service learning will likely also require a higher-than-average degree of flexibility in sharing goals and methods and an ongoing commitment to revisit objectives and actions. Faculty leadership is essential to support this sort of complex, long-term objective. However, because of the dedication required to foster external collaboration and the relatively long period needed to observe and measure impact, involvement must be considered carefully in light of institutional promotion and tenure requirements. This may be achieved through mentoring of junior faculty and/or drawing on supplemental faculty, staff, and student support. Broad involvement may be particularly beneficial for large-scale projects. As Yontz and McCook describe, "service learning projects can be a vehicle for reducing the isolation of individual professors and for facilitating meaningful collaboration across disciplinary lines, thus helping create more diverse and nurturing communities within a campus."[9]

Robert Sigmon describes a variety of types of service learning, from service learning, in which the goals of service and learning are completely separate, to SERVICE LEARNING, in which the goals of service and learning are balanced and integrated.[10] Balancing the need to establish community partnerships and identify authentic community needs that are in line with university interests and structures is a challenge in reaching a fully integrated state of SERVICE LEARNING. Given that it can take years to develop trusting relationships between university and community members, in a very real sense early engagement in service learning can only provide an introductory understanding to working within a community.

Although involvement in advanced SERVICE LEARNING projects may be highly desirable, waiting until ideal conditions exist to embark on them may not. Starting small offers some advantages. For example, it may help to develop initial experience and trust. A flexible approach to engaging in service learning can facilitate the development of additional opportunities as conditions emerge. At GSLIS, faculty and students are involved in a wide range of initiatives. Several large-scale GSLIS service learning initiatives are presented in the following sections, as well as in chapter 3 in this volume. First, highlights from a few smaller approaches are shared.

Service Learning and the Administration of Online Student Education

Although much service learning is based on participation emphasizing a physical location, not all students, faculty, or community members are able to come together regularly. For example, more than 50 percent of GSLIS master's students pursue courses online. Most students seeking their degrees online through Illinois do so because they are place-bound. GSLIS faculty and staff strive to incorporate robust and authentic learning opportunities into online courses. Such is the case with LIS 504 Reference and Information Services, where students contribute to the Internet Public Library by responding to reference questions.[11] This is perhaps an extreme example of distributed community interaction based on information needs. Service learning activities may be developed in other ways with online classes, too, for example, by promoting engagement with students' local communities. As Kazmer notes, "course knowledge shared in the social world is enhanced by all students' community embeddedness and by the fact that each student is embedded in a different local community."[12]

An Administrator's View of Practical Engagement

At GSLIS, as in many other LIS programs, students may incorporate supervised practical experience into their learning programs through a practicum course, alternative spring break placement, or internship. Sometimes this may also be an opportunity to participate in a service learning initiative through involvement with local organizations such as Books to Prisoners.[13] This may extend to service learning opportunities in remote communities via partnerships such as the collaboration between the GSLIS Community Informatics Initiative and the Puerto Rican Cultural Center.[14] Ongoing opportunities for involvement are also fostered through participation in student organizations such as the Progressive Librarians Guild.[15]

McCook describes a number of options and approaches for fostering positive community growth based on service learning. This may begin by partnering with existing organizations such as those named above or others like Libraries for the Future or the Urban Libraries Council.[16] As McCook notes, LIS faculty and students have much potential to contribute to community building in developing understanding of opportunities, sincerity of commitment, relationships based on trust, experience with collaboration, and flexible and adaptable strategies.[17]

In the following section, our understanding of service learning is enhanced through consideration of faculty experience based on multiyear engagement in developing a service learning course to meet a large-scale community technology goal.

Service Learning: A Faculty Perspective

For twenty years, residents of East St. Louis, Illinois, have participated in the East St. Louis Action Research Project (ESLARP) with the University of Illinois to address the needs of their economically disadvantaged community.[18] In 1999 these residents suggested that a high priority for the partnership was to bridge the prevalent digital divide. Community partners requested support through ESLARP in reaching their goal of establishing a community technology center (CTC) within a five-minute walking distance of anywhere in East St. Louis, a community of 30,000. Help from the Prairienet Community Network, an outreach unit of GSLIS, was enlisted based on a track record of addressing the digital divide in east-central Illinois.[19] Martin Wolske, a technical advisor for Prairienet, was approached with a challenge to make it happen. His response, "me and what army?" turned into the redesign of the GSLIS master's-level course LIS 451 Introduction to Networked Systems and an eight-year journey with 389 students across fifteen semesters that has brought CTCs to fifty-seven different organizations throughout East St. Louis and adjacent communities. The journey itself illustrates a range of benefits that have been realized through the use of service learning as a pedagogical tool beyond the original driving force of meeting a community need.

Focus and Incentive

Prior to the inclusion of the service learning component, LIS 451 was primarily a lecture-oriented course that included a handful of brief labs providing hands-on opportunities with the actual technology. From 1996 through 1999, three different GSLIS faculty members taught the course. It underwent a number of changes in an attempt to more effectively teach core concepts by adding hands-on exercises. For the fall 2000 semester, a service learning final project was added and the course was redesigned with a focus on the question: "What do students need to know to refurbish used computers and build networked community technology centers?" Lab exercises were taken directly from instructions used by Prairienet staff and volunteers to refurbish donated computers for work within east-central Illinois. This new focus provided students with a more meaningful way to approach the material, helping them to grasp the important technology skills involved. However, as a graduate-level course, students needed to go beyond learning basic technology skills and grapple with broader issues. Lab exercises themselves do not use checklists to teach skills but instead are set up in a way to foster student discovery of how technology works and how to troubleshoot when it does not work. Additionally, reflective exercises at the end of each lab help students consolidate learning; lectures and readings are used to place activities within a broader conceptual context.

Equally important, partnering with residents in economically disadvantaged communities as part of their coursework provides students an added incentive to immerse themselves in the material. Many students who take LIS 451 do not enter GSLIS with particular experience or interest in information systems. At the same time, they realize that even in more traditional library roles, they will be expected to have a basic understanding of hardware, operating systems, and networking. Course evaluations completed by the students each semester indicate they feel they invest more time in this course than in other LIS courses, in part because they are "afraid to let their community partners down."

Real-World Experience

Prior to the implementation of service learning, students' final projects in the course had them working in groups to design a computer lab for a fictional library in a fictional town. Their final presentations were to a fictional board comprising the instructor and their classmates. With the addition of the service learning component, students began learning additional important lessons with the real-world application of their newly developed skills. As part of their final presentations, students are asked to describe the lessons learned. These regularly include phrases like "We were surprised at the challenges in coordinating with our community partners," "We found that the work took far longer than we expected, even though we were told at the outset to multiply our estimates by three to four times," and "What works in the lab does not always work in the field." Further, while individual lab exercises break skills and concepts into digestible chunks, the final project provides an opportunity to integrate the learning into a whole practice and, as one student described it, "cement the process in my head." More broadly, the service learning project provided lessons in how to "achieve a balance between seeking friendship, imparting our classroom knowledge, and taking into account [the community partner's] expertise of her own library."

One objective of the course is to provide "insights into the strengths and weaknesses of computers and networks as tools used to meet the needs of 'the community' in which they find themselves."[20] Effective needs assessment can be a significant challenge, particularly when the community members, as one student described it, "do not share my background and reference points." As a classmate explained, "We came into the experience with our own thoughts on what the project would be, but when we stopped and started to listen, we started to pick up on what it was the community needed and what it was the lab needed." Students learn that what they think makes a good computer, a good operating system, and a good network might be quite different than that of their site coordinators. Clear descriptions of expectations on both parts and effective negotiation of what will be accomplished with the limited resources available are difficult and important lessons learned as part of the service learning experience.

People-Oriented Technology

In his address "Beyond Vietnam," Martin Luther King Jr. stated:

> We must rapidly begin the shift from a thing-oriented society to a person-oriented society. When machines and computers, profit motives and property rights, are considered more important than people, the giant triplets of racism, extreme materialism, and militarism are incapable of being conquered.[21]

Ongoing course revisions to LIS 451 increasingly emphasize that the effective implementation of technology, more than anything else, is a social issue rather than a technical one. In her recent ethnographic study of this course, Junghyun An reflected on the significant challenges of helping students move beyond an emphasis on skills development to a broader conceptual understanding of the potential positive and negative connotations of technology implementation for individuals and communities.[22] This sentiment is echoed in information schools' focus on connecting information, technology, and people, which Larsen characterizes as "a commitment to learning, centered on understanding the role of information in all human endeavors."[23]

As part of the reflective process following lab exercises, recent revisions to the course added additional guiding questions that further emphasized a people-oriented implementation of technology. In some cases, the questions were as simple as "was this a good computer?" after the completion of an early exercise in which computers were disassembled and reassembled by students. The discussion led to a consideration that "good" depends on what is needed by a community. After an exercise that compared the Windows and Linux operating systems, the students were asked to consider the similarities and differences of "corporate-based choice vs. community-based choice in the development of operating systems."

Most recently, LIS 451 was offered in the summer session, when the amount of time spent in East St. Louis could be increased from the usual four days to nine days. This additional time gave students greater freedom to work with community partners to define project goals. More time was also available to meet with many different community leaders, both formally and informally. Initial feedback from students indicates that investing more time on-site facilitated a deeper understanding of technology and community than previously achieved. For instance, one student commented, "After only a few days, I realized that technology is just like many other aspects of librarianship in that you must consider the particular community. It won't do to think of community and technology as separate. There is no such thing as a 'right' operating system, network setup, etc. There are only operating systems and such that are right for your community." Another student added, "We all need to understand the importance of community in implementing technology and we all need the experience of putting our learning into context by working with a community that can benefit from this learning."

Advancing toward service learning has been an iterative process focused on integrating pedagogical and community interests. Ideas and actions have been rewritten to more tightly integrate service learning into the entire fabric of the course. The first trip to East St. Louis is taken earlier in the semester. Lab exercises are now more directly related to the needs of community goals, with lab work and fieldwork becoming a more integrated whole. It has meant that more planning for lab exercises must take place during the semester. As a result, students and community partners take more control in defining what will be done within those exercises as they define projects. It has required additional support from the teaching assistant and student volunteers to be on-site to provide immediate facilitation of learning within the field. It has meant less lecture material emphasizing conceptual learning. And yet, the result appears to be a greater level of learning both basic skills and higher concepts that begs further study.

Faculty Perspective Summary

Service learning was first implemented as a means of serving the East St. Louis community in their stated goal of bridging the digital divide. It also provided a way to organize course content that proved meaningful to students by offering them incentives to invest more deeply in the learning process. Real-world engagement through service learning has given students a means for internalizing concepts. Such lessons have required course modifications to ensure that students developed essential skills to effectively carry out the assigned work. This was supported by the university organizations ESLARP and Prairienet, whose staff identified and coordinated projects.

The full objective of the course is to integrate skills development with a deep appreciation of the need for community-oriented implementations of technology. This is possible when the university and community are brought fully into the process of project development as equal partners, and when all are integrated into the learning process.

As challenges emerge and energies are invested to investigate and develop a curriculum that tightly integrates service and learning, the payoff is an educational environment that, in the words of one student, allows everyone to "bring their whole selves to the course." Wolske also reflects on his experience as the instructor of record for LIS 451:

> In my faculty role, I have experienced this, too. I find I have grown significantly as I look for ever richer ways to see communities through the kaleidoscope of community members' and students' eyes. Community members not only receive much-needed help, they also act as both learners and leaders in the course as the classroom becomes an open people-oriented forum.

One student's final reflection describes her amazement at her ability to apply newfound skills within the service project. She offers this additional perspective of the process:

> It made me see how we've become so used to remaining in our comfort zones—learning about the world at arm's length, yet not venturing out from our insular ivory towers and actually engaging with it. I've learned that there is gratification in giving and a genuine motivation to learn when real-world situations and communities are involved, and not simple academic assignments that will be quickly forgotten once the semester has ended. I've come to realize that the past is still so with us, that the legacy of slavery and racism lingers on, and that unless we make genuine steps towards recognizing and resolving these issues, things will not change.

Service Learning: A Student Experiences International Engagement

After considering these insights based on developing a service learning course, the final section of this chapter moves to extend the student perspective. Here Beth Larkee, a GSLIS alumna, shares detailed insights of her experience as a student involved in two major service learning initiatives—a debut with East St. Louis and a subsequent transition to São Tomé e Príncipe in West Africa.

In my first class, on my first day of graduate school in 2005, I met Dr. Martin Wolske. I didn't know at the time that one course he taught would end up shaping my education and my career. The class was LIS 451 Introduction to Networked Systems. Honestly, I was a bit nervous about even signing up because I thought I might lack some needed technical skills. As we began, I found out the course focused around a group service learning project in East St. Louis, in which we would build a computer lab from scratch for a site. My group was paired with a community center that offered job training and computer classes.

Dr. Wolske's course was hands-on, and I learned a tremendous amount about taking apart and putting back together computers, lessons that I use frequently in my library job to this day. Moreover, the service learning portion of the course stayed with me, as well as what we've come to call the East St. Louis model. In LIS 451, we view the community of East St. Louis as our partner, and we make an effort not to descend on the community as experts from the university. Although we are graduate students, we are not, for the most part, technology experts, so we both begin with a lot to learn while working together toward a common outcome. While the demographics will tell you that the East St. Louis area is economically depressed, what the demographics leave out is the variety of talented, vibrant people who reside there. I enjoyed interacting with the community a great deal, and when the semester was over I asked Dr. Wolske if I could continue traveling to East St. Louis with his class as a volunteer. He obliged.

As a volunteer my role changed somewhat. Instead of building computer labs for sites, I became a coordinator to refurbish machines for individual distribution. I worked in East St. Louis throughout my master's studies, for a total of five semesters. It was because of my experience in East St. Louis that Paul Adams, the director of Prairienet, asked me to participate in a new service learning project. This project was in Africa.

A Student Experiences International Engagement

I should probably back up and explain how a library school makes the leap from service learning in East St. Louis to service learning abroad. One student in Dr. Wolske's class in 2000 was an international student named Jorge Coelho. Originally from São Tomé e Príncipe, he completed LIS 451 as part of his studies. After graduation, Coelho was offered a position in the ESLARP offices on-site in East St. Louis. When he returned to Africa he worked in several positions, eventually rising to become the director of airports. Coelho understood the positive effects the ESLARP service learning project had on his education and the community in East St. Louis, and he thought a similar program could be started in São Tomé e Príncipe. He contacted Adams to explore the possibilities.

São Tomé e Príncipe is an island country in the Gulf of Guinea in West Africa and one of the smallest countries in Africa. The national language is Portuguese, and French is a common second language. The majority of the people live in the capital city, São Tomé, located on the larger island of the same name. The capital is urban, crowded, and crisscrossed with small winding brick streets, much like old European cities. The rural areas are in sharp contrast, jungle villages and plantations often without electricity and plumbing. Many homes are built upon wooden stilts, and inside the single bed is often draped in mosquito netting to ward off malaria. The division between the very poor and the very, very rich is great, with little middle class. This is true of East St. Louis as well. The crowded schools and libraries do not have computers for the students to use, the few machines being reserved for administrators, if any exist at all.

Adams visited São Tomé in February 2006 to assess the potential and feasibility for partnering. Like East St. Louis, the city of São Tomé had many places where a computer lab could make a huge difference, such as the Biblioteca Nacional (National Library), the main library for the city of São Tomé. It was recently built by the Taiwanese and had plenty of space for a lab. They only had a few computers in the whole building, and those were needed for staff. The director hoped to have a publicly accessible computer lab, since a free one did not exist in the city. In addition to the Biblioteca Nacional, there were regional libraries in four of the five districts of the country; these were located in the villages of Guadalupe, Trinadade, and Santana on the island of São Tomé and on the island of Príncipe. Adams identified several other sites that would be excellent places for computer labs, such as the Liceu Nacional (National High School) in São Tomé city.

When Adams returned from this initial visit to São Tomé, he asked me if I would be interested in building computer labs in West Africa. I jumped at the opportunity.

One lesson quickly learned when beginning an international project was the focus on logistics. Even though I had experienced a huge array of challenges in East St. Louis, we worked hard to anticipate potential difficulties in São Tomé. The LIS 451 course takes an initial trip to East St. Louis at the beginning of the semester to meet the site coordinators, measure the lab location, and find out the mission and goals of the site in order to better prepare the computers with appropriate software and setup. It was not exactly in our budget to fly to Africa for meet and greet. Also, since Coelho was the only person we knew on the island who spoke English, his role was critical. We basically arranged everything through him. For the first trip, it was not feasible to ship our computers in advance, because of cost and time, so we decided we would need to bring the computers along as checked luggage. Carrying over 400 pounds of equipment through an international airport with heightened security is another lesson. We kept an inventory of what was in every single piece of luggage to give to the security screeners.

Before we could pack a single thing, we needed passports, visas, and shots. The University of Illinois student health center was a helpful resource. We purchased student travel insurance and researched health information for the area. It was particularly helpful that Adams had visited São Tomé before because he could prepare us for cultural differences and customs. Because few people in the United States know of São Tomé, it was not surprising that I could not find guidebooks on the country. I was able to search the Internet and find maps on sites like Google Earth, photographs on Flickr, and several websites in Portuguese. Despite making careful preparations, there were many surprises, and one of the most important lessons I learned was to temper my expectations. I had wanted to meet with tons of people and visit many places. After a few days, I learned to follow the community lead, including heeding a common Saotomean saying, *Levé, Levé,* which translates to "Slow, Slow."

During this trip, which took place between February 24 and March 10, 2007, our team of five did meet many people, through Coelho and through a growing circle of partners.[24] The project was expanding both in Illinois and in São Tomé. We started by building a computer lab at the Biblioteca Nacional, as well as one at the airport for the staff. We also began planning for a subsequent summer trip by visiting the regional libraries and schools, the future lab sites. Despite being as prepared as possible, there were many surprises. For example, one of the schools we visited had eighty students per teacher. The students were packed into desks and classrooms built for half as many. The schools had open-air cement rooms built with a central courtyard. The schools we visited did not have any computers available to either students or teachers—only the administrators had desktop computers for record keeping. The students shared books and paper and struggled to hear the teacher over the noise of other students in the courtyard.

One of the schools we visited in the village of Guadalupe housed sixth through eighth grades. Helcio, our interpreter, had taught at this school, which he attended as a youth. Despite the crowded conditions, he succeeded and continued on to the national high school in the capital city. Like other students from the villages, he had to make the 20-kilometer (12.4-mile) trip each way. Until recently there was not a bus, and most students biked or walked. Conditions at the high school were very crowded, with over 5,000 students in a building the size of a city block. Still, the students there all seemed excited about their education, and many talked of attending college in Portugal, since the country of São Tomé does not have a university. A few students asked about college in the United States. I told them to study hard, keep practicing their English, and take the Test of English as a Foreign Language (TOEFL). There is not an exam center on the island, but they hope to have one. The first requirement to become an exam center is to have fifteen computers with Internet access. During our first visit, the high school did not have that many.

Installing computer labs was one of our major projects on both the first trip and on the second trip, from June 28 to July 15, 2007, when we returned with a team of ten. Our group was growing in number and scope, including representatives from the University of Illinois Architecture and Urban and Regional Planning programs. In all, we upgraded and installed labs in nine locations: Biblioteca Nacional, Guadalupe Library, Trinadade Library, Santana Library, the Liceu Nacional, the Coast Guard, the airport, STeP UP (a nongovernmental organization), and the Teachers College. We also repaired broken computers found at the school in Santana and at the Guadalupe

Municipal Offices. Originally, we had wanted to install more computers at the Biblioteca Nacional, but we ran into problems with the building infrastructure. The library did not have enough power to run fifteen computers needed for a TOEFL lab, and monitors and step-down converters and the fuses were continuously blowing out. Even when an electrician was brought in, the team decided that only four computers would be possible during the first trip. The library power supply was increased, and during the second trip four more computers were installed.

In addition to working in the city, we wanted to test the viability of setting up computers in remote regions of the island. We traveled with Roberta dos Santos, currently with STeP UP and formerly with the Peace Corps, south to a mountain plantation above the town of Santana. The road was unpaved and dangerous, but the views were breathtaking. When we finally reached the co-op, we were met by village leaders, children, and free-roaming pigs and dogs. Many had never met Americans before and were excited about the computer we brought. Most of the villagers crowded into the community center to watch Adams and me set it up and then plug it into the generator. I had selected the smallest computer for this site, one running at only 1.5 amps. The monitor, donated by STeP UP, required 2 amps of power. The room became crowded, with the excited audience getting larger. When we powered up the generator, we discovered that while both the computer and the monitor could run independently, they could not run at the same time, as the generator was only 3 amps. Although this proved disappointing, my broken Portuguese was improving and I was able to talk a bit with the women of the plantation. They asked me about my family and if I had children. I used my best Portuguese to tell them I was studying to be a librarian.

We took the computer back to STeP UP and installed it in their offices so the staff could have an additional computer. I also helped Roberta install Skype, the voice-over IP technology, in her office. She had received an e-mail from the United States asking her to install the program in order to talk via the Internet instead of over the phone. It took over two hours to download. Since the bandwidth was extremely limited, it was unclear how well the software would work, if at all, during peak times. During the February trip I had used Skype nightly to call the United States, but I had some trouble maintaining a connection the following summer. It seems in the few months between trips the number of people using the Internet had increased, squeezing the bandwidth.

We found several places that offered Wi-Fi, mostly hotels catering primarily to Portuguese tourists, as well as one café. The café was in the city center and was run by an American named Maria Joao, or simply MJ. Musicians as well as locals and the few Americans on the island frequented the café. I would guess that there were fewer than a dozen Americans who were permanent residents of São Tomé. In fact, I met most of them at a party hosted by the American ambassador in honor of the Fourth of July. MJ catered the event, which included hot dogs, hamburgers, and Bud Light. We were also given straw cowboy hats to wear, which was a first for many of us from the Midwest. I gave mine to Helcio at the end of the night, because he is a huge fan of American Western films. He said John Wayne helped him improve his English.

São Tomé achieved independence from Portugal on July 12, 1975. Some of the people we met talked about what it was like being a colony. They saw the present as a time of recovery. All over the country there is evidence of a lack of infrastructure. The plantations in the surrounding mountainside have continued, though not at the impressive production rates they once had. The people are poor, but hardworking and determined to succeed. The Saotomeans are keen to learn and understand technologies to help the community advance. We can measure some of the small changes around the island by how many labs we install and by how many people have access to the Internet, but one factor that is more difficult to grasp and measure is the impact on the students involved in the service learning projects.

Student Perspective Summary

My own education was impacted from the first day of graduate school by one class. I started a master's program with minimal technology skills. My first service learning project prepared me for a technical assistantship. Continued engagement in East St. Louis prepared me for working in Africa. These combined experiences prepared me for a career in library and computer technologies. Soon after returning from the second trip to Africa, I was hired at Hollins University in Roanoke, Virginia, as the information technology librarian. I doubt that I could be confident in my current position without the education I received at the University of Illinois. I know that without my service learning experience, my career would have looked very different. I feel prepared for work and life and intend to continue looking for ways to foster positive community change.

In her dissertation research on the impact of LIS 451 on GSLIS alumni careers, Nazarova emphasizes the span of this extended effect, noting that "a very important aspect of the impact of the course is the fact that beyond the skills that the students have been applying to their careers, many also adopted a vision and philosophy of the service-learning model."[25]

Conclusion

Integrating service learning opportunities into LIS education involves confronting complex issues and challenges. It also provides new opportunities for student, faculty, and community growth. Based on these vital outcomes, service learning is best understood as an essential element of LIS education. Because implementation and project evolution involve establishing new paths and encountering unanticipated options, and the impact may be difficult to measure using preexisting criteria, engagement in this realm requires significant multi-tiered investment. Commitment must come from individual, departmental, and campuswide levels within universities; individual, organizational, and community-wide levels within communities; and may also draw on the resources of additional partners, for example, nongovernmental organizations, corporations, and consortia.

Starting with small course components or other school projects may ease the transition. However, as Bishop, Bruce, and Jeong discuss in chapter 3 in this volume, there is a critical need to invest in larger-scale holistic approaches by bringing university and community members together to set goals, conduct studies, and build new structures and processes. As the collaborative culture grows, diverse participants will have more opportunities to engage as peers.

To conclude, we look toward the next phase of service learning planned for the summer of 2008. This is when a group from the university will return to São Tomé e Príncipe. For this trip, three youth and a community leader from East St. Louis will form part of the team. In this phase, community and university members and Saotomeans will embark on creating new paths of learning, discovery, and engagement.

NOTES

1. University of Illinois, Board of Trustees, "Welcome to the Chancellor's Office" (2004), www.oc.uiuc.edu/welcome/index.html.

2. Kellogg Commission on the Future of State and Land-Grant Universities, "Renewing the Covenant: Learning, Discovery, and Engagement in a New Age and Different World" (2000), www.nasulgc.org/NetCommunity/Page .aspx?pid=305&srcid=751.

3. Leigh S. Estabrook, "Distance Education at the University of Illinois," in *Benchmarks in Distance Education: The LIS Experience,* ed. Daniel D. Barron (Westport, CT: Libraries Unlimited, 2003), 63–73.

4. Learn and Serve, America's National Service-Learning Clearinghouse, "Service-Learning Is . . . ," www.servicelearning.org/what_is_service-learning/ service-learning_is/index.php.

5. Elaine Yontz and Kathleen de la Peña McCook, "Service-Learning in LIS Education," *Journal of Library and Information Science Education* 44, no. 1 (Winter 2003): 58–68.

6. Mary Alice Ball and Katherine Schilling, "Service Learning, Technology, and LIS Education," *Journal of Library and Information Science Education* 47, no. 4 (Fall 2006): 277–90.

7. American Library Association, Office for Accreditation, "Standards for Accreditation of Master's Programs in Library and Information Studies" (2008), www.ala.org/ala/educationcareers/education/accreditedprograms/standards/ standards_2008.pdf.

8. Stephen T. Bajjaly, "Contemporary Recruitment in Traditional Libraries," *Journal of Library and Information Science Education* 46, no. 1 (Winter 2005): 53–58.

9. Yontz and McCook, "Service-Learning in LIS Education."

10. Andrew Furco, "Service Learning: A Balanced Approach to Experiential Education," in *Expanding Boundaries: Service and Learning* (Washington, DC: Corporation for National Service, 1996).

11. Internet Public Library, www.ipl.org.

12. Michelle M. Kazmer, "Community-Embedded Learning," *Library Quarterly* 75, no. 2 (2005): 190–212.

13. UC Books to Prisoners, www.books2prisoners.org.

14. University of Illinois Community Informatics Initiative, www.cii.uiuc.edu.

15. Progressive Librarians Guild, GSLIS Chapter, www.lis.uiuc.edu/plg/.

16. Libraries for the Future, www.lff.org; Urban Libraries Council, www .urbanlibraries.org.

17. Kathleen de la Peña McCook, *A Place at the Table: Participating in Community Building* (Chicago: American Library Association, 2000), 52–53.

18. University of Illinois, The East St. Louis Action Research Project, www.eslarp .uiuc.edu.

19. University of Illinois, Prairienet Community Network, www.prairienet.org.

20. Martin Wolske, LIS 451 Introduction to Networked Information Systems (2008), http://courseweb.lis.uiuc.edu/lis/2008su/lis451al1/syllabusLIS451SU08 .xhtml.

21. Martin Luther King Jr., "Beyond Vietnam," 1967, www.mlkonline.net/ vietnam.html.

22. Junghyun An, "Service Learning in Postsecondary Technology Education: Educational Promises and Challenges in Student Values Development" (Ph.D. dissertation, University of Illinois, 2007).

23. Ronald L. Larsen, "Groups of Leading Colleges Launch Major Effort to Put the Information Field on the Map," *News for the iWorld,* August, 21 2007, www .ischools.org/oc/news.html.

24. *University of Illinois and São Tomé e Príncipe Partnership* blog, http:// saotomeproject.wordpress.com.

25. Muzhgan Nazarova, "Service Learning and Career Development: A Case Study in Library and Information Science" (Ph.D. dissertation, University of Illinois at Urbana-Champaign, 2007).

Chapter 5

Experiential Education
The Student Role and Experience
Sara Albert and A. Arro Smith

For a library and information science student, experiential education can be a vital component of her graduate studies. While in school, participating in a fieldwork experience can help reinforce the lessons learned in the classroom and demonstrate real-world applications of the basic foundations of library education. In this way, experiential education can improve the overall quality of a program of LIS coursework. There are not only direct benefits to the student during the LIS program, but practical experience will put the student ahead in the job search following graduation. Students with library experience have an advantage over those without it when it comes time to find that first job out of graduate school.

In any fieldwork experience, there are three major players: the student, a faculty advisor from the LIS program, and a field supervisor from the fieldwork site. This chapter addresses the role of the student within this scheme, while the other chapters examine the roles of the faculty advisor and touch on involvement by the field supervisor.

Examples of Fieldwork Programs

Modern fieldwork and internship programs are as varied as the individual institutions that sponsor them. These programs have many diverse names as well: experiential learning, service learning, practicum, and "capstone" all refer to components of the LIS degree that take place outside the walls of the classroom, often as part of an independent study. Some are a mandatory component of the master's degree, and others are optional. Some are paid internships, and others are considered a community service component of the curriculum.

The University of Alberta's School of Library and Information Studies offers its students an optional three-credit practicum. It is available to students who have completed the first half of their master's degree program and requires 100 hours of fieldwork. Working with a professor who visits the site after the first fifty hours, the students keep a journal and submit a final paper about the experience.[1] Students may take on practica involving "reference, collection management, cataloging and indexing, technology applications, interlibrary loan and circulation, meetings, programming, and customer relations."[2]

In California, two LIS schools share a common fieldwork program that places students in paid internships in Los Angeles–area public libraries. Students at San Jose State University's School of Library and Information Science and UCLA's Department of Information Studies share the From Interns to Library Leaders (FILL) program.[3] This program was conceived to promote public librarianship in two schools that were experiencing a marked disinterest in public library work. They found that the majority of students were "opting to apprentice at movie-studio libraries and other venues they considered more alluring."[4] The students are paid to work between 120 and 135 hours during the course of the public library internships. The stipends—provided through a Library Services and Technology Act grant—make the internships more competitive and popular, and "both the students and their supervisors agree that the fiscal incentive adds a sense of professionalism that is often missing in unpaid internships."[5]

At the University of Texas at Austin School of Information, students pursuing a master's degree must choose a capstone course to fulfill graduation requirements. Options include a report, a thesis, or fieldwork; depending on the field of study, fieldwork may be a Practicum in School Libraries, a Practicum in Preservation Planning, a Conservator Internship, or, the most general, a Professional Experience Project (PEP). Students participating in the PEP are expected to complete 125 hours of work and demonstrate their progress or results using journals, portfolios, papers, oral reports, or other methods of evaluation. In addition, a poster session at the end of each semester is held to showcase the students' work.[6]

The above fieldwork program descriptions are just a few examples of what exists in library schools today. Chapter 10 in this volume, entitled "Highlights of Service Learning Experiences in Selected LIS Programs," elaborates on service engagement options for students attending nine graduate LIS programs.

Preparing for a Fieldwork Experience

In some library programs, a fieldwork experience is a required component of the master's degree. In other programs, such as the School of Information at the University of Texas at Austin, students have the option of doing a fieldwork experience to fulfill part of the degree requirements. In still other programs, pursuing fieldwork may be left up to the initiative of the student, who may be able to earn credit through a petition for independent study.

Some institutions will want a discrete, defined project, while others may be satisfied with a fieldwork experience that is more reflective of a host site's ongoing projects or services. Students should be sure they know what they are expected to accomplish and should consult with their faculty advisor to be sure their project meets the requirements, if any, of their program.

Choosing a locale for a fieldwork experience may be the responsibility of the student. Locating leads may be facilitated by the library school in the form of fairs or open houses designed to bring students into contact with potential fieldwork sites, as well as through postings of fieldwork opportunities in a database. The School of Information at the University of Texas at Austin is fortunate to have such a database. It is browsable and searchable by various fields, including type of library or institution and area of the project, such as archives, cataloging, or reference. In addition, the school maintains the JobWeb, a database of career opportunities, including student jobs, internships, volunteer calls, and professional positions from around the world. Both of these resources are freely available to the public through the school's website at www.ischool .utexas.edu. With careful selection, many of these types of postings could be potential fieldwork experiences. In any institution, the faculty advisor should be able to assess the student's career goals to determine if fieldwork would contribute to her program of study.

One of the initiatives of 2007–2008 ALA President Loriene Roy is conceptualizing the development of a national capstone database. Chapter 18 in this volume, by Krichten, Stohr, and Warlick, addresses how recent graduates of LIS programs respond to this idea. Once such a database has been implemented, LIS students across the country can refer to it in order to locate fieldwork opportunities.

Besides locating fieldwork opportunities through established databases or career offices, students often propose projects they find on their own. In some cases, students may choose a fieldwork site where they have some work or volunteer experience already. Students at a loss for where to complete their fieldwork can first consider the type of institution they are most interested in, then make a list of potential sites that meet that criterion.

The type of institution that serves as a fieldwork site for an LIS student can vary widely. The most obvious possibilities are nearby public, academic, and school libraries. These sites are easily located through the Internet or local phone book. Moving beyond these options requires more research. A student's city may contain law firms, technical companies, hospitals, museums, research labs, association headquarters, women's shelters, and numerous other groups or companies that maintain private libraries or archives. Other groups may not maintain libraries but have a current need to disseminate or organize compiled information. It may be up to the student to choose a field or site that matches his professional interests, make contact with staff at potential sites, and propose a project to his faculty advisor. The regional chapters of professional organizations such as the Special Libraries Association may be able to assist students desiring an internship.

Faculty advisors serve to guide the students through their fieldwork experiences, ensuring that the work is a relevant and worthwhile part of their graduate education. Therefore, when given a choice, it makes sense to select a faculty advisor with expertise in the area of the fieldwork experience. For example, a student completing fieldwork in a cataloging department should consider a faculty advisor who is knowledgeable about cataloging practices. Likewise, a student designing and building a website could benefit from an advisor capable of answering digital media design questions. Students should approach their desired faculty advisor as soon as possible. Professors have many obligations, including teaching, publishing, traveling, advising, serving on committees, and so forth, and may accept only the first few students who ask them to serve as their faculty advisor for fieldwork experience.

During the Experience

A student will likely work with one or more staff members at the field site, including the field supervisor who directs, or at least monitors, the student's work. Although it may seem like common sense, the student should remember to approach the experience in a professional manner, which involves using appropriate behavior and language, dressing in a way suitable for the site, and being punctual, respectful, and dependable. The site staff may not be responsible for the student's grade in the fieldwork course, but the importance of making a good impression with them remains. These very staff may serve as references for the student or may even become a future employer.

A student's fieldwork experience may or may not require a specific number of hours dedicated to the project. In either case, it is probably a good idea to lay out a time line of dates when specific components should be completed. Keeping a written record of completed work will ease the preparation of a final report of activities if one is required. Students completing practicum courses at the University of Illinois Graduate School of Library and Information Science have been advised to use a daily log, not as "an itemization of activities performed but rather a reflection on the personal and professional lessons of the day."[7]

Reporting the progress and results of a student's fieldwork experience will again depend on the specific requirements of the degree program and other circumstances of the fieldwork experience; for instance, whether it is a required course or an optional independent study. During the course of the project, the student may be required to meet periodically with the faculty advisor, who should make sure the student is on track and that the project is remaining relevant to the student's education and is meeting program expectations. Even within a particular school, different faculty advisors may expect or require different amounts of collaboration between advisor and student. Based on individual teaching styles, some advisors will be more hands-on and involved in their students' fieldwork experiences, while others may leave much of the monitoring responsibilities to the students themselves.

Whether a student works hand in hand with a faculty advisor throughout the course of the project or not, some sort of final report to the advisor and/or the school will almost certainly be required. This final report could take many forms: an oral presentation, a poster session, a portfolio such as a notebook of gathered resources, a written report of activities, or a website. In most cases, the student's final product will be shared not only with the faculty advisor or LIS program but also with the field site. Examples of this could be a pathfinder to meet an outside client's research needs, a database of integrated library system specifications under consideration for purchase by a library, or a training manual for new reference volunteers.

Benefits of Fieldwork

John N. Berry III in a *Library Journal* editorial has said that "some kind of library practice gives a new graduate an immense edge in an extremely com- petitive employment arena and adds substantially to the educational value of the coursework" in LIS programs.[8] The benefits gained from fieldwork may therefore be both immediate and long-term.

One obvious benefit of student fieldwork is the opportunity to learn new practical skills. Many courses in library and information schools address theory but perhaps do not address actual tools and practices used in the field—these tools are likely to change, whereas the theory lays a foundation for the career. A student's fieldwork experience is the opportunity to learn current and local practices at a field site and apply the theory learned in the classroom.

Working in the field can be an opportunity to try out the type of job the student may be considering. A student's choice may reinforce her interest in the library field or in a particular size or type of library, or conversely it may reveal a mismatch between the student's strengths or personality traits and the fieldwork environment. Either way, the fieldwork experience can provide feedback to the student regarding future job searches.

Consider the following three examples and the lessons that simply cannot be acquired in the classroom:

1. *Young adult reference.* The experience of interviewing a young adult who needs to read a "coming-of-age" story for her summer reading assignment is far different from learning that "bildungsromans" is the correct LC subject heading for that genre in the librarian's young adult literature class. The finer points of that reference interview involve intangible—and virtually unteachable— qualities, such as gleaning the reader's maturity, interests, reading ability, attention span, and whether she would object to sexual content. Sometimes the interview needs to take into account the young reader's family. Is the reader's mother going to object if she finds the librarian has recommended S. E. Hinton's *Rumblefish*—a classic of the genre that includes young characters smoking cigarettes and fighting?

2. *Cataloging.* The experience of cataloging a monograph for a library is also different from learning descriptive cataloging and classification in library school. Because each library serves a different population of patrons, each library's collection demands its own cataloging rules and policies. Learning

cataloging and classification theory—and even cataloging exercises within a class—are clearly different from analyzing a new accession in hand and deciding which rules, subject headings, and call number to apply to it. Although knowing and understanding cataloging theory is essential to be an effective cataloger, nothing can replace the actual discipline of studying a real library collection and choosing the best access points and classification for a new item to be included in the existing collection.

3. *Children's services.* Nothing in graduate school can truly prepare a librarian to confront her first storytime. Here is a *short* list of skills impossible to acquire in the classroom:

- learning to improvise when your audiovisual equipment fails
- learning the hokey-pokey
- learning how to deal with hand fatigue during puppet shows
- learning to judge the attention span of a room of toddlers and knowing when to stop before reaching a critical mass of crying children
- learning to organize two months of entertaining activities for the annual summer reading program

Here we have just discussed three disparate library positions that are impossible to fully prepare for in the context of a classroom. After participating in a fieldwork program, a student may actually learn more useful information about her future career by *eliminating* certain positions simply because they were a bad fit. A student who has entered graduate school with the notion of being a reference librarian may find that she, in fact, does not enjoy working with the public—or only enjoys working with children.

Likewise, a practicum may also force students to entertain a clearly different type of library career than they had originally been interested in. One of the authors of this chapter participated in an internship at the Texas State Law Library and then held a part-time position at the Texas State Archives while finishing his degree. Although both experiences proved very useful—and enjoyable—he was able to make a categorical decision to not pursue law librarianship or archival work. The fieldwork was an exceptionally useful heuristic—trial and *error,* in this case—that propelled him to public librarianship.

Similarly, the FILL program reports that its internships have a profound effect on the students' professional outlook. "First-year alumna Natale Majkut was contemplating a career as an archivist before interning in a children's department. 'FILL made me realize that I enjoyed working with children,' she relates. Today, Majkut works as a full-time children's librarian at the Glendale Public Library."[9]

Completing a fieldwork experience allows a student to reveal her abilities—and potential—to the site staff. Knowing the student's strengths and abilities may enable the staff members to become valuable professional references during the student's job search. If a job opening is available at the site itself when the student begins the job search, she may have an advantage over other applicants if she has demonstrated potential value to the institution.

A mentor can be extremely valuable to any new professional, and students completing a practicum may find a new mentor in their field supervisor. Keri Botello, the internship program coordinator at the UCLA Department of Information Studies, has described this type of mentoring as "another major component of the practical experience" that "often offers the intern a glimpse at the larger professional world by sharing the thoughts, expertise, and wisdom of a seasoned information professional."[10]

As Berry pointed out, library experience can be critical to landing a first professional library job. Completing fieldwork can provide a student with relevant experience that can be listed on his résumé or job applications. If the fieldwork project has resulted in a tangible product such as a report, pathfinder, or website, this item can be added to either a physical portfolio or e-portfolio to provide examples of one's work. Some projects may be innovative enough to serve as the basis for a conference presentation or publication. Sharing work with the professional library community further increases the student's network of contacts. If the project is related to the faculty advisor's research interests, he may choose to co-present or coauthor with the student, and in this way further mentor the student.

There are other intangible benefits of fieldwork involving the mental transition from student to professional. Botello has described the internship experience as an "opportunity for the interns to begin developing their own philosophy or personal style as an information professional."[11] Fieldwork concurrent with library school coursework can enable students to construct a professional identity even before they have entered their first postgraduate job. Silver has described another related future benefit of a practicum experience: professional confidence, which she says "is bound to transfer over to the job interview as well as to the start of a new job."[12]

Conclusion

Service learning experiences have great potential to augment the classroom education of graduate library school programs. One of us is a recent graduate and highly values the opportunities she had for service learning while in school, including a paid internship at a technical corporate library, volunteer work at the local public library information desk, and a capstone course completed at a community college library. Therefore, before graduation, she had experience in academic, public, and special libraries that provided her with firsthand knowledge of a range of library settings, along with flexibility in the types of libraries to which she might apply in the job search.

Any student in library school can participate in experiential learning—required or optional. It may be up to the student to create her own fieldwork opportunities through independent study courses, volunteer work, or part-time employment. Whether or not this work leads to a career in the specific area of the study, it will prove to be an invaluable experience by providing an immersion into the real world of library careers.

NOTES

1. Dianne Oberg and Toni Samek, "Humble Empowerment: The LIS Practicum," *PNLA Quarterly* 63, no. 3 (1999): 20–22.

2. Ibid., 20–21.

3. Cindy Mediavilla, "FILLing in the Public-Librarian Ranks," *American Libraries* 34, no. 6 (2003): 61–62.

4. Ibid., 61.

5. Ibid., 62.

6. University of Texas School of Information, "Capstone Information," www.ischool .utexas.edu/programs/capstone/.

7. Isabel Dale Silver, "The LIS Practicum: An Internship with Academic Credit," in *Public Library Internships: Advice from the Field,* ed. Cindy Mediavilla (Lanham, MD: Scarecrow, 2006), 24.

8. John N. Berry III, "The Practice Prerequisite," *Library Journal* 130, no. 15 (September 15, 2005): 8.

9. Mediavilla, "FILLing in the Public-Librarian Ranks," 62.

10. Keri S. Botello, "Library School Internship Programs: How UCLA Does It," in Mediavilla, *Public Library Internships,* 14.

11. Ibid., 15.

12. Silver, "The LIS Practicum," 32.

Chapter 6

The School Library Media Practicum as Service Education

Johan Koren

The school library media profession can only be described in terms of the Norwegian expression "å falle mellom to stoler," literally "falling between two chairs." While we might say "falling between the cracks" in English, the Norwegian saying captures the essence of school library media: it falls between the two chairs of teaching and librarianship and has elements of both, but at the same time, school media librarianship is neither wholly teaching nor is it wholly librarianship. The school media librarian teaches classes, it is true, but she does not usually teach the same class on a regular basis as a classroom teacher does, at least not in the ideal view of the role of the school librarian as presented in *Information Power* or Danielson's *Enhancing Professional Practice.*[1] The school media librarian organizes and manages a collection of print and nonprint materials that enhances and supports the curriculum of the school, and she must provide both intellectual and physical access to these materials. She is at once a leader in providing and advocating for education in information literacy and a service professional in supporting the classroom teacher and the school's administration in their mission.

This delicate balancing act between time, role, and resources cannot be easily learned in formal education for school library media, where classes are of necessity compartmentalized into the separate aspects of professional procedure and theory. The elephant has to be eaten one bite-sized chunk at a time after all. The task of integrating theory with practice falls, therefore, to the practicum. In an interview entitled "Learning for the 21st Century," John Abbott, director of the British Education 2000 Trust and the leader of an international effort to search for new learning strategies that "go with the grain of the brain," as it was put in the interview, affirmed that "people worldwide need a whole new series of competencies," and added:

> I doubt such abilities can be taught solely in the classroom, or be developed solely by teachers. Higher order thinking and problem-solving skills *grow out of direct experience,* not simply teaching;

they require *more than a classroom activity.* They develop through active involvement and *real-life experiences in workplaces and the community.*[2]

Research on the School Library Media Practicum

Both Shannon and Mardis note the paucity of literature and research on education for school library media specialists (SLMS) and the practicum in particular.[3] Only three publications have some relevance to a discussion of the practicum as service learning.

1. Lyders and Wilson's 1991 national survey "Field Experience in Library Education" concluded with a call for joint planning of the field experience between the supervising media specialist and the university supervisor in order "to help the professor and the practitioner share new ideas in theory and practice and inspire fresh interest in the larger worlds of education and libraries."[4]

2. Vansickle focused on the development of pre-service media specialists as school leaders and likewise advocated that "university professors and supervising media specialists should work together to ensure that the preservice internship is centered around activities that will provide leadership, collaboration, and professional involvement experiences," leaving the more mundane and routine duties of media center management to actual on-the-job training.[5]

3. Mardis looked specifically at the role of the practicum for two cohorts of a total of nine students in their transition from classroom teachers to school media specialists. Although her small sample and inadequately edited paper make for some uncertain results, her descriptions of the implications of her findings do suggest some interesting ways of organizing the practicum that can aid students in their transition to school media librarians. Mardis asserts:

> Despite the prior research that suggested that practicum experiences should focus on instructional partnering experiences or an equal exposure to all Information Power roles, once the participants experienced the unique library-related aspects of the SLMS job like cataloging, weeding, and ordering books before they felt comfortable acting as instructional partners and program leaders [sic] . . . By allowing students to experience dismiss [sic] information specialist and program administrator early in their practicum, they experience valuable opportunities to embrace the aspects of their new roles with which they are least confident.[6]

The awkwardness of these two sentences notwithstanding, the implication is that there is a need to structure the practicum in such a way that students with prior experience as classroom teachers can gain confidence in the more librarian-specific competencies of their position as early as possible. This, together with Mardis's earlier observations gleaned from the literature concerning the problems of candidates working full-time in fitting in the demands of a culminating practicum or internship, suggests that the practicum might be more rewarding and fruitful if spread over the span of the library media program. Despite this objection, she asserts that "defining the practicum in terms of transition, the results of this project have the potential to reposition and embrace the field experience as crucial culminating coursework."[7]

The Practicum and the Busy Practitioner

What exactly is a practicum, then? Vansickle's investigation of how pre-service media specialists view the leadership role only fleetingly refers to the practicum and appears to use the concept interchangeably with "preservice internship." A 2004 survey of the preparation of SLMS does not include the word *practicum* at all, preferring instead to use *internship*—defined, as it was in the 1991 national survey of field experience, as "field experience under the supervision of a professional."[8] Mardis, on the other hand, consistently refers to the practicum, though without formally defining its meaning, while explicating its purpose as "grounded in the theory that students should experience their new professions as part of the endorsement process."[9]

A "Library Education Update" from *Mississippi Libraries* makes the distinctions clear, however: an internship is traditionally a "relatively long-term paid position," while a practicum is "generally shorter and more specialized in purpose than an internship" and is "normally part of a student's academic program, taken for credit, and involves no remuneration." In addition, "a practicum normally lasts for one semester; it is not necessary to formulate a long-term agreement between the university and institution (although formal agreements are required for each placement); and institutions do not normally pay the students."[10]

Whatever the supervised field experience might be called, there are concerns about the way the school library practicum has traditionally been organized. Vansickle pointed to the brevity of the experience, arguing, as noted above, for the exclusion of some practice activities in order to provide more opportunities for focusing on leadership and collaboration. In addition, it can be challenging for graduate students to fit the required experience into a busy, often full-time working schedule. Shannon notes that students are often forced to negotiate for leaves of absence in order to complete their practica. Another problem, touched on obliquely in the literature, is the lack of guidance for students and their library media supervisors from library educators during the practicum experience. Shannon reported that several of the schools that required a supervised field experience did not include visits from the supervising university faculty.

The Library Media Program at Murray State University has instituted one solution that helps to alleviate some of these concerns. The program requires a practicum totaling 150 contact hours in exchange for 3 hours of university credit. Students are offered a choice between the traditional, less focused culminating practicum that squeezes all 150 hours into one semester, or spreading the practicum out over the course of their studies in a series of three practicum courses of one credit hour each, linked to the three central core courses. LIB 626 Library Practicum: Administration is paired with a theoretical course, LIB 620 Library Administration, and must be taken either concurrently or after taking the theory course. Similarly, LIB 636 Library Practicum: Cataloging has LIB 630 Classification and Cataloging as its pre- or corequisite, and LIB 646 Library Practicum: Information Skills is paired with LIB 640 Information Sources and Services. Each of the three practicum courses requires fifty contact hours. This arrangement allows the student some flexibility in a small program. With only one instructor of record, the theory courses must of necessity be offered according to a fixed schedule.

Feedback on this arrangement has generally been positive. One student commented: "I like the fact that the practicums have been broken down into three one-hour practicums. This is somewhat easier to work into an already busy daily schedule for an elementary teacher."

Service Learning and the Practicum

What is service learning? There appears to be no single accepted definition of the concept. Loriene Roy cites a formal definition that is also found in slightly modified form on the Northern Kentucky University website's "Public Engagement Terminology" page:[11]

> a course-based, credit-bearing educational experience in which students participate in an organized service activity that meets identified community needs and reflect on the service activity in such a way as to gain further understanding of course content, a broader appreciation of the discipline, and an enhanced sense of civic responsibility.[12]

Does the practicum constitute a form of service learning? Fisher and Finkelstein strongly argue that "properly designed practica placements ... meet the requirements of service-learning if students maintain a focus on the recipient and service as they develop professional skills which help them to become better service providers to those recipients."[13] Indeed, service learning has been called both "methodologically and philosophically appropriate" as a strategy to match the needs of pre-service teachers and of the local community.[14] One can argue that the practicum is the ideal setting for a service learning experience, precisely because the practicum integrates the theoretical curriculum into a practical professional context. The editor of the American Association for Higher Education's recent eighteen-volume series on service learning in the disciplines emphatically declared:

> To conceptualize service-learning only in terms of individual course design is to overlook its potential as a vehicle of general curricular

reform, as a way of addressing a variety of pressing educational and institutional needs. Because well-designed service-learning activities naturally and effectively lead to a deeper understanding of the learning process even while they provide an opportunity to create larger units of curricular coherence, they can simultaneously address the challenges of facilitating deep learning and of overcoming piecemeal implementation of reform.[15]

A South African perspective on the importance of service learning in the context of the practicum makes reference to Zlotkowski and puts it this way:

> In the Library and Information Science arena the traditional pre-professional fieldwork can incorporate structured reflection sessions on service-related as well as discipline-specific concerns in the fieldwork period in order to enhance the fieldwork experience. These reflective activities will aid to turn simple "exposure" into a deliberately constructed learning opportunity.[16] Service learning can then be labelled as enhanced fieldwork.[17]

The Bringle and Hatcher definition of service learning includes three requirements: a course-based, credit-bearing educational experience; an organized service activity that meets identified community needs; and reflection on the service activity. The practicum adds a fourth activity: practical professional experience. This allows us to create a 2 × 2 matrix, a problem-solving and planning instrument that could be called a "squaral," making it possible to design a practicum that fills all the requirements (see figure 6-1).

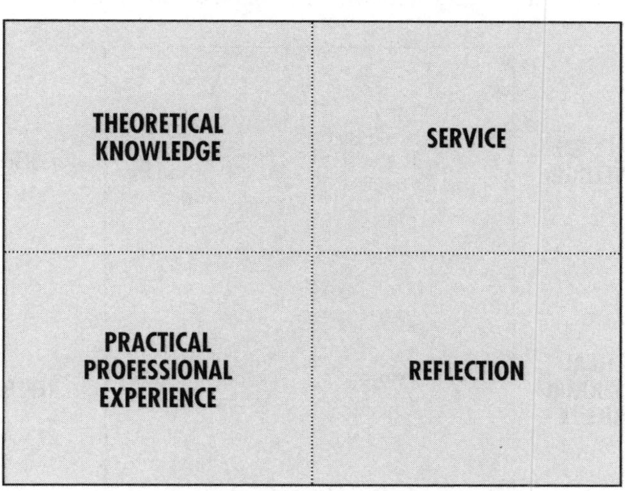

THEORETICAL KNOWLEDGE	**SERVICE**
PRACTICAL PROFESSIONAL EXPERIENCE	**REFLECTION**

Figure 6-1. The service learning practicum squaral

For example, the application of the squaral can be seen after the fact in figure 6-2, an analysis of the structure of a gerontology practicum that sought to fulfill a university's emphasis on service learning as the result of a newly introduced shift in the legislated mission to public affairs.[18] Here specific course requirements are embedded within the squaral.

In the same way, the semester-long Professional Experience 3 described by Vickers and others, involving the participation of pre-service teachers in an alternative education setting where they mentored an at-risk student, can be analyzed as a squaral in figure 6-3.

Proposing a School Library Service Learning Practicum

The literature of the field does not report on school library practica that specifically incorporate a service learning component; it reports on only a few in the broader LIS arena as well. Roy's If I Can Read, I Can Do Anything project and other endeavors with her students at the School of Information at the University of Texas-Austin are often student activities conducted outside of regular classes, but they do provide much-needed opportunities for LIS students to engage with "non-majority cultures" and provide "a social context for students to acquire and share new skills."[19] On the other hand, they do not provide the same kind of institutional context that a service learning experience as part of a practicum placement provides.

Fiona Bell of the University of KwaZulu-Natal, Pietermaritzburg, South Africa, describes something that appears to fit our criteria in an application of South Africa's Community-Higher Education Service Partnerships project, in which two modules of the postgraduate diploma in information studies (PGDIS), "Information Users and Use" and "Information Delivery Systems," were applied to a rural high school with little or no school or public library service.

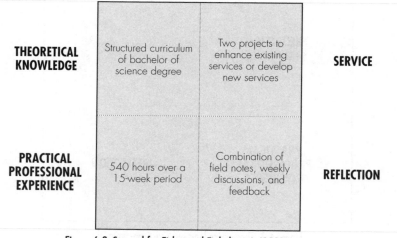

Figure 6-2. Squaral for Fisher and Finkelstein's (1999) practicum

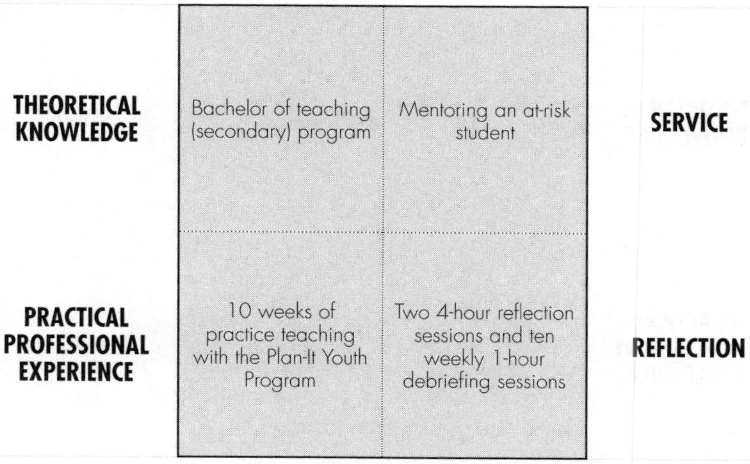

THEORETICAL KNOWLEDGE	Bachelor of teaching (secondary) program	Mentoring an at-risk student	**SERVICE**
PRACTICAL PROFESSIONAL EXPERIENCE	10 weeks of practice teaching with the Plan-It Youth Program	Two 4-hour reflection sessions and ten weekly 1-hour debriefing sessions	**REFLECTION**

Figure 6-3. Squaral for Vickers and others' (2004) Professional Experience 3 practicum

Using information needs assessment techniques learned in the first module, the PGDIS students interviewed the high schoolers in order to gather data on their information needs and, by extension, community information needs. The results were analyzed and incorporated into the production of pamphlets and what we would call bulletin board displays providing information on topics such as child abuse and AIDS education, as well as career information.

> The research and investigation into the lack of information provision at Emzamwemi High School and the Inadi community provided the PGDIS students with a real-life situation, very similar to many other rural areas, where there is no school library or information provision of any kind in the community . . . The research and practice embarked upon will ultimately serve to inform both the needs of information provision and literacy to the Inadi, Delft and Bellville communities respectively and the need to build up a body of service-learning research which will be unique to the South African context but remain relevant to the international context.[20]

This example may be conceptualized in our squaral as figure 6-4.

The United States can also provide contrasts as stark as those described by Bell, both in inner-city urban schools and in rural schools. It would not be hard to find service learning opportunities and needs similar to those of Emzamwemi High School. But even the suburbs provide community and individual situations that a pre-service school librarian can turn into a service project. In fact, one can design a practicum that combines the desiderata noted above, with the collaboration of a supervising and media specialist to "share new ideas in theory and practice."[21] This will "ensure that the preservice internship

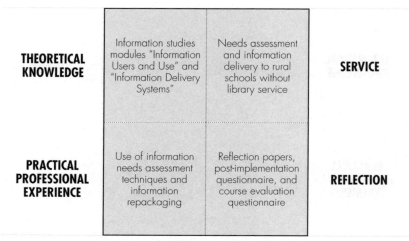

	Information studies modules "Information Users and Use" and "Information Delivery Systems"	Needs assessment and information delivery to rural schools without library service	
THEORETICAL KNOWLEDGE			**SERVICE**
PRACTICAL PROFESSIONAL EXPERIENCE	Use of information needs assessment techniques and information repackaging	Reflection papers, post-implementation questionnaire, and course evaluation questionnaire	**REFLECTION**

Figure 6-4. Squaral for Bell's (2007) Inadi initiative

centers around leadership, collaboration and professional involvement" while "allowing students to experience [the roles of] information specialist and program administrator early in their practicum."[22]

As reported earlier, Murray State University's Library Media Program offers the student a choice between a culminating practicum of three credit hours involving 150 contact hours of work in a library media center, or three practicum courses of one credit hour and 50 contact hours each, linked with each of the three library media core courses. These practica do not currently include a service learning component, but one is conceivable in the form of a project developed in collaboration between the student and the university educator, library media supervisor, classroom teachers, and school administration that meets concrete, identifiable needs within the school and community. Taking the one-hour course LIB 646 Library Practicum: Information Skills as an example, we can devise a squaral similar to that of figure 6-5.

LIB 646 is intended to give the student an opportunity to focus on the provision of reference and information services and the teaching of information skills, covered in LIB 640 Information Sources and Services, the theoretical knowledge that is incorporated into the practicum. The practical professional experience in this practicum would therefore involve answering student and staff reference questions, matching reference sources with reference queries, practicing the reference interview, teaching information skills in collaboration with classroom teachers, and so forth. Reflection is already built into the structure of the practicum in the form of the practicum log and opportunities to reflect on Blackboard online. The instructor is in the process of adding blogs as reflective tools to the students' repertoire. That leaves a service learning project that could very well be modeled on the Emzamwemi project: assessing

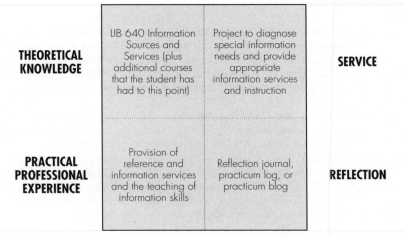

| THEORETICAL KNOWLEDGE | LIB 640 Information Sources and Services (plus additional courses that the student has had to this point) | Project to diagnose special information needs and provide appropriate information services and instruction | SERVICE |
| PRACTICAL PROFESSIONAL EXPERIENCE | Provision of reference and information services and the teaching of information skills | Reflection journal, practicum log, or practicum blog | REFLECTION |

Figure 6-5. Squaral for LIB 646 Library Practicum: Information Skills

special information needs and providing appropriate information services and instruction.

The Murray State Library Media Program is taught almost completely online, with the exception of the practica. This combination of linked online courses and practica appears to be an effective one, as suggested by the results of a comparison between the provision of a course alone and a combination of a course and a three-hour practicum. Three implications were identified in the study:

1. The use of a project-based practicum provides needed structure and facilitates reflection by practicum teachers.
2. Practica and coursework that are integrated provide valuable opportunities for teachers to engage in professional experimentation that can lead to teacher change.
3. Collaborative learning communities can serve as important support systems for teachers completing a practicum experience.[23]

There is an indication that the introduction of a service learning component to such an online course-practicum combination can afford additional educational benefits.

Conclusion

SLMS programs have long employed service learning largely in the format of a practicum. While not an object of study, it is felt that this is an essential component of professional preparation.

NOTES

1. American Association of School Librarians and Association for Educational Communications and Technology, *Information Power: Building Partnerships for Learning* (Chicago: American Library Association, 1998); and Charlotte Danielson, *Enhancing Professional Practice: A Framework for Teaching,* 2nd ed. (Alexandria, VA: Association for Supervision and Curriculum Development, 2007).

2. Interview with Ted Marchese, *AAHE Bulletin* (March 1996), as quoted by Edward Zlotkowski in "Mapping New Terrain: Service-Learning across the Disciplines," *Change* 33, no. 1 (January/February 2001): 25–33.

3. Donna Shannon, "The Education and Competencies of School Library Media Specialists: A Review of the Literature," *School Library Media Research* 5 (2002); and Marcia A. Mardis, "From One-to-One to One-to-Many: A Study of the Practicum in the Transition from Teacher to School Library Media Specialist," *Journal of Education for Library and Information Science* 48, no. 3 (Summer 2007): 218–35.

4. Josetta Lyders and Patricia Jane Wilson, "A National Survey: Field Experience in Library Education," *School Library Journal* 37 (January 1991): 31–35.

5. Sharon Vansickle, "Educating Preservice Media Specialists: Developing School Leaders," *School Libraries Worldwide* 6, no. 2 (July 2000): 18.

6. Mardis, "From One-to-One," 233.

7. Ibid.

8. Lyders and Wilson, "A National Survey"; Donna Shannon, "Preparation of School Library Media Specialists in the United States," *School Library Media Research* 7 (2004), www.ala.org/ala/aasl/aaslpubsandjournals/slmrb/slmrcontents/volume72004/shannon.cfm.

9. Mardis "From One-to-One."

10. Thomas D. Walker, "Learning on the Job: The Value of Internships and Practica," *Mississippi Libraries* 64, no. 3 (Fall 2000): 83–84.

11. Northern Kentucky University, Office of the Associate Provost for Outreach, "Public Engagement Terminology," www.nku.edu/~nkuope/definitions.html.

12. Robert G. Bringle and Julie A. Hatcher (1995), as quoted by Loriene Roy in "Diversity in the Classroom: Incorporating Service-Learning Experiences in the Library and Information Science Curriculum," *Journal of Library Administration* 33, no. 3–4 (2001): 213–28.

13. Bradley J. Fisher and Marvin S. Finkelstein, "The Gerontology Practicum as Service-Learning," *Educational Gerontology* 25, no. 5 (July/August 1999): 393–409.

14. Margaret Vickers, Catherine Harris, and Florence McCarthy, "University-Community Engagement: Exploring Service-Learning Options within the Practicum," *Asia-Pacific Journal of Teacher Education* 32, no. 2 (July 2004): 130.

15. Zlotkowski, "Mapping New Terrain," 33.

16. Ibid., 28.

17. S. L. Witbodi, "Service Learning in the Library and Information Studies Curriculum at the University of the Western Cape: An Exploratory Study," *Mousaion* 22, no. 1 (2004): 101.

18. Based on Fisher and Finkelstein, "Gerontology Practicum."

19. Roy, "Diversity in the Classroom," 224.

20. Fiona Bell, "Service-Learning in LIS Education: The Case of the University of Natal's Inadi Initiative," *South African Journal of Librarianship and Information Science* 73, no. 2 (2007): 154.

21. Lyders and Wilson, "A National Survey."

22. Vansickle, "Educating Preservice Media Specialists"; and Mardis, "From One-to-One."

23. Timothy Frey, "Determining the Impact of Online Practicum Facilitation for Inservice Teachers," *Journal of Technology and Teacher Education* 16, no. 2 (2008): 201.

Chapter 7

Service Learning and International Students
Gilok Choi

According to a report by the Association of Library and Information Science Education, student enrollment in library and information science programs totaled 22,786 in 56 schools during fall 2004, with 1,329 (6 percent) being international students from around the world, including China, South Korea, India, Canada, France, Russia, and the United Kingdom.[1]

Under current U.S. regulations, international students are required to obtain special authorization to work outside the university.[2] The authorization procedure is fairly tedious, and the work period is limited to fewer than twelve months during the students' full study period. International students also need to take classes that are directly related to their employment, with the approval of their professors while they are working.

Due to legal restrictions and practical situations, service learning offers international students an alternative to the traditional internships and summer jobs that are popularly used by American students. This may be the only option for international students to acquire preprofessional experience and to learn about real-world needs and challenges.

When integrated into the academic curriculum, service learning benefits international students as well as American communities. Service learning opportunities provide students with a "substantive [and] varied learning experience."[3] Service learning is particularly meaningful to students from other countries because it offers an effective vehicle for international students to maximize academic learning, to enhance their understanding of American communities, and to promote goodwill worldwide. Additionally, the different voices of international students bring new insights and valuable opportunities for communities that benefit from global richness and cross-cultural exchanges.[4]

Advantages of Service Learning to International Students

International students gain multiple benefits from service learning. First, the students are able to leverage their classroom learning by applying the knowledge they have acquired to the real-world environment.[5] Second, in terms of sociocultural issues, service learning immerses international students in U.S. work environments so they can experience cultural differences such as group dynamics, interpersonal communication, and work practices at firsthand.[6] Third, service learning provides international students with hands-on skills and field experience.[7]

Real-World Experiences

With regard to academic goals, service learning allows international students to combine their studies with practical and concrete experience. Service-based education has been an integral component of LIS curricula from the beginning.[8] Melvil Dewey, the founder of the first School of Library Economy at Columbia in 1894, acknowledged that class lectures and reading are not enough to accomplish the best learning goals and results.[9]

The new knowledge that students acquire in the classroom needs to be supplemented by an understanding of how this knowledge can be applied in libraries and other information settings. In order to fully internalize the new knowledge, international students in particular need to understand work environments and situations in the United States, where most of the LIS structures and procedures have been developed, and the basis on which LIS academic curricula and course materials have been designed.

This is important because the work environment of many international students in their home countries is often very different. Because of cultural differences, international students often lack the necessary social and workplace approaches that are unique to the United States and, therefore, often find it difficult to comprehend course materials apart from the American work environment. Even when international students are assigned class projects and perform cooperative work in the classroom, their academic experience is not sufficient for them to truly make sense of real-world problems and needs such as routines, workflow, and organizational structure. Therefore, service learning offers a valuable opportunity for students from other countries to acquire not only practical experience but also a much broader understanding of the profession.

Among the challenges that international students may not be familiar with is the need to deal with multiple stakeholders for the successful management of library systems in the United States and the relevant factors as well as the dynamics that affect relationships among stakeholders.[10] Because the topic of multiple stakeholders is not one that students can learn about from course readings and class lectures, service learning provides an ideal opportunity to fill the gap between theoretical knowledge and the practical reality of library work. As students apply the information from their courses to real-world settings, they are able to maximize opportunities for thoughtful engagement in learning and for insightful integration of theory and practice.[11]

Cultural Differences

Service learning meets the multicultural needs of international students by helping them to identify different cultural factors and work practices. Recognizing cultural differences in the U.S. work environment is probably the most valuable benefit that international students acquire through the service learning experience.[12]

According to Schein, culture is the accumulated learning shared by a group of people who have the same history. In his book *Organizational Culture and Leadership,* Schein points out the importance of culture for comprehending the rules, norms, and common values of organizations.[13] Because the core of culture is implicit and invisible, students can easily recognize and internalize a different culture as a result of personal experience and direct interaction. Therefore, the students' actual use and observation of cultural factors that are specific to U.S. libraries and other organizations are often more valuable and far-reaching than mere technical skills acquired in service learning.[14] Opportunities to work with people who have had different life experiences also enrich the international students' overall education and lives.

Peters and Waterman describe the U.S. organizational culture as having eight characteristics that include autonomy and entrepreneurship, productivity through people, and being close to customers.[15] These unique cultural factors are also prevalent in library operations and services. For example, libraries in the United States are much friendlier and more easily accessible compared to libraries in most Asian countries. More specifically, university libraries in the United States are basically open to the public, whereas libraries in Asian countries are usually limited to university students. Similarly, public libraries in the United States are an integral part of community life where people read magazines, meet friends, and take children to story hour, whereas public libraries in Asian countries are places for students to study and are furnished with many desks and chairs.

Hands-On Skills and Practical Knowledge

Oftentimes, service learning equips international students with field-related skills and practical knowledge that give them a competitive edge in their career development and that enhance the educational value of their coursework.[16] In fact, real-world experience is frequently considered as important as the degree itself in today's employment market.[17]

Actual work within a variety of library and information settings also "provide[s] students with both managerial and front-line experience."[18] For example, students can make direct contact with users who have a wide range of needs, abilities, and personal styles and, as a result, can come up with creative ways to approach various categories of users. This is important not only for international students with little or no work experience but also for those students who have had experience in their own countries, because they are able to compare multiple systems in terms of the nature of information work and work environments.

Moreover, service learning may help students to interact with more advanced systems than have been covered in their courses and will provide them with confidence in their emerging skills.[19] For example, as part of their service learning experience, students may become familiar with a wide range of software and systems.[20] In an ever-changing information marketplace, it is increasingly important for library and information professionals to keep current with and informed about new practices and issues.[21]

In a similar vein, through service learning, international students are given opportunities to experience not only the employment of technical skills but also to recognize professional aspects of information work. Service learning offers useful social networks and professional connections that might be difficult for international students in particular. In these ways, service learning adds substance for international "students [to] realize the dynamic and complex nature of the [library and information] profession" as well as to understand their roles as information professionals.[22]

Benefits of Service Learning to American Communities

The information revolution has intertwined geographically dispersed and culturally disparate constituents in a globally networked macrocommunity.[23] In this fast-changing, closely knit "global village," it is becoming ever more important to be familiar with the dynamics of global interdependence and cross-cultural collaboration.[24] In this respect, international students bring a valuable perspective for U.S. communities to benefit from the global richness and multicultural diversity in concrete, person-to-person ways. Service learning offers a unique chance for international students to share their experiences and knowledge with LIS professions in general and with U.S. communities in particular.

International students can help shape a more ecocentric, instead of egocentric, viewpoint of the world, by bringing an international flavor to LIS issues and concerns.[25] The experience and knowledge offered by international students provide new insights to U.S. communities on specific services, systems, and policies and, therefore, allow for comparisons and contrasts between the United States and other nations. Information professionals are required to be acquainted with topics of international interest in order to collaborate successfully with and participate in global information flow and exchanges.[26] In the realm of a continuously changing global marketplace, only an international-minded information workforce can provide quality service, participating in the exchange of information on professional issues and developments and employment opportunities worldwide.[27]

International students are also able to bring to service learning situations a wide range of cross-cultural perspectives that are capable of introducing new approaches to projects, based on their various backgrounds and experience. For example, in the Korean culture, Koreans have a strong tradition of reciprocal family relationships that require a lot of time and attention. To minimize the effort required to keep in touch with everybody, Koreans created Cyworld, the first social networking system in the world that includes individual home pages and automated systems for contacting friends and relatives. Cyworld, in turn, has led to the creation of other extremely popular social networking sites in other countries such as Facebook and MySpace in the United States. The Ranganathan Colon Classification system from India is another example that illustrates how librarians can learn from practices in different parts of the world. The Ranganathan Colon Classification system provided inspiration to modify the Dewey Decimal system and is leading to the creation of faceted hierarchies for management of the Web.[28]

Issues and Challenges of Service Learning for International Students

There are several issues and challenges that international students confront when they join service learning programs in U.S. communities. First of all, service learning combines theory and practice with a strong emphasis on civic duty, the philosophy that students "serve to learn" and "learn to serve."[29] Many international students may not be familiar with such theoretical and pedagogical concepts in their own countries, and academic discussions that are a part of service learning should include these and related issues. To support a diverse group of students, it is also necessary that service learning seek to broaden its philosophical framework to emphasize global citizenship that responds to human needs and incorporates responsibilities to serve.

Because team dynamics and interpersonal communication in professional arenas are often different due to cultural variations, misunderstandings can occur. For example, in some cultures, employees are encouraged to explicitly express ideas to participate fully in group work, while in other cultural settings employees are expected to follow the direction of a group leader without significant disagreement as a more polite way to participate. Observing such cultural differences can potentially help international students to gain a deeper understanding of issues related to human nature, privacy, negotiation, and group dynamics.

Apart from the above-mentioned issues, international students may sometimes tend to unconsciously adopt the prejudices and biases of U.S. work environments where they participate in service programs. For that reason, there should be a mechanism to help students to avoid overgeneralizing or oversimplifying based on their limited experience. Classroom discussions about this and related topics can, therefore, expand the learning of international students with regard to U.S. work environment and culture.

Conclusion

Due to visa restrictions, international students can have difficulty in finding opportunities to work in real-world environments as part of their studies in the United States. As a viable alternative to classroom-based approaches, service learning offers international students invaluable hands-on learning possibilities in different cultural environments. In service learning programs, international students can acquire practical experience as well as a much greater understanding of the U.S. work environment where much of the new knowledge in LIS has been developed.[30] Direct and personalized experience of cultural factors in U.S. workplaces is, therefore, another valuable benefit of service learning.[31] Finally, service learning provides hands-on skills and in-depth learning experiences for library and information professionals worldwide.[32]

At the same time, international students who participate in service learning can make significant contributions to U.S. communities with culture-specific knowledge from their own countries and new insights on LIS issues based on their own disciplinary backgrounds and cross-cultural experience.[33] International students have tremendous potential, and in order to realize that potential, there should be more systematic and careful support for their participation in and involvement with actual work environments. In these various respects, service learning offers valuable opportunities for American communities to share their experience with international students, some of whom will remain in the United States and some of whom will take what they have learned in the United States back to their own countries.

NOTES

1. Jerry Saye and Kathy Wisser, "Library and Information Science Education Statistical Report" (2003), http://ils.unc.edu/ALISE/2004/Students/Students.htm.

2. Code of Federal Regulations, 8 CFR 214.2(f).

3. John N. Berry III, "The Practice Prerequisite," *Library Journal* 130, no. 15 (September 15, 2005): 8.

4. Bharat Mehra and Ann Bishop, "Cross-Cultural Perspectives of International Doctoral Students: Two-Way Learning in Library and Information Science Education," *International Journal of Progressive Education* 3, no. 1 (2007): 44–64.

5. Dianne Oberg and Toni Samek, "Humble Empowerment: The LIS Practicum," *PNLA Quarterly* 63, no. 3 (Spring 1999): 20–22.

6. Mary Alice Ball and Katherine Schilling, "Service Learning, Technology, and LIS Education," *Journal of Library and Information Science Education* 47, no. 4 (Fall 2006): 277–90.

7. Berry, "Practice Prerequisite."

8. Loriene Roy, "Diversity in the Classroom: Incorporating Service-Learning Experiences in the Library and Information Science Curriculum," *Journal of Library Administration* 33, no. 3–4 (2001): 213–28.

9. Melvil Dewey, "School of Library Economy at Columbia College," *Library Journal* 9, no. 7 (July 1894): 118.

10. Ball and Schilling, "Service Learning."

11. Oberg and Samek, "Humble Empowerment."

12. Ibid.

13. Edgar Schein, *Organizational Culture and Leadership* (San Francisco: Wiley, 2004).

14. Ball and Schilling, "Service Learning."

15. Thomas Peters and Robert Waterman, *In Search of Excellence: Lessons from America's Best-Run Companies* (New York: HarperCollins, 2004).

16. Loriene Roy, "Supporting LIS Education Through Practice," www.ala.org/ala/hrdr/abouthrdr/hrdrliaisoncomm/committeeoned/EdForum2007Roy-SRA.pdf.

17. Berry, "Practice Prerequisite."

18. Ibid.

19. Roy, "Supporting LIS Education Through Practice."

20. Oberg and Samek, "Humble Empowerment."

21. Ibid.

22. Ibid.

23. Mehra and Bishop, "Cross-Cultural Perspectives."

24. Katherine Cveljo, "Internationalizing LIS Degree Programs: Internationalizing Library and Information Science Degree Programs—Benefits and Challenges for Special Librarians" (April 25, 1996), www.sla.org/content/SLA/professional/businesscase/acteng/cveljo.cfm?style=text; Marshall McLuhan, *Understanding Media* (London: Routledge, 2006).

25. Mehra and Bishop, "Cross-Cultural Perspectives."

26. E. J. Josey, "Meeting the Challenge: Educating for Universal Library and Information Service," in *Translating an International Education to a National Environment,* ed. Julie I. Tallman and Joseph B. Ojiambo (Metuchen, NJ: Scarecrow, 1990), 1–12.

27. Cveljo, "Internationalizing LIS Degree Programs."

28. Mehra and Bishop, "Cross-Cultural Perspectives."

29. Robert G. Bringle, Richard Games, and Edward A. Malloy, *Colleges and Universities as Citizens* (Boston: Allyn and Bacon, 1999).

30. Oberg and Samek, "Humble Empowerment."

31. Ball and Schilling, "Service Learning."

32. Berry, "Practice Prerequisite."

33. Mehra and Bishop, "Cross-Cultural Perspectives."

Chapter 8

Service Learning Connecting Diverse Communities and LIS Students and Faculty

Loriene Roy

In the realm of service engagement, it is logical that students will be interested in working with communities unlike their own. Students and their faculty supervisors may seek out opportunities—or be invited to participate at settings—that serve patrons from varying social, economical, ethnic, or cultural backgrounds. This chapter addresses the conceptual framework of such work by discussing our motivations for interacting with cultural communities, the roles of community outsiders and insiders, interaction behavior as defined by etiquette or protocol, a draft protocol for engaging with indigenous communities, and suggestions for the products of such collaborations. Because the author and her students engage in service work with Native peoples, the examples provided are most appropriate for working with those audiences. The author also speaks from the perspective of an indigenous person: she is Anishinabe, enrolled on the White Earth Reservation, a member of the Minnesota Chippewa Tribe, Pembina band, makwa or bear clan.

Motivation to Work with Communities of Color

Motivation to serve others may be explained by understanding altruistic motivation. In 1975 Hoffman posited that a feeling of "sympathetic distress" might motivate individuals to engage in helping behaviors.[1] This motivation to act is also influenced by whether or not an individually felt intervention is the responsibility of a larger group or whether an individual on his own might make a difference. In fact, perceiving that someone is in need might prompt someone to experience a sympathetic distress that will continue until action is taken or until the observer is able to justify his reasons for not taking action. Empathy—rather than sympathy—is an even more accepted explanation for why people engage in altruism.[2] Empathy implies a level of circumspection where people express a caring concern about the welfare of others that is more sympathetic than demeaning.

Those attracted to careers in the fields of library and information science are often motivated by a desire to make a difference in the world. Typically, applicants to LIS programs note two explanations for why they are seeking a degree: love of books and reading and love of people. These enduring sentiments can sustain students in their programs of study and help them identify a specialization area within the field. From the beginnings of formal education for librarianship, students have been provided with options—or even have been required—to use their developing skills in the workplace.[3] The volunteer ethic continues once students graduate and enter the field. In 1896 a Massachusetts public librarian reminded his colleagues that "it is the duty of every man to set apart some of his time and strength to be devoted to the welfare of the community in which he lives."[4] The rationale for "doing good" was also felt to be based on internal rewards: "no librarian can enter into the improvement of the social and intellectual life of the community without gaining strength himself."[5]

Roy found that the experiences of LIS program master's student interns at tribal community centers were "impacted by role identification, scheduling, communication, skills set, expectations, and personal attributes."[6] Successful interns were those who displayed initiative, maturity, flexibility, and persistence. While no intern left the program, their enthusiasm and commitment for the work increased when they were able to physically visit their communities of service.

The challenge within the LIS professions is to arm students with the skills to actualize their intrinsic altruism. Such sentiments must be tempered with reality and a perspective that places user needs at the center of any efforts. Thus, students might have to challenge their own motivations by humbling themselves to serve.

Insider and Outsider Relationships

Through service learning, LIS students may serve as a bridge between communities of service and sources of information they might find of value. The task is often perceived as one of bringing opportunity to those who lack it. These actions may be taken in response to patron needs or even in anticipation of need. In return, students find personal meaning and value and forge a commitment to their newfound careers. This liaison role sets up an insider/ outsider relationship with information workers living and working outside of the world of those inside the cultural communities they serve. As Kusow notes, the insider/outsider dichotomy might reflect more the characteristics of a specific service environment than the characteristics of the liaison.[7] That is, socioeconomic differences between LIS students and the individuals they serve do not demarcate the insider/outsider relationship. The distance between liaison and recipient is created more from the settings where interaction takes place.

Typically, each role—insider or outsider—claims certain advantages and weaknesses. This dichotomy was often described by characteristics such as the following. Insiders' strengths were described as "easy access, the ability to ask more meaningful questions and read non-verbal cues, and most important, be able to project a more truthful, authentic understanding of the culture under study," while outsiders benefited from "curiosity with the unfamiliar, the ability to ask taboo questions, and being seen as non-aligned with subgroups."[8] Insider researchers within indigenous communities "also need to define closure and have the skills to say 'no' and the skills to say 'continue.'"[9] In reality, insider/outsider roles often overlap and are more likely defined by the influences of "positionality, power, and representation."[10]

Insider/outsider role assignment may result from perceptions. Library researchers may view the community insiders as impoverished. Chatman defined an impoverished life as one that involved and valued "risk-taking, secrecy, deception, and situational relevance."[11]

Risk taking is tied closely to the concept of trust: community insiders tie their ability to trust an outside source with the perceived risk of danger or personal compromise. Secrecy is seen in the private ownership of cultural expressions. For example, within tribal communities there may be social expressions, such as dance, that can be witnessed by anyone, while the communities might hold their own observances or sacred dances that can only be witnessed by tribal members. Deception, or deliberate misinformation, may be an act to protect community knowledge or lead outsiders away from community areas of concern. When an exchange with an outsider is perceived as useful, then an insider might justify that it is situationally relevant. The notion of situational relevance then becomes a screen through which outsiders and their connections must pass through in order to be found acceptable.

LIS faculty and students will want to consider their insider/outsider roles when reflecting on service learning experiences. These deliberations will help elevate discussions above case-specific or even gossip-ridden conversations. The inclusion of theoretical modeling of group dynamics may diminish a feeling of intrusion on the part of students involved in service learning activities while still allowing for social bonding.

Protocol and Etiquette

Protocol and etiquette refer to the ethical structures that govern human interactions, especially those that are research or study based. Communities other than one's own have locally and culturally based mores and frameworks of behavior. Some of these behaviors can be described as etiquette: "the practices and forms prescribed by social convention or by authority."[12] Etiquette is respectful human contact, often learned and culturally specific. Other behaviors follow cultural protocols and can be tied to historic ritual or contemporary negotiation of performance. Protocol not only guides community members in their interactions with each other, but increasingly explains the expected behaviors of outsiders working within communities. Cultural protocol "controls interpersonal relationships, provides ways for groups to meet and interact, and even determines how individuals identify themselves."[13]

Today, academics are familiar with following research protocols through seeking approval from institutional review boards (IRBs). This process generally consists of submitting a research proposal, with details on how the research participants provide informed consent. Often, researchers must document their preparation for conducting such studies. Preparation generally includes the completion of research methods classes, research conducted in well-known laboratories or with recognizable researchers, and the completion of human subjects research training, such as online courses available through the National Cancer Institute of the U.S. National Institutes of Health.[14] Such awareness of the needs of research subjects evolved from cases of severe abuse, such as Nazi-sponsored medical experiments conducted during World War II and the Tuskegee syphilis study conducted from the 1930s until 1972.

Although IRBs might require stringent review for work with vulnerable populations such as minors, women, and incarcerated individuals, they might not recognize special considerations in working with communities of color. One exception is Northern Arizona University, which states that for "research being conducted with Native American people or groups . . . additional review by the appropriate Tribal entity may be required."[15]

Students engaged in service learning should be aware that their involvement may be governed by both institutional and cultural protocols. They may need to develop skills that enable them to walk confidently on the narrow, sometimes contradictory margins between these perspectives. For example, students who routinely gather evidence through photography and/or audio will need to abide by tribal regulations regarding such documentation.

Resistance to outsider visits in tribal lands is linked to histories of mis-behavior and opportunism on the part of researchers. Smith frames the writing of her critical text, *Decolonizing Methodologies: Research and Indigenous Peoples,* by stating: "The word itself, 'research,' is probably one of the dirtiest words in the indigenous world's vocabulary."[16] The presence of sometimes well-meaning outsiders is tied to the history of colonialism, where the impact of strangers with strong belief systems led to the loss of Native language, appropriation of cultural symbols and belief systems, loss of land, and permanent alterations in traditional ways of life.

Although presented as a public good, those involved in service learning must be cognizant that their work will be equated with research in the minds of many and that "research is not an innocent or distant academic exercise but an activity that has something at stake and that occurs in a set of political and social conditions."[17] Smith describes how indigenous and Western views differ regarding sets of concepts such as race, gender, individuals, societies, space, and time.

There are dangers in service work. One is that of potential dilettantism. Service work with communities of color should not be undertaken merely to sample cultures or gather a good story to tell. Once students start to communicate and work with user communities, they may be expected to maintain those relationships indefinitely. Indigenous people often had research or service foisted upon them. They have often been forced into the role of passive objects of research. Efforts should be made to share authority in the work, share credit, and equate levels of power and decision making.

Students should also be cautioned against overgeneralization. Smith describes how indigenous people respond to generalized research statements: "It galls us that Western researchers and intellectuals can assume to know all that it is possible to know of us, on the basis of their brief encounters with some of us."[18] This is one way to assure community members that one's intentions are not solely for personal gain. Although American Indian tribes may share some common characteristics, such as a type of teasing humor and a strong reverence for military service, they are sovereign nations that can vary greatly from each other with regard to language, history, customs, and contemporary life. Those working with tribal communities should emphasize specificity in their communication with members of the service learning community by, for example, referring to the tribe by its preferred name.

Process

Documents that provide guidance in working with Native peoples have been developed by individual research groups, tribal cooperatives, and sovereign Native nations. These materials are especially useful in illustrating how to gain trust among members of a Native community. Past models of working within these communities have been built on one-on-one alliances whereby individual researchers worked with individual members of tribal communities. These relationships, while personal and social, often raised specters of suspicion because Native information providers were vulnerable to the sometimes undisclosed motives of the researcher. Awareness is building that consent by individual tribal members is not equated with respecting community-held knowledge and approval. Cultural content is often owned by the entire community and is not at the disposal of one community member.

One such guiding document is the Alaska Native Knowledge Network's *Guidelines for Respecting Cultural Knowledge*. This document delineates the responsibilities of both tribal and nontribal members in respecting culture. Native elders are called on to "seek out information on ways to protect intellectual property rights and retain copyright authority over local knowledge that is being shared with others for documentation purposes," and authors and illustrators are advised to "arrange for copyright authority and royalties to be retained or shared by the person or community from which the cultural information originated and follow local protocols for its approval and distribution."[19] Advice is also given to curriculum developers and administrators, educators, editors and publishers, document reviewers, researchers, Native-language specialists, Native community organizations, and the general public.

Researchers and volunteers working in cultural communities are usually well schooled in Western research methodologies. In many cases, observers in indigenous communities will have to moderate research skills in order to successfully interact with communities of color. Smith identifies an agenda for indigenous research based on the actions of healing, decolonization, transformation, and mobilization.[20] She delineates a number of case studies that employ specific methods that intersect and support this indigenous research agenda, including efforts involving claiming, testimonies, storytelling, celebrating survival, remembering, indigenizing, intervening, revitalizing, connecting, reading, writing, representing, gendering, envisioning, reframing, restoring, returning, democratizing, networking, naming, protecting, creating, negotiating, discovering, and sharing.

Roy and Larsen described adapting Cajete's model of indigenous learning styles in a graduate class with a large service learning component. An indigenous person's journey through life is a series of interconnected circles of explorations, encompassing those actions of being, asking, seeking, making, having, sharing, and celebrating.[21] Take, for example, the act of questioning. Cajete described how asking questions is just one step in the process of living a fulfilled life as an indigenous person.[22] One way to prepare students for work in tribal communities is to model their classroom experiences along this indigenous model of learning, starting with being or deep understanding of themselves and their genealogy. In starting an educational experience with this stage, students might introduce themselves to each other and to their service community "culturally, and by learning style and cardinal direction, specific content contributed, and/or technological applications utilized."[23] At another meeting, LIS students might discuss their reflections on indigenous values, such as the Native Hawaiian values of belonging, mastery, observation, listening, reflection, questioning, independence, and generosity.[24]

Henare describes how barriers are maintained between the Maori, the indigenous peoples of New Zealand, and the Pakeha, those of European descent in that country: "Barriers are being created unnecessarily by the hypersensitivity of the Maori and the insensitivity of the Pakeha to Maori aspirations. But with goodwill, greater understanding, and better knowledge of each other's values and culture, these barriers can be demolished."[25]

While issues of protocol might at first seem unusual, time-consuming, or overly structured, they present means for students to learn about culture firsthand. By carefully and respectfully following cultural protocols, students learn to negotiate environments, develop deep connections, and learn about themselves.

LIS educators, community members, and students can create their own protocols for establishing productive and satisfying service learning environments. A sample protocol might include the following statements, drafted after years of connecting students with indigenous communities.

LIS educators may contribute to the service learning experience through

    a.   Seeking opportunities to collaborate with tribal communities on service learning options for students

b. Following tribal protocol for access to community members and cultural materials
c. Helping students prepare for working with tribal communities by assigning background reading and attending community social events
d. Thoughtfully matching students and cultural community sites
e. Carefully delineating the roles of all partners in the service learning program
f. Providing tribal members with opportunities for input and evaluation
g. Providing a continuous evaluation component of the service engagement, including recording of students' private reflections as well as group sharing
h. Providing tribal community members with copies of any products and/or information gathered
i. Thanking tribal communities for their involvement

LIS students may contribute to the service learning experience through

a. Reading culturally appropriate materials about the tribal community and attending public social events hosted by Native communities
b. Respectfully receiving cultural content without demanding to learn culturally protected information
c. Challenging their personal motivations for working with tribal communities
d. Reflecting on their own cultural heritage
e. Weighing student schedules with tribal community calendars
f. Crediting contributions of community members in documenting the development of products of the service engagement experience
g. Thanking tribal communities for their support

Tribal communities may contribute to the service learning experience through

a. Leading the LIS educators and students to any available guidelines or protocol governing the access and use of cultural material
b. Protecting cultural knowledge, including retaining access to relevant material
c. Informing LIS educators and students about cultural calendar events and restrictions

    d.   Sharing news about the service learning engagement with relevant tribal members and/or organizations

    e.   Sharing service engagement results and products with relevant tribal entities

    f.   Participating in the evaluation of the service learning experience

Products

The days are long gone when it was acceptable for researchers and community volunteers to elect to share what they learned when working with cultural communities with those community members. Work is now much more collaborative and might best be described by the process of shared authority. Oral history methodology recognizes that "collaborative oral history—sometimes called 'reciprocal ethnography'—involves the process of engaging our interviewees in the analysis of the interviews we generate and/or the creation of any products drawn from those interviews."[26] Shopes describes the challenge of shared authority:

> Collaborative work is personally and intellectually demanding, requiring an ability—even the courage—to deal with people and situations that can be difficult; a certain tolerance for ambiguity and uncertainty about how a project will work out; a willingness to take risks, not follow established protocols, and make decisions based on the logic of the work itself.[27]

In most cases, research and collaboration with communities of color results in some textual document. Value is attributed to these materials, whether it is seen as a line on a researcher's résumé, a book contract, or resulting invitations to present research findings at conferences or other venues. In some cases, researchers have abused their collaborative relationships by disclosing cultural content, withholding copies of products from the community, or conducting studies in ways that community members did not sanction. These cases create suspicions between communities that might only be settled through years of negotiation. As a result, communities of color might want to be excluded from some projects or efforts, especially those that purport to document their heritage or depict a desirable or average way of life. Until there are sufficient tribal community members who are trained, available, and interested in conducting research and coordinating service activities in their communities, we will continue to need to forge productive, sincere, and generous communities of service.

Conclusion

The intersection between service learning, LIS educators, LIS students, and communities of color is rich, rewarding, and intensely experiential. These settings form unique environments that not only have the potential for creating meaningful end products but may also promote self-reflection. In many ways, such work replicates the creations of family or even clan units, with individuals connected to each other through shared purposes despite their individual differences.

Student reflections perhaps best state the impact of collaborating on cross-cultural service learning initiatives. Students in a graduate Library Instruction and Information Resources class prepared a virtual library of education resources for pre-service teachers at Northwest Indian College, a tribal college located in Washington State. Comments in their reflective essays illustrate the students' skills acquisition as well as the deeper learning that took place:

> Building the virtual library taught me much more than how to manipulate software applications; it taught me to listen to people and to keep others' wishes ahead of my own as I created a work that was not for me alone . . . Now, I am truly invested in my and my classmates' creation and am proud of my work.

> I am emerging from this class with new experiences, skills, and interpersonal connections. At the center of my being, I have changed for the better, and created out of this experience a fuller understanding of life. As I apply the skills I have learned and new experiences to other aspects of my life, another cycle will begin.

> Our group came together and negotiated a large project that will have a life beyond our class, and it thus stands in my mind as a singular event in my library school career.[28]

These comments illustrate that service learning is not only useful but brings excitement and purpose to the educational experiences of both instructors and students.

NOTES

1. Martin L. Hoffman, "Developmental Synthesis of Affect and Cognition and Its Implications for Altruistic Motivation," *Developmental Psychology* 11, no. 5 (1975): 607–22.

2. Miho Toi and C. Daniel Batson, "More Evidence That Empathy Is a Source of Altruistic Motivation," *Journal of Personality and Social Psychology* 43, no. 2 (August 1982): 281–92.

3. Loriene Roy, "Diversity in the Classroom: Incorporating Service-Learning Experiences in the Library and Information Science Curriculum," *Journal of Library Administration* 33, no. 3–4 (2001): 213–28.

4. Charles Knowles Bolton, "The Librarian's Duty as a Citizen," *Library Journal* 21, no. 5 (May 1896): 219.

5. Ibid.

6. Loriene Roy, "Building Tribal Community Support for Technology Access," *Electronic Library* 24, no. 4 (2006): 517–29.

7. Abdi M. Kusow, "Beyond Indigenous Authenticity: Reflections on the Insider/ Outsider Debate in Immigration Research," *Symbolic Interaction* 26, no. 4 (Fall 2003): 591–99.

8. Sharan B. Merriam and others, "Power and Positionality: Negotiating Insider/ Outsider Status within and across Cultures," *International Journal of Lifelong Education* 20, no. 5 (September/October 2001): 405–16.

9. Linda Tuhiwai Smith, *Decolonizing Methodologies: Research and Indigenous Peoples* (New York: Zed Books, 1999).

10. Merriam and others, "Power and Positionality."

11. Elfreda A. Chatman, "The Impoverished Life-World of Outsiders," *Journal of the American Society for Information Science* 47, no. 3 (March 1996): 193–206.

12. *The American Heritage Dictionary of the English Language.*

13. Ibid.

14. U.S. National Institutes of Health, National Cancer Institute, "Human Participant Protections Education for Research Teams," http://cme.cancer.gov/ clinicaltrials/learning/humanparticipant-protections.asp.

15. Northern Arizona University, "Institutional Review Board for the Protection of Human Subjects: The Informed Consent Procedure," www.research.nau.edu/vpr/ IRB/icdprocess.htm#D.

16. Smith, *Decolonizing Methodologies.*

17. Ibid.

18. Ibid.

19. Assembly of Alaska Native Educators, *Guidelines for Respecting Cultural Knowledge* (Anchorage, AK, 2000), www.ankn.uaf.edu/publications/knowledge .html.

20. Smith, *Decolonizing Methodologies.*

21. Loriene Roy and Peter Larsen, "Oksale: An Indigenous Approach to Creating a Virtual Library of Education Resources," *D-Lib Magazine* 8, no. 3 (March 2002), www.dlib.org/dlib/march02/roy/03roy.html.

22. Gregory Cajete, *Look to the Mountain: An Ecology of Indigenous Education* (Skyland, NC: Kivaki, 1994).

23. Roy and Larsen, "Oksale."

24. Malcolm Naea Chun, *Pono: The Way of Living* (Honolulu: University of Hawaii, Curriculum Research and Development Group, 2006).

25. Hiwi Tauroa and Pat Tauroa, *Te Marae: A Guide to Customs and Protocol* (Auckland, NZ: Reed, 1986).

26. Alicia J. Rouverol, "Collaborative Oral History in a Correctional Setting: Promise and Pitfalls," *Oral History Review* 30, no. 1 (Winter/Spring 2003): 61–85.

27. Linda Shopes, "Commentary: Sharing Authority," *Oral History Review* 30, no. 1 (Winter/Spring 2003): 103–10.

28. Roy and Larsen, "Oksale."

Chapter 9

Puentes de la Comunidad
Exploring the Impact of LIS Service Learning on Library Services to Latino Youth in the Carolinas

Jamie Campbell Naidoo

This has turned out to be a marvelous networking opportunity . . . one of the results of the [service learning component] has been to instigate the forming of a bond between one of the elementary schools and the public library in our county.

—Susan Suárez

Susan and I stay in touch and hope to continue to work together to help our Latino community. Thank you for helping me find a way to do this!

—Susan Hansen

On July 1, 2002, Latinos became the largest ethnic minority in the United States, with 38,800,000 residents identifying themselves as Latino.[1] More recent estimates indicate that 44,300,000 U.S. residents identify themselves as Latino.[2] Further predictions suggest that the Latino population will make up 36 percent of the total U.S. population by the year 2125.[3] In the meantime, they continue to be the youngest and fastest-growing ethnic minority in the country.

According to U.S. Census Bureau data, South Carolina's Latino population increased over 350 percent between 1990 and 2005, from roughly 30,000 to 135,000. Similarly, the Pew Hispanic Center reports that Latinos make up 3.5 percent, or almost 150,000, of the population in South Carolina and 6.7 percent, or over 595,000, of the population in North Carolina. However, based on immigration rates, school enrollment data, and birthrates, researchers at the University of South Carolina's Consortium for Latino Immigration Studies estimate that South Carolina's Latino population is actually between 400,000 and 500,000, with many of these Latino immigrants being undocumented. The Pew Hispanic Center also reports that the Latino school-age population of individuals ages 5 to 17 in the new settlement areas of the South, which include both North and South Carolina, grew by 322 percent between 1990 and 2000.[4] During this same period, the Latino preschool population of those age 4 and under in the new settlement areas increased by 382 percent. As a result of this influx, an increasing percentage of young library patrons in the Carolinas are of

Latino origin. Unfortunately, little information is available on the current level of services for Latino youth in public libraries throughout either state.

Through a new course offering entitled Literacy Materials and Services for Latino Youth, the University of South Carolina's School of Library and Information Science (SLIS) has attempted to facilitate understanding of Latino youth services in school and public libraries in the Carolinas and to equip future and current library professionals with the essential skills needed for planning services to Latino youth and their families. A component of the graduate course involves community engagement between SLIS students and children's librarians.

This chapter outlines the current service learning component of this new course, highlighting examples of the collaborative engagement between students and children's librarians to create a shared knowledge and socialization network among information professionals throughout the Carolinas interested in serving Latino youth. It also describes another service learning opportunity in which future students of the course share their knowledge of library services and the literacy needs of Latino youth with educators, teachers, and librarians from across the nation. The chapter then details how the initial service learning component of the course led to a subsequent collaboration between the course instructor and the South Carolina State Library in a new grant-supported initiative entitled SPLASH! Launching Successful Library Services for South Carolina's Spanish Speakers. This initiative examines the current services and programs for Spanish speakers and Latinos in all of the state's public libraries. Finally, the chapter concludes with a discussion of the preliminary findings from the SPLASH! survey and details the future training efforts of SLIS to prepare librarians and educators in the Carolinas to serve Latino children and young adults.

Literacy Materials and Services for Latino Youth

Initiated in the summer of 2007, Literacy Materials and Services for Latino Youth is one of the first graduate courses in the United States designed to specifically educate librarians on how to select materials and plan programs and services for Latino youth and their families.[5] The course introduces a wide variety of print and nonprint resources suitable for Latino youth from birth to age 14 and provides the appropriate techniques for their effective evaluation. In addition, the course explores literature-based activities and programs for Latino youth, with an emphasis on helping future and current librarians learn strategies for successfully working with diverse Latino populations in both public and school library settings. Among the topics the course addresses are the following ones: understanding Latino cultures; the growing Latino population in the Carolinas; origins and development of juvenile literature about Latinos; notable Latino youth authors and illustrators; distinctive genres and their characteristics; cultural authenticity; the nature and function of illustrations; social issues addressed in multicultural literature today; problematic aspects in contemporary youth literature about Latinos; critical approaches to choosing developmentally and culturally appropriate, quality youth literature about Latinos; and suggestions for designing library/literacy programs and services that connect Latino youth, their families, and high-quality books.

Description of the Latino Youth Service Learning Project

A key component of the graduate course is community engagement between graduate students and children's librarians in public and school libraries throughout the Carolinas. This component is developed through a service learning project that bridges classroom theory and current practice to connect students with practicing librarians. Students have the opportunity to learn how actual libraries in the Carolinas serve Latino patrons. Current librarians share their expertise about serving Latino populations and learn innovative ways from students on how to select materials or plan programs. Boyle-Baise affirms this pedagogy, stating that "service learning offers a structure for community-based learning, collaborative in intent, responsive to local needs, reflective upon experience, and integrated into course content."[6]

Students select a "partner library" that serves Latino youth or is located in an area with a growing Latino population. They then must interview the children's librarian or school library media specialist, depending on the type of library, to determine the current level of programs and services available to Latino youth and their families. Students also examine the partner library to identify potential cultural barriers between library staff and Latino youth and suggest improvements to the current services offered. Using their knowledge of appropriate environments for Latino patrons, students further examine the partner library's collections, signage, programs, and so forth, to ascertain the friendliness of the library for Spanish-speaking Latino patrons. The results of the observations and interviews are compiled and reported to classmates and the professor via Blackboard, an online classroom management software system.

These results serve multiple purposes. First, they alert students to the practices in local libraries for serving Latino youth. This allows the students to compare current practice with their background knowledge from their readings and other coursework and make suggestions for improvement. Suggestions are incorporated into a report shared directly with partner libraries. This provides a snapshot of their current services and helps them understand ways to improve their library services to Latino patrons. Students who are engaged in creating this report are using higher-order thinking skills to synthesize information from the field with classroom knowledge. Consequently, they develop a deeper understanding of the concerns involved in developing programs and services for a targeted audience.

The results of the observations and interviews are also used by the professor to determine the specific needs of local libraries in relation to serving Latino children. This information is incorporated into workshops and conference sessions aimed directly at training librarians about Latino services. In addition, the professor uses the information to develop questionnaires on library services that are distributed to children's librarians across the state via a cooperative alliance with the South Carolina State Library, an effort discussed later in this chapter.

Student Outcomes of the Service Learning Project

Students participating in the service learning component of the course have the opportunity to create a shared knowledge and socialization network with other information professionals. They are making connections with librarians who can serve as their mentors or collaborative partners once they enter the profession. As with other service learning projects, the student learning outcomes vary according to the amount of time students dedicate to the project. Those students enrolled in the initial course offered in summer 2007 experienced various levels of involvement that ranged from maintaining contact only through the duration of the assignment to creating enduring cooperative alliances between school and public libraries.

Obtaining Employment

One student in South Carolina received her current public library position through a contact she made through the service learning project. In a personal communication to the professor, she wrote, "The librarian that I interviewed for the Latino course is currently my immediate supervisor. The fact that I had to interview someone is what prompted me to volunteer at this library, and the fact that I was volunteering here made me a better candidate for a job when one became available." The student also explained that her knowledge of materials and services for Latino youth was another important factor in obtaining her current employment.

Building Community Partnerships

Another student, a school library media specialist at East Elementary School in Monroe, North Carolina (Union County Public Schools), developed a rich relationship with the Hispanic services librarian at the Union County Public Library. This partnership has led to various visits from the public library to the school for Latino-focused programming. Public librarian Susan Suárez remarks that the service learning project has "turned out to be a marvelous networking opportunity."[7] She met with the student, answered her interview questions, gave her a tour of the public library, explained her job functions, and introduced her to the department assistant, Oscar Ortiz. Then they set up a tentative date when Oscar and Susan would visit the student's elementary school library media center to share knowledge about their Hispanic heritage. Later in November 2007, Oscar and Susan conducted their Hispanic Heritage program four times for an audience of over 125 Latino children in the first through fifth grades. The children were excited to see adults who shared their same heritage, spoke their language, and enjoyed sharing culturally relevant stories. After the event Susan Hansen, the school library media specialist and student in the Latino Youth course, remarked, "The children enjoyed their time with Susan and Oscar so much that they are asking for more visits. They loved meeting bilingual friends!"[8]

This initial visit from the public library to the elementary school library media center sparked a synergy that led to other programs. Following the success of the first event, Susan Suárez and Susan Hansen made another appointment in which the student was introduced to another librarian who conducts the Every Child Ready to Read program, an ALA early literacy initiative. Using East Elementary's school library media center, the librarian later conducted four early literacy programs with Spanish-speaking Latino parents and their preschool children. Again, this program was a huge success, as it brought Latino parents into the school library media center and introduced them to a librarian from the local public library. A connection such as this is essential for motivating Latino families to visit the public library and to become involved in the education of their children. If they know there is someone at the library who speaks Spanish and truly wants them to visit, then the likelihood of Latino families using the library and its services significantly increases.

In January 2008 Susan Suárez, Oscar Ortiz, and another librarian visited the elementary school library media center again with another program for Latino kindergarten students. During this event, the librarians read stories and shared music and danced with Latino children. Other programs have been planned for the future, including an assembly for all of the children to promote bilingual literacy in honor of "El día de los niños/El día de los libros" (Children's Day/Book Day), observed throughout the United States on or around April 30. The team is also working on several cooperative grants related to library services that would assist Latino parents in both settings.

Additional Student Outcomes from the Latino Youth Course

Students enrolled in the summer 2007 section of the course participated in pre- and post-tests, follow-up surveys, and interviews to help the professor ascertain their level of comprehension in relation to literacy materials and services for Latino youth. These measures suggest that participants acknowledge many practical implications of the service learning project and course content but desire further assistance in learning Spanish and developing community partnerships with local Latino agencies. Additionally, results of the assessments indicate an overall increase in student knowledge across the various areas relating to literacy materials and services for Latino youth. Table 9-1 presents these findings.

Table 9-1. Synthesis of pre- and post-test data of student knowledge outcomes

	% Increase in Student Knowledge	
Knowledge Areas	No Knowledge to Some Knowledge	Some Knowledge to Extensive Knowledge
Developmental needs of Latino youth	100%	33%
User needs of Latino youth	100%	75%
Library services for Latino youth	100%	60%
Youth literature about Latinos	100%	83%
Planning library programs for Latino youth	100%	75%
Locating print and electronic resources about library services to Latinos	All participants had at least some knowledge in this area	33%
Planning library services to the Latino community	100%	100%
Concerns in selecting translated materials	100%	67%

Future Service Learning and Community Outreach Opportunities for SLIS Students

In spring 2008 students enrolled in the Literacy Materials and Services for Latino Youth course will be encouraged to develop deeper connections from their service learning projects as they create not only outcome reports of their interviews and observations to share with their partner libraries, but also a list of the ten best resources for helping the library better serve Latino youth. These resources will be drawn from information that students have learned in the course.

Students will also share their knowledge of Latino services with educators, teachers, and librarians from across the nation as they create research posters to be presented at the University of South Carolina's first annual Celebration of Latino Children's Literature Conference.[9] This inaugural event represents a joint partnership between the College of Education and SLIS to prepare future and practicing educators, teachers, and librarians for the exciting career prospects of serving Latino youth. Concurrently, the conference provides a forum for presenting current research related to the education and information needs of Latino children and the social influences that Latino children's literature has upon the developing child. Students who participate in this event have a unique opportunity to share their course-related knowledge with practicing librarians and educators. Students' expertise will move beyond the boundaries of the Carolinas and influence library services to Latino youth nationally.

Making a Big SPLASH!

The service learning project of the Literacy Materials and Services for Latino Youth course also led to a collaborative project for the professor. Using the results of the student service learning projects, he created survey questions to measure the level of service that public libraries offered Latino youth and their families. Specifically, the professor addressed the following:

1. What programs and collections are being developed in public libraries in South Carolina to specifically target the Latino population?
2. What training is available to help the library staff discern how to serve Latino children and their families?
3. Is the physical environment of the children's department inviting to Latino children and their families?
4. Do the children's librarians collaborate with local Latino agencies and/or parent groups to learn how to better serve Latino children and their families?

These questions were combined with a survey administered by the South Carolina State Library to public libraries across the state. The survey is part of a project with WebJunction, an initiative funded through the Bill and Melinda Gates Foundation entitled SPLASH! Launching Successful Library Services for South Carolina's Spanish Speakers. This initiative examines the current services and programs for Spanish speakers and Latinos in all of the state's public libraries. In addition, SPLASH! offers workshops that discuss cultural diversity as well as suggestions for serving Latino residents.

For the professor, the partnership with SPLASH! allowed his survey questions to be integrated into an existing instrument distributed to all public libraries in South Carolina. The collaboration between the professor and the state library also afforded an opportunity for the professor's input related to the workshops conducted under the SPLASH! initiative.[10]

Preliminary Results from SPLASH! Surveys

Only preliminary data from the SPLASH! surveys are available. However, initial results indicate a huge disparity in the level of library services to Latino youth and highlight the urgent need for additional training related to serving this diverse population. Fewer than 25 percent of the libraries provide exceptional programs and services to Latino youth and their families, and the majority of South Carolina's libraries fail the informational and recreational needs of the state's majority minority. The subsequent paragraphs detail some of these deficiencies as related to programming, collections, and services to the Latino community. Potential barriers faced by libraries serving Latinos are also mentioned.

Areas of Concern

REFORMA (the National Association to Promote Library and Information Services to Latinos and the Spanish-Speaking), an affiliate of the ALA, is dedicated to (1) providing library services and programs to the Latino community; (2) building and promoting high-quality Spanish, bilingual, and culturally relevant collections; and (3) recruiting Latino and Spanish-speaking library professionals who will effectively serve the growing Latino population. The Carolina chapter of REFORMA is very active in creating an awareness of serving Spanish-speaking and Latino populations throughout libraries in the Carolinas. According to the initial results of the SPLASH! surveys, 70 percent of the public librarians in South Carolina were familiar with REFORMA and the association's objectives. However, the survey also suggested that the majority of these librarians do not adopt REFORMA's goals. For instance, half of the librarians indicated they are familiar with the developmental needs of Latino youth, yet 75 percent of South Carolina's libraries do not offer storytimes in Spanish or related to Latino themes, nor do they offer bilingual programs. Similarly, almost all of the libraries surveyed do not offer Spanish or bilingual programs for young adults. These practices contradict child and adolescent psychologists who maintain that youth learn best in their own language and need to be exposed to experiences that positively represent their culture.

Survey results further imply that many of the libraries in South Carolina may own collections that do not meet the needs of Latino youth. Over half of the librarians acknowledged that they have collections that include bilingual children's books as well as Spanish-language books for all age levels. Unfortunately, almost half of the librarians admitted that they cannot attest to the quality of the Spanish-language children's materials they purchase. The aforementioned problem is also applicable to children's and young adult materials about Latino cultures. It would seem that while many libraries do hold culturally specific or Spanish-language materials for youth, the librarians selecting and promoting these materials need additional training to ensure their accuracy.

One final concern highlighted by these preliminary findings relates to the level of services that Latino youth and their families receive from South Carolina public libraries. The survey results intimate that none of the librarians surveyed had detailed knowledge of how to find resources for serving Spanish-speaking and Latino populations. If librarians are not knowledgeable about the resources available to libraries serving Latino populations, how can they plan successful programs or ensure that they meet the needs of the Latino community?

Potential Barriers

The SPLASH! survey results emphasized barriers that could potentially influence the level of library services offered to Spanish-speaking and Latino patrons. Some librarians stated that they would not plan services for Latinos until "native" citizens such as African Americans also received high-quality service. These librarians noted that other populations in the state were not receiving adequate library services; thus, Latinos should not have preferential treatment over other minority groups.

Library funding is certainly a problem that libraries in South Carolina face, but it is not the only issue that prevents library services to Latino youth and their families. Several of the librarians surveyed indicated considerable concern in relation to the political ramifications of serving South Carolina's Latinos. Currently, a bill is being considered that prohibits services supported by tax dollars to undocumented individuals. If passed, this law would make it illegal for librarians to assist undocumented residents who make up a large portion of South Carolina's Latino population. Another bill—an English-only law—could eliminate bilingual and Spanish-language signage, brochures, and other documents integral to public libraries serving Spanish-speaking Latinos. The law would also influence Spanish and bilingual library programs and materials, restricting information access to all patrons who are not English literate. Librarians are worried that if they actively serve Latinos through specific library collections and programs, they will lose funding from local governments when anti-immigration legislation is passed. The prospect of financial cutbacks is not a gamble libraries are willing to take.

Additional Opportunities for Librarians Serving Latino Youth

The preliminary results of the survey underscore the need for culturally specific training for librarians across South Carolina on how to select materials and plan programs and services for the Latino community. In addition to the state library's SPLASH! workshops and SLIS's Literacy Materials and Services for Latino Youth course, there are numerous other efforts being launched by the University of South Carolina's SLIS program to prepare librarians and educators in the Carolinas to better serve Latino youth.

Celebration of Latino Children's Literature Conference

As mentioned previously, the University of South Carolina's Celebration of Latino Children's Literature Conference is an annual event to educate as well as celebrate. Teachers, librarians, educators, academicians, and college students have an opportunity to learn strategies for celebrating Latino culture through literature. At the same time, conference participants can learn approaches for working with Latino children in a classroom or library setting. The conference will invite researchers and practitioners from all over the world to visit South Carolina and share their expertise on serving Latino children and their families.

Through this avenue, librarians in South Carolina can learn how librarians in other states—such as Arizona, New Mexico, California, and Texas—successfully meet the needs of their Latino youth.

¡Imagínense! Latino Youth Literature and Literacy Initiative

Another project aimed at preparing educators in the Carolinas to serve Latino youth is the ¡Imagínense!: Latino Youth Literature and Literacy Initiative. This forthcoming multifaceted program combines current research and practice to assist librarians and teachers in meeting the literacy needs of Latino children and adolescents. Several key objectives outline the purpose of ¡Imagínense! These include

1. Emphasizing research on the literary and literacy needs of all Latino youth
2. Promoting early childhood and adolescent literacy among Latino families
3. Fostering acceptance of Latino cultures through the use of culturally relevant children's and young adult literature and resources
4. Educating librarians, teachers, and child-care workers about literacy services for Latino youth and their families
5. Supporting collaborative community-based projects that promote Latino literacy (understanding of the Latino culture)

Four smaller initiatives underscore the purpose of ¡Imagínense! These are research in the areas of Latino youth literacy and literature; training workshops for teachers, educators, and librarians on how to effectively work with Latino youth; a material evaluation collection that provides an opportunity to assess Spanish, bilingual, and culturally specific Latino print and nonprint resources; and community outreach to local Latino families and those agencies serving these families.

¡Imagínense! will allow engagement and connections among pre-service and practicing teachers and librarians, Latino literacy researchers, literacy agencies serving Latino youth, and the Latinos throughout the Carolinas and the East Coast. Through its initiatives, this program can help build community bridges and create a better future for our Latino youth.

Conclusion

The service learning project of the Literacy Materials and Services for Latino Youth course allows SLIS students to become advocates for Latino library services while assisting current libraries in finding needed resources for planning these services. The project will inevitably grow and change along with the needs of the students and partner libraries serving Latino youth. However, bridging classroom learning with current practice will always be at its core.

Implemented successfully, the service learning project is a win-win situation, with students gaining a current understanding of the challenges faced by librarians who are serving Latino youth and their families. At the same time, the project allows practicing librarians to benefit from students' current knowledge about library services to Latino youth. Collaboratively, the two groups can make libraries throughout the Carolinas environments where Latino youth and their families can hear a resounding *¡Bienvenidos!*

NOTES

The epigraphs for this chapter come from personal communications with Susan Suárez, Hispanic services librarian in the Union County (NC) service learning project, and Susan Hansen, school library media specialist in the Union County (NC) service learning project.

1. *Latino vs. Hispanic:* the terms *Latino* and *Hispanic* are labels often used interchangeably in U.S. society to refer to the same population of people who live in Mexico, Central and South America, and the Caribbean. However, each of the terms is a label loaded with both social and political implications and is accepted or rejected in various degrees by the people they purport to describe. It is important to note that the labels *Latino* and *Hispanic* are only used in the United States to describe this ethnic population. Jorge J. E. Gracia, in *Hispanic/Latino Identity: A Philosophical Perspective* (Malden, MA: Blackwell, 2000), provides a lengthy discussion on the issues and politics behind each term and describes the rationalizations used by the people who adopt one label over the other to describe themselves. Similarly, Suzanne Oboler, in "The Politics of Labeling: Latino/a Cultural Identities of Self and Others" (in *Transnational Latina/o Communities: Politics, Processes, and Cultures,* ed. Carlos G. Vélez-Ibàñez and Anna Sampio [Lanham, MD: Rowman and Littlefield, 2002]), describes the resistance of Latino people to the labels, stating that this minority of over 40,000,000 interprets the labels to be derogatory terms used by white American Anglos to describe the group as dirty and lower class. John M. Kibler, in "Latino Voices in Children's Literature: Instructional Approaches for Developing Cultural Understanding in the Classroom" (in *Children of La Frontera: Binational Efforts to Serve Mexican Migrant and Immigrant Students,* ed. Judith LeBlanc Flores [Charleston, WV: ERIC, 1996]), maintains that the term *Hispanic* is linked to conservative policy issues, while *Latino* is linked to liberal policy issues, and he reiterates that these labels are only used in the United States. Accordingly, in this chapter the term *Latino* is used to describe the people from Mexico, Central and South America, and the Caribbean in order to affirm the cultural heritage of the group and to adopt a more liberal approach to library services for this majority minority.

2. U.S. Census Bureau, 2007.

3. Jorge Ramos, *The Latino Wave: How Hispanics Will Elect the Next American President* (New York: Rayo HarperCollins, 2004).

4. Rakesh Kochhar, Roberto Suro, and Sonya Tafoya, "The New Latino South: The Context and Consequences of Rapid Population Growth" (2005), Pew Hispanic Center, http://pewhispanic.org/reports/report.php?ReportID=50.

5. This course was designed by the author; additional information on the learning goals, objectives, and assignments for the Literacy Materials and Services for

Latino Youth course can be found on the author's website (www.libsci.sc.edu/fsd/naidoo/jn.htm).

6. Marilynne Boyle-Baise, *Multicultural Service Learning: Educating Teachers in Diverse Communities* (New York: Teachers College Press, 2002).

7. Susan Suárez, personal communication.

8. Susan Hansen, personal communication.

9. Additional information about the Celebration of Latino Children's Literature Conference is available at www.libsci.sc.edu/latinoconf/index.htm.

10. SPLASH! workshops are managed by the Library Development unit of the South Carolina State Library as a joint project with WebJunction, which is generously funded by the Bill and Melinda Gates Foundation in partnership with OCLC. For additional information on SPLASH! consult the South Carolina State Library (www.statelibrary.sc.gov).

Chapter 10

Highlights of Service Learning Experiences in Selected LIS Programs

Sara Albert

In this chapter we describe required and optional service learning experiences in selected library and information science master's programs accredited by the ALA.[1]

McGill University, School of Information Studies

The School of Information Studies (SIS) at McGill University in Montreal, Quebec, offers an elective three-credit practicum.[2] A distinctive aspect of their practicum course is its flexibility in terms of being project based, operational based, or a hybrid. As one might assume, the project-based practica allow students to complete a project or multiple projects, while the operational-based practica focus on the day-to-day processes and services at the site. Regardless of the practicum type, students are expected to complete 120 hours of work, at least half at the practicum site. Practica may cover the areas of knowledge management, archival studies, or librarianship.

Students interested in the practicum course must submit an application to SIS staff, including a cover letter and curriculum vitae. Next, the practicum coordinator connects students with potential sites, and the site supervisors conduct student interviews. After a site supervisor has accepted a student, the two collaborate on a work plan for the semester. Students must maintain weekly log reports, provide midterm and final reports, and give a presentation at the end of the semester. Additional deliverables may be required, depending on the student's individual work plan. The practicum coordinator determines a pass or fail evaluation for each student.

San Jose State University, School of Library and Information Science

The School of Library and Information Science (SLIS) at San Jose State University (SJSU) is strongly focused on distance learning, with classes offered entirely online or in a hybrid online/on-site format.[3] In addition to three core courses, a research methods course, and electives, all students must fulfill the university requirement of a "culminating experience." This is accomplished by completing either a thesis course or an Advanced Topics in Library and Information Science course. A typical Advanced Topics course focuses on the students' development of an electronic portfolio (e-portfolio).

The e-portfolio is an online portfolio of written statements and evidentiary items that allows students to address how they have achieved the dozen or so core competencies of the program. Examples of these core competencies are to be able to "design, query, and evaluate information retrieval systems" and to "use service concepts, principles, and techniques that facilitate information access, relevance, and accuracy for individuals or groups of users."[4] Students are expected to spend at least 135 hours developing their e-portfolio and can earn three credits upon successful completion of the course. The course should be completed at the end of the program, but students can work on their e-portfolio as they move through their program of study. A major goal of the e-portfolio is to allow the students to make connections between LIS theory and practice. The last core competency is to be able to "contribute to the cultural, economic, educational, and social well-being of our communities," which demonstrates the program's emphasis on community involvement.[5] Students address their achievement of this competency in a "statement of professional philosophy" as part of the e-portfolio.

LIBR 294 Professional Experience: Internships is an elective course for San Jose State SLIS students desiring fieldwork in a credit course. Students can complete up to two internships, each from two to four credits, following the guideline of forty-five hours of work per credit. One faculty member serves as faculty advisor for all students in non-archival internships, and a second faculty member supervises archival internships. Students select a potential internship site and submit an application to the appropriate faculty supervisor. LIBR 292 Professional Experience: Projects is another elective fieldwork course supervised by an information professional. Students completing this course can earn three credits by working on a large project for an individual or organization.

In 2005 SJSU began its Executive MLIS program, a two-year program designed for experienced librarians without master's degrees. The program incorporates one- to three-week residency periods with distance learning courses. Each year a new cohort begins, and students follow the prescribed course progression with the other members of their cohort. The first four cohorts have all been required to complete the Executive MLIS Organizational Consulting Project, which comprises both a "culminating experience" Advanced Topics course and a Professional Experience: Projects course. Students individually choose a client (who may be their current employer), complete a project proposal for faculty and client approval, analyze the client's situation, perform relevant research, and ultimately make recommendations for improving the client's situation. The project is expected to take at least 320 hours of work time and to result in a 60- to 100-page report and presentation to the client.

Another special MLIS program with additional service learning requirements is the Teacher Librarianship specialization. Two capstone courses are required: the Advanced Topics course as well as School Library Fieldwork. The latter consists of supervised fieldwork in at least two different school library settings.

Syracuse University, School of Information Studies

The School of Information Studies at Syracuse University offers a variety of master's degrees, including the MSLIS, the MS in information management, and the MS in telecommunications in network management.[6] For our purposes here, we are only considering the MSLIS experience.

In addition to core courses and total credit hours prescribed for the MSLIS, students are also obligated to fulfill an exit requirement that can be either an internship or a cooperative education experience (co-op). An internship is worth three credit hours and requires that the student complete 150 hours of fieldwork. The guidelines are relatively flexible, especially in that there can be a special project or not. There is not a standard contract; instead, the internship contract is jointly developed by the student, the site supervisor, the faculty internship supervisor, and the student's advisor. A co-op is also worth three credit hours but involves more work time from the student and includes a paycheck. Internships, on the other hand, can be paid or not. For both internships and co-ops, students can consult with the career office or make their own contact with potential sites. A student's advisor can approve an independent study or a readings and research course instead of the internship/co-op requirement if the student already has sufficient work in the field.

For students desiring a school media specialization along with their MSLIS, there are more stringent service learning requirements, including two fifty-hour segments of fieldwork and two practicum courses. The practica are necessary for New York State certification for school media students. Students may begin the noncredit fieldwork portion after they have completed one semester in the program and may complete one or both fifty-hour segments in a semester. Each fifty-hour segment can be divided into one to three independent projects that can help the student fill in gaps or improve scores on her competency checklist. At the end of each fifty-hour experience, students submit a one-page summary of the project and any related deliverables. Students are encouraged to consider deliverables they create during their fieldwork for their professional portfolio.

School media students enroll in the practicum courses following completion of the fieldwork and at least twenty-five hours of credit. Each practicum requires 150 hours of actual work time and is worth three credit hours. The practica can both be undertaken in the same semester if desired. Students can work between two and five full days per week at the site until they have worked 150 hours in a professional apprentice role under a school media-certified, MSLIS-degreed site supervisor. At the completion of a practicum, the student submits a journal, a one-page summary of at least one major project, and a video of the student teaching. The site supervisor completes a student performance evaluation as well. Again, students are encouraged to include deliverables in their professional portfolio.

The fieldwork and practicum requirements are designed to give school media students exposure to different working environments. Fieldwork guidelines prescribe a combination of urban, suburban, and rural experience, and an urban setting is required for one practicum if possible. Half of the fieldwork hours and one of the two practica must be completed in an elementary setting and the remainder in a secondary setting.

University at Albany (State University of New York), Department of Information Studies

The Department of Information Studies at the University at Albany offers an MS in information science (MSIS) with five areas of concentration: archives and records administration, library and information services, library and information services/school library media specialist, information management and policy, and information systems and technology.[7] Although each of these concentrations entails specific curricula, all require the completion of a three-credit, 150-hour internship course or appropriate experience to waive or reduce the requirement.

Before enrolling in the internship course, students should have completed twenty-four graduate credits and should have completed or be enrolled in a set of specific courses depending on their chosen area of concentration. Students work with an assigned faculty advisor to come up with internship options and submit an application along with a current résumé to the internship coordinator. The internship coordinator reviews the application, consults with the student, and arranges a tentative placement to be confirmed after an interview between the student and the mentor or site supervisor. The internship should include a project and mostly professional-level responsibilities. Off-site, students may have additional assignments such as journals, reports, or assigned readings and/or individual or class meetings with their faculty supervisor. At the end of the internship, students receive a satisfactory or unsatisfactory evaluation.

Like Syracuse school media students, University at Albany school media students must complete 100 hours of fieldwork and two internship courses as part of their degree program to receive New York State certification. Albany students, however, can obtain the fieldwork hours via fieldwork components in their course sequence. Literature for Children, Literature for Young Adults, Technology in School Library Media Centers, The Curriculum and Supportive Resources, and Administration of School Media Centers are all required courses for school media students that include fieldwork hours to fulfill the 100-hour requirement.

School media students, unlike other MSIS Albany students, must take two rather than one three-credit internship course, each made up of 150 work hours, with one being in a school considered high needs. One of the two internships may be waived if a student has at least one year of experience as a full-time school library media specialist. Like Syracuse students, the Albany students are supposed to divide their fieldwork and internships equally between elementary and secondary settings.

Other service learning courses that can be taken as electives in the department include completing an approved field project as an independent study and an Advanced Internship in Information Science and Policy.

University of Michigan, School of Information

To earn the forty-eight-credit MS in information (MSI) at the University of Michigan School of Information, students must complete six credits that qualify for the Practical Engagement Program (PEP).[8] These Practical Engagement credits or "PEP points" are earned through internships, courses with service learning components, or the University Library Associates program.

All students must complete SI 501 Contextual Inquiry and Project Management as a core course for the MSI degree. This three-credit course provides one PEP point and is a prerequisite for enrolling in any Internship/Practical Experience course.

Summer internships must be sanctioned by the PEP office to be eligible for PEP credits, and students must enroll in the appropriate Internship/Practical Experience course in the summer semester or in the fall semester following the summer internship. To earn six credits (both toward the total number of credits as well as PEP credits), students are expected to work full-time for a minimum of ten weeks, with 360 hours of work being the minimum requirement. Internships during any term of the school year can earn one credit per sixty hours of work, up to six credits. Students are encouraged to consult iTrack, the school's online job search tool, as well as the university's Career Center, for potential internship opportunities; they can check with the PEP office to make sure a particular internship qualifies for PEP credits. All internships are undertaken with the cooperation of a faculty supervisor and a mentor professional in the field. Students do not earn a letter grade, but credit is determined based on a student's online e-portfolio containing biweekly reports, weekly blog entries, and a reflection/self-evaluation. The fieldwork supervisor also completes an evaluation. Student work is showcased on the School of Information website where each student has submitted a synopsis of his project, including objectives and outcomes.

Certain courses at the School of Information that involve service learning projects can provide a PEP credit as well. Examples of three-credit courses with a project component equivalent to one PEP credit include the aforementioned Contextual Inquiry and Project Management as well as Database Application Design, Evaluation of Systems and Services, Outcome-Based Evaluation of Programs and Services, and Computer-Supported Cooperative Work. Several three-credit Practical Engagement Workshop courses offer the opportunity to earn three PEP credits, with topics including Digital Librarianship, Information Technologies in Small Nonprofit Organizations, and Archives and Records.

A final way students can earn PEP credits is through participation in the University Library Associates program. In this program, full-time School of Information master's students selected for a two-year appointment work half-time for the university library and are compensated with a stipend, full tuition coverage, and benefits. As a snapshot example, at the time of this research there were eight students listed as current program participants. Library Associate students can enroll in the internship course during the fall and winter terms to earn one PEP credit for their work.

University of North Texas (UNT), School of Library and Information Sciences (SLIS)

For students without prior professional library experience, the UNT SLIS practicum is required for most students in fulfillment of the UNT graduate school requirement of an exit examination for master's students.[9] There are multiple sections and professors listed for the SLIS 5090 Practicum course, and students register for the appropriate section depending on their chosen course of study; for instance, public libraries or health informatics.

For students in the general section of the practicum, which envelops the areas of public libraries, school libraries, academic libraries, many special libraries, and information centers, the role of the faculty supervisor is minimized, with the responsibility for selecting a site and supervisor falling upon the student. Once a potential site has been located and a preliminary verbal agreement has been made between student and site supervisor, the student submits an application to the course professor. Other communications from student to professor take place online throughout the semester. The student completes assignments such as practicum objectives, a personal statement, a site description, and a final paper including personal reflection. This section requires students to complete 120 hours of work at the site.

The health informatics section of the practicum course has different specifications. Students in this section must complete 180 hours of fieldwork along with a project during the course of the experience, either with or without additional duties at the fieldwork site. The faculty advisor for this section maintains a more involved role, collaborating with the student to select a field site and site supervisor.

Unlike many other programs, the UNT SLIS practicum course (or previous fieldwork used to waive the practicum requirement) does not count toward the number of credits required for the degree.

University of Texas at Austin, School of Information

The School of Information (iSchool) at the University of Texas at Austin stipulates that all master of science in information studies (MSIS) students must take a capstone course, after completion of at least thirty-two credit hours in the program and typically during their final semester.[10] The capstone course can be any one of the following: Professional Experience Project (PEP), Master's Report, Master's Thesis, Practicum in School Libraries, Practicum in Preservation Planning, or Conservator Internship. Four of these six—all but the Master's Report and Master's Thesis—represent fieldwork experiences.

The PEP option involves a minimum of 125 hours of work at a library or other professional setting related to the student's course of study. Students select a faculty advisor, a site, and a site supervisor, while working with the Capstone Experience Office to follow specific guidelines. Project opportunities are listed in the capstone database, or students can propose their own ideas for approval. Evaluation methods vary case by case but are decided upon before the project commences and can include a journal, portfolio, oral or written report, site visits by the faculty advisor, and other methods. In addition, the field supervisor completes a performance evaluation and submits it to the faculty advisor at the end of the project. Ultimately students receive a credit or no-credit assessment, with three credits awarded for a successful experience.

The Practicum in School Libraries is also offered as a credit/no-credit three-hour course and is designed for students seeking a Standard School Librarian Certificate from the Texas State Board of Educator Certification. School library students must have completed or registered for Introduction to Information Resources and Services, Materials for Children or Materials for Young Adults, Descriptive Cataloging and Metadata, and School Library Management before beginning their practicum. This practicum requires 100 hours of work at a school library. Again, the field supervisor submits a performance evaluation, and the faculty supervisor determines if course credit has been earned.

The Practicum in Preservation Planning is the capstone course for students pursuing an MSIS with a Certificate of Advanced Study in Preservation Administration of Library and Archival Materials and consists of fieldwork in a library or archives lasting approximately five to six weeks.

Students seeking a Certificate of Advanced Study in Conservation of Library and Archival Materials in addition to the MSIS must complete specialized fieldwork following the successful completion of all other required conservation coursework. First is a fieldwork course focused on collection care in a library, archives, or other related setting. Next (or concurrent) is the nine-month conservator internship, which takes place in a conservation laboratory. Both the fieldwork and internship courses are credit/no-credit only. Some students may be able to do an independent study in lieu of the conservator internship.

At the end of the semester, students in all capstone courses at the iSchool must present their work at a poster session, which includes a ninety-second summary presentation for the audience followed by a traditional poster session, with students standing by their posters to discuss their work in more depth with interested attendees.

University of Washington, Information School

The Information School at the University of Washington offers the MLIS degree among a few others.[11] One graduation requirement for MLIS students is either a thesis or, more popularly, a portfolio, which, like the e-portfolio at San Jose State, allows students to provide evidence of their efforts in areas specified by the graduate program. At the University of Washington iSchool, the items in the portfolio should move beyond minimum course requirements but must be completed during the student's course of study. Among the five "essential areas" each student must address is "significant practical or service experience."[12] A review of sample portfolios on the school's website shows that students have submitted volunteer experiences, internships, directed fieldwork, and paid positions as evidence. This method of evaluation impresses upon students the importance of learning in the field while giving them freedom in how they pursue the experience. For those desiring guidance from the school as well as academic credit, the Directed Fieldwork course (LIS 590) is a natural choice.

Prerequisites for the Directed Fieldwork course are thirty hours of credit and an information session offered once or twice per quarter. Depending on the area of the fieldwork, students may also be expected to have completed subject-specific coursework such as reference or cataloging courses. Each Directed Fieldwork course typically lasts one quarter term and can take 100, 150, or 200 hours of work time from the student for two, three, or four credits, respectively. Students can undertake a second Directed Fieldwork course for additional credit, but it must be a different experience at a different location. The MLIS academic advisor can help students identify potential sites, and a list of over 100 suggested host sites is provided on the iSchool website. An information professional at the site serves as supervisor/mentor during the fieldwork. Students and site supervisors discuss progress and submit a midterm report to the faculty coordinator during the term. At the end of the term, site supervisors submit a final evaluation, and students submit a descriptive and self-evaluative report and complete an exit interview with the faculty coordinator for the fieldwork program.

Directed Fieldwork is popular but not required for most MLIS iSchool students. MLIS students seeking Washington State Library Media Endorsement, on the other hand, must take Directed Fieldwork and must do so under the supervision of a certified K–12 teacher librarian. Law MLIS students, too, are required to complete a Directed Fieldwork course for four credits and under the guidance of the director of the Law MLIS program. Law MLIS students have the added opportunity of the Law Library Intern program, in which the students are paid for working at local law libraries during the school year, typically ten hours per week. The intern program is optional but encouraged.

Valdosta State University, Master of Library and Information Science Program

The Master of Library and Information Science Program at Valdosta State University in Georgia offers an optional Supervised Fieldwork course (MLIS 7960) worth three credit hours. The online course description details the requirements of the course and expectations for the student, the faculty fieldwork coordinator, and the site supervisor.[13] As in many other programs, the fieldwork component is typically undertaken near the end of the student's studies in the graduate program.

At Valdosta State, the faculty fieldwork coordinator plays a large role in the planning of the fieldwork experience, including selecting a site and choosing a site supervisor for the student based on the student's professional interests and educational goals. The student is expected to complete 120 hours of work for the course and submit the required tangibles of a biweekly log and a final paper to the faculty coordinator. The field supervisor is also asked to complete an evaluation at the end of the experience.

The student's final paper must address several points, both descriptive and reflective. The reflective portions help to focus the student's attention on how the fieldwork experience has affected the student personally and could help the student relate the experience to her educational background as well as to advancement into the professional arena.

Wayne State University, Library and Information Science Program

To earn the MLIS degree offered by the Library and Information Science Program at Wayne State University, students are not required to complete a practicum or other service learning experience, but it is encouraged as a way to attain library experience.[14]

The program offers six different practicum courses with options including public, academic, health science, special, archives, and school media. To enroll in any of these practicum courses, students must have completed twenty-four hours toward their degree, including all but one of the core classes. In addition, the archives-focused practicum requires students to have completed the basic Archival Administration course as a prerequisite. There are graduated requirements for earning either two or three credits in a practicum course: 90 hours at the field site are required for two credits, while 135 hours are required for three credits.

Evaluation of the students is based on many factors. Students report their progress through a journal, work examples, and a critical analysis, and the site supervisor provides a performance evaluation.

Specializations in school media and archives do require a practicum. Students seeking a Graduate Certificate in Archival Administration must take a practicum in archives. MLIS students seeking Michigan School Library Media endorsements must take the School Media Practicum as part of the additional requirements of their specialization. Students must obtain prior consent from their advisor and have a teaching certificate if enrolled after April 1, 2004. This practicum option also stipulates that students develop a project to be completed at the site. This option, unlike the other Wayne State practica, awards students a letter grade rather than a pass/fail assessment.

Conclusion

The examples in this chapter illustrate the variety of service learning opportunities in selected LIS programs today: required or optional, credit or noncredit, closely supervised or largely self-directed. What ties them together is how they allow LIS students to extend their education beyond the classroom. Clearly, many LIS programs have recognized the value of such experiences in preparing their students for their professional careers.

NOTES

1. The information in this chapter is deemed current at the time of research, but program requirements or offerings are subject to change.

2. Information for this section was gathered from the Practicum section of the McGill SIS website at www.mcgill.ca/sis/practicum/.

3. Information for this section was gathered from the SJSU SLIS website at http://slisweb.sjsu.edu.

4. San Jose State University, School of Library and Information Science, "Statement of Core Competencies," http://slisweb.sjsu.edu/slis/competencies.htm.

5. Ibid.

6. Information for this section was gathered from the Syracuse University School of Information Studies website at http://istweb.syr.edu.

7. Information for this section was gathered from the University at Albany, State University of New York, Department of Information Studies website at www.albany.edu/cci/informationstudies/.

8. Information for this section was gathered from the University of Michigan SI website at www.si.umich.edu.

9. Information for this section was gathered from the UNT SLIS website at www.unt.edu/slis/.

10. Information for this section was gathered from the University of Texas iSchool website at www.ischool.utexas.edu.

11. Information for this section was gathered from the University of Washington iSchool website at www.ischool.washington.edu.

12. University of Washington Information School, "Portfolio Guidelines," www.ischool.washington.edu/mlis/portfolioguidelines.aspx.

13. Valdosta State University, Master of Library and Information Science, "Supervised Fieldwork: MLIS 7960: Policies and Procedures" (revised February 26, 2004), www.valdosta.edu/mlis/syllabi/documents/MLIS7960GUIDELINES.pdf.

14. Information for this section was gathered from the Wayne State LISP website at www.lisp.wayne.edu.

Chapter 11

Working from Within
Critical Service Learning as Core Learning in the MLIS Curriculum

Clara M. Chu

The Students Diversity Action Group (SDAG), a group of students at the University of California Los Angeles (UCLA) Department of Information Studies (IS) who wanted to have access to an antiracist and twenty-first-century education based on social justice, submitted a proposal in spring 2003 to the faculty for two core courses: one on technology and the other on cultural diversity. The adoption of these two new courses resulted in the decision to drop an existing core course, Design of Library and Information Services.[1] However, more important, this put UCLA IS in the position of being the only library, archival, and information studies program, nationally and internationally, to offer a required course addressing cultural diversity. Here I will focus on this course, its development into a service learning course, and experiences with the course.

Although past research has shown that institutional missions of LIS programs value cultural diversity, this is not necessarily substantiated in action.[2] In this particular case, the offering of a cultural diversity core course adheres to both our school mission and departmental vision and goals.[3] Appendix A includes these full statements. The mission statement for the Graduate School of Education and Information Studies (GSE&IS) is the scaffolding for the development of our vision and goals:

> GSE&IS is dedicated to inquiry, the advancement of knowledge, the improvement of professional practice, and service to the education and information professions. We develop future generations of scholars, teachers, information professionals, and institutional leaders. Our work is guided by the principles of individual responsibility and social justice, an ethic of caring, and commitment to the communities we serve.

There was much discussion about what would be a meaningful diversity course to prepare our students to work in a multicultural, technological, and information-overloaded globalized society. The professional challenges faced by current and future information professionals include technological, institutional, social, and ethical ones. The faculty made the decision that the coverage of ethics was an important component in addressing information services in our twenty-first-century multicultural communities and tasked a committee to develop this core course. With colleague Virginia Walter, then doctoral student Romelia Salinas, and I serving as a committee, we recognized that the course should not just be an intellectual exercise within the confines of the classroom but should provide students the opportunity to engage with real community information needs that could lead to their professional transformation. Through this transformative process the students would learn the power of information institutions to collect or exclude information, the importance of knowing actual community information needs, and the value of reflecting on the key role information institutions play in providing equity of information services. Thus, community participation or engagement was considered critical and resulted in the course not only addressing cultural diversity and ethics, but requiring service learning. This service learning course emphasizing ethics, diversity, and transformation was adopted by the faculty with the title Ethics, Diversity, and Change in the Information Professions (IS 201). The current goals of our Master of Library and Information Science (MLIS) program speak directly to the scope and nature of this course:

1. To educate MLIS students to become the top leaders, policy makers, and designers of information systems and services within the information professions
2. To educate MLIS students with strong professional ethics and a sense of individual, institutional, social, and professional responsibility
3. To educate MLIS students with the skills to become change agents within their institutions and professional communities
4. To educate MLIS students who are able to work effectively in culturally diverse environments
5. To educate MLIS students who are committed to their own lifelong continuing professional education
6. To redesign our curriculum continuously to reflect faculty strengths and rapidly changing environmental demands

It should be noted that service learning is contrasted to internship, in that internship serves to provide an opportunity for professional development, that is, learning on the job, and requires a substantive time commitment. In the case of UCLA, this is 120 hours per quarter. Additionally, service learning is not limited to this core course, as other faculty may and have chosen to require students to work on community projects and other learning experiences that have similar characteristics to service learning.

Theoretical Orientation of the Service Learning Core Course:
Adding the "Critical" to Service Learning and "Working from Within"

As the faculty member with the responsibility to develop a pilot course and to begin its formal offering in spring 2005, I imagined the course would give students an opportunity to learn and give back by engaging with the community. They would also understand their particular role in the process and be involved with redistributing the power to those involved in the learning process. Although there are many different interpretations of service learning as well as different objectives and contexts, many can agree on the following definition:

> Service-learning combines service objectives with learning objectives with the intent that the activity change both the recipient and the provider of the service. This is accomplished by combining service tasks with structured opportunities that link the task to self-reflection, self-discovery, and the acquisition and comprehension of values, skills, and knowledge content.[4]

In order for students to identify their particular role in terms of the attitudes, skills, and knowledge that they bring, I wanted to find a service learning approach that would provide a model incorporating reflection, dialogue, and understanding of these areas in order to identify their privileges, gaps, biases, and contributions. It is for this reason that I have adopted Masucci and Renner's critical service learning approach. They note that in adding "critical" to frame service learning, it becomes

> an important opportunity to integrate and facilitate the ideals of a more radical democratic engagement with one's society. In other words, democracy can be viewed as a radical social practice that requires one to take a critical inventory of one's social location in terms of power and privilege and by understanding our relationship and responsibilities to others.[5]

They define critical service learning as a four-step process of pre-reflection, theory, action, and reflection, further elucidated below:

1. Pre-reflection. In this step of the process, "one should reflect upon and politicize oneself (i.e., investigating who we are and what we stand for, as well as investigating our past service experiences, our preconceptions about the project and our predictions as to its outcome)."[6] Theories assist in gaining an understanding of individual subjectivities, identities, positions, and localities.

2. Theory. The second step helps students to understand the construction of the world in theoretical terms and examine its relation to action (service learning). Potential theories to be examined are those posited by Bourdieu (habitus, meaning-construction), Foucault (in relations to power), Freire and others (in pedagogy), Gramsci (organic intellectual and hegemony), and Matsuda and Crenshaw, Delgado, and others (critical race theory) on feminist, postcolonial, and queer theories.[7]

3. Action. The action step is described as "drawing from a cultural studies tradition, action must be the accompanying harmony that helps inform and update theory." Action in service learning can take on many forms as are particular and appropriate in the community partnership. It is suggested that the "action include some type of dialog and/or dialectical understanding with those whom you are partnering in order to assure that the voice of that partnering organization is evident in the action."

4. Reflection. The final step is the foundation for the entire endeavor: "through critical reflection one has the opportunity to integrate and personally contextualize the experience of service learning." A sharing space is created with the instructor and fellow students.

Implicit in the learning process are the relationships that are forged and the need for them to be egalitarian and bidirectional. In short, all involved in the process are working with and learning from each other. These relationships include the student, instructor, and community to reflect community solidarity, and they offer the opportunity for bidirectional academic (student-to-student and instructor-to-student) and community (student-to-community and instructor-to-community) engagement. Figure 11-1 illustrates these concepts. These relationships lend themselves to particular forms of action—community engagement, participatory learning, reflection—that impact both individuals and a community of learners, resulting in personal and professional transformation, as well as social change.

As a person of color, I am also cognizant of the challenges for all involved in the process of working in or with and serving culturally diverse communities. Whether one is an insider or outsider of a community, engaging with community requires cultural competence that is based on an emic perspective (insider knowledge), participatory engagement, cultural respect, and professional integrity. I wanted to move from a "drive-by" approach to education, research, and professional practice to the engagement of praxis. I call this engagement with culturally diverse communities "working from within." This pedagogy or framework aims to resist a positivistic or superficial approach to multicultural

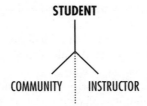

STUDENT

COMMUNITY   INSTRUCTOR

» Community engagement
» Participatory learning
» Reflection—individual and
  community of learners
» Personal and professional
  transformation
» Social change

Figure 11-1. Associations and action by participants engaged
in critical service learning

community engagement, to acknowledge an insider/outsider perspective, and to insert counter-narratives. This positionality recognizes the duality of insider knowledge gained as a community member and outsider perspective as one from the academy or a different sociocultural status. Grounded on critical theory and reflection, and epistemological understanding, this mode of multicultural community engagement is posited as appropriate to working with oppressed or underserved communities. "Working from within" enables engagement with culturally diverse communities in learning, research, and practice; that is, engagement that may lead to community building, organizing, and empowerment, whether the extent of participation of the information institution/professional is as active collaborator or facilitator of information.

Ethics, Diversity, and Change: A Critical Service Learning Class

IS 201 Ethics, Diversity, and Change in the Information Professions (EDC) is a "service-learning course that serves as a forum to discuss, learn and understand the ethical challenges of a multicultural information society that shape societal, professional community and individual views, and impact professional practice, decision making and public policy."[8] As I teach it, EDC offers a means for bidirectional academic (student-to-student and instructor-to-student) and community (student-to-community and instructor-to-community) engagement. As such, the course has the following goals:

1. To introduce students to the meaning of ethics and what it means to be ethical from multiple perspectives: societal, professional, and personal

2. To acquaint students with the purpose of a professional code of ethics

3. To have students recognize an ethical dilemma, examine it critically, and apply a code of ethics using a decision-making model to solve an ethical dilemma

4. To use service learning to help students understand the importance of community collaboration and outreach in order to address equity of information access

5. To provide students with the opportunity to address the information needs of underserved groups

6. To have students examine information ethics issues and policies developed to address them

The learning objectives that I have set for the course are as follows:

1. Students will study various ethical frameworks and develop a personal approach to being ethical information professionals.

2. Students will use service learning experiences to develop their understanding of issues of equity and information services in diverse and/or underserved communities.

3. Students will develop a critical perspective of diversity and information practices.

4. Students will learn about strategies for effecting change in information institutions.

5. Students will consider approaches to advocacy and social justice in the information professions.

The essential topics that are covered by the course are ethics, values, and LIS; ethical decision-making; professional codes of ethics; critical service learning; issues related to a changing multicultural, technological, and globalized society such as identity, difference, power, social responsibility, and social change in information practices and institutions; change strategies; and critical perspectives on information practices and professionalism, including information representation, neutrality, politics, advocacy, justice, change, and policy.

Optional areas that the course can cover are information policy issues including, but not limited to, access, digital divide and community, intellectual freedom (free speech), open access and open source, ownership (intellectual property), plagiarism, privacy, security, spam, whistle-blowing, and replevin.

In order to engage a critical service learning approach and a "working from within" framework, the students have the following requirements that result in particular forms of learning and practice. Appendixes B and C are the course requirements and student responsibilities for EDC. In summary, students are evaluated through the following assignments:

1. Service learning (twenty hours)—practice within community (application and praxis)
2. Journal (25 percent)—looking within self (reflection)
3. Paper (50 percent)—probing within profession (application and praxis)
4. Class discussion and presentation (25 percent)—learning within classroom community (dialogue and praxis)

In the context of the course, service learning, or community partnerships, has the following characteristics:

- It is either arranged by instructor or student.

- Community partners have been identified based on prior working relationships with the instructor or through referrals. Prior experience with the instructor or UCLA address the development of productive working relationships based on familiarity, trust, communication, reciprocity, and confidence.

- Criteria for selecting sites dictate that they should be ones where the community environment would either be new to the students *or* is a community-based or nonprofit organization. Such informational, social service, government, cultural, or educational organizations need assistance because they do not have the resources to achieve all their priorities or because they rely on a volunteer base to implement many of their activities. Students must conduct information-related work.

- Partner responsibilities include coordination, supervision, and facilitation of student activities, as well as communication with the class instructor with any concerns, and evaluation of the service learning experience.

Critical Service Learning in Action

Since the class has been taught there have been a variety of community partners, some of whom have participated from the start and others who have chosen to participate in particular years. The concerns for most sites in deciding to participate are whether they can offer a meaningful experience and whether they have staff to adequately serve as liaison or facilitator. The instructor may be concerned about the quality of student-to-partner relationships. Especially worrisome are partners who are not selected by students, partners who do not offer a meaningful experience, and partners who are not responsive and delay student engagement in the short time frame of a ten-week quarter. The primary student concern is selecting a partner and/or site that fits her needs.

Each spring quarter when the class is offered, I arrange for about 25 community partners to be available to the 70–90 students. Throughout the years, the students have had the opportunity to choose from minority group–specific or non-minority-group-specific libraries, archives, museums, cultural centers, labor organizations, community organizations, historical societies, animal shelters, civil rights and advocacy organizations, detention centers, homeless shelters, children and family centers, media centers, health organizations, and literacy and educational institutions.

Two community partners/sites that stand out in terms of the contributions and continued engagement that students have had are the Rae Lee Siporin LGBT Library at UCLA and the Barry J. Nidorf Juvenile Detention Facility in Sylmar, California. The relationship and work of our MLIS students are noted on the LGBT Library website.[9] Students helped organize and develop the collection into a working library with an automated catalog:

> The UCLA LGBT Center Library is home to over 4000 books, films/DVDs, and journals. With a generous grant from the Liberty Hill Foundation, Candace Lewis was hired in 2004 as a graduate level librarian, to catalogue the library and prepare it for use. Since then, Candace has encouraged the UCLA [Department of Information Studies] to establish the LGBT Library as a training site for other graduate level Information Science students who have made the Library accessible via our website. We are deeply grateful to those very talented and dedicated students.

The Barry J. Nidorf Juvenile Detention Facility (Nidorf) does not have a library, but it does have a staff that recognizes the community's interest and need for reading materials and other library services. Over the years the students have been very committed to Nidorf, and the Young Adult and Children's Services at UCLA student organization has developed the Nidorf Project, allowing them to provide continued services to Nidorf throughout the year.[10] Graduates involved with Nidorf have founded an allied funding and development initiative named the Nidorf Collective, a group that collects book donations for booktalks and distribution at Nidorf, which houses over 600 incarcerated children and teens, ages 10–17.

Service Learning Experiences and Outcomes

What are students learning in EDC, and what do they think about service learning? These questions will be addressed using several sources of data. In addition to students' discussions in class regarding their service learning and other matters, their journals are useful to understand their attitudes and experiences. They are told that only the instructor and reader(s) would read them and that they should be open and thoughtful in their reflection. I inform them that there is no expectation of expression of particular views, that they should be safe to not self-censor, as their grades do not depend on their writings, and that honest reflection is critical for their learning experience. The course is graded on an Satisfactory/Unsatisfactory scale. As a result, I have been moved by many journals because the students have been earnest, have challenged themselves, and have been truly introspective. Here I include excerpts from Amy Guy's journal. She completed the course in spring 2007 and provides a glimpse of the inner struggle, openness, and enrichment of critical service learning:

I. Journal Entry: April 11, 2007

Tomorrow I will begin my service learning at the Chicano Studies Research Center (CSRC). I, along with several other MLIS students, will attend an orientation meeting with the center's librarian and archivist, Yolanda Retter Vargas. Before attending the orientation I need to honestly reflect on why I chose this particular site, beyond the fact that lack of transportation restricts my choices to the UCLA campus. While location is a great motivation, I did forgo my first choice, UCLA's Asian American Studies Center, because I feel that I have a responsibility to learn about Chicano/Chicana history in order to better serve academic library users. I anticipate that the Chicano Studies Research Center will allow me to learn more about Chicano history, culture, and reference sources.

Next, I ask myself: why do I know so little about Chicano history? After all, I undertook rigorous efforts to learn about the histories and cultures of Asian Americans and Americans of Middle Eastern descent. Why have I not done the same for Chicano history? This question leads me back to my childhood in Ellwood City, Pennsylvania, a defunct steel town established and inhabited mainly by Italian Americans and a small population of individuals of Scottish, Irish, and Welsh descent. Homogeneous in nature, the city lacked cultural and ethnic diversity with the exception of two African American families. I was well into my twenties before I ever encountered or met an individual of Asian or Chicano/Latino descent, at least as far as the eye could discern. Of course "race" undeniably exists as a social construction, yet the myth of race as a biological "fact" invokes a mine-ridden landscape, where physical markers are not reliable indicators of an individual's ethnic and cultural background. Can physical appearances constrain a person's sense of self or can they liberate, allowing marginalized peoples to identify as members of a collective group all seeking the same rights? This seems to be the crux of identity politics. Do individuals identify along ethnic lines and embrace the strength provided by community, or are these communities so narrowly drawn that they divide communities into separate, isolated spheres? After studying the work of Chandra Talpade Mohanty, I came to the opinion that individuals can find strength in identifying with particular ethnic identities and yet still find solidarity with other ethnic and cultural groups in fighting against injustices in the neighborhoods or communities in which they reside. But then of course, the question comes up, is whiteness an ethnic identity? Is a Euro-American identity ethnic? Yes. Of course "whiteness" is yet another social construct cobbled together by disparate and often conflicting groups from various European nations. Whiteness is a privilege and yet perhaps to many "whites" or "European-Americans," whiteness lacks an ethnic, exotic feel because it is the face of the majority, the "dominant" culture expressing its power institutionally through government institutions, advertising, and a monopoly on the institutional production of knowledge.

. . . I often wish I had something to identify with and I greatly appreciate that many cultural groups take comfort in their ethnic identities, not forgetting that they have done so as a result of collective exploitation. Of course, it's a double-edged sword in the sense that many minority groups have experienced great injustice and have greatly benefited from identification through shared ethnic pride and history. This is a powerful force in fighting invisibility and erasure from mainstream history and political representation. At any rate, I hope that I can learn more about Chicano history and especially how Chicano culture and history have shaped U.S. mainstream culture. Because whiteness too has been shaped by Chicano/Chicanas, as the mainstream culture has regularly appropriated knowledge, art, and cultural practices from the peoples it has tried to colonize. At the end of this reflection, I realized that everything came back to me and my positionality, and I don't think this is necessarily a positive activity.

. . . The CSRC provided me a vehicle in which to acquire an acute awareness of the exigency of the issues of access, diversity, power, and social justice. My brief stay at CSRC helped me acquire a greater appreciation for the need of specialized research centers to house, highlight, and excavate the texts of marginalized peoples. Without this important information archaeology, voices can slip into the dark recesses of history, reducing the fullness and clarity of our historical narratives.

From the initial test trial of the course and its initial offering, the journals and class evaluations demonstrated that there were more cases of transformation than resistance. A few students revealed that if it was not for service learning, they would not have learned of the collective struggles of minority groups and their longtime and continued fight for social justice. Transformation was taking place, and those who were skeptical had an opportunity to examine their own attitudes and perceptions regarding service learning from an ethical framework. Also, initial offerings of the course provided less opportunity for in-class reflection on service learning, so students had to seek me out when problems arose. Now, these are discussed in class as they are taking place, and the class as a community has the opportunity to problem-solve.

This class has also been a learning experience for readers who are Ph.D. students. They were given reader assignments as part of their funding offer. Readers have to either complete the course or have a related background in order to qualify to grade student papers and serve as a resource during small-group discussions. Shari Lee, one of the readers in spring 2008, observed every class meeting for her section as well as occasionally sitting in at the other section. She made the following commentary recently as I was discussing the course with her:

> Based on classroom responses and journal entries, I think the class is an intervention that worked—engaging the complexity of diversity through service learning and ethics as a core requirement. By the end, many had a shift in thinking or seemed open to rethinking biases they initially held. This was evident in the words they used and the way they approached difficult topics. It seems the class provided a comfort zone—a safe environment—where people felt that they would be respected. No one seemed visibly upset when hard issues, such as racism, were raised; students saw the value in discussing things openly and honestly, even though they may not have agreed with everyone or everything. I also think that the deliberately and thoughtfully inserted voices of the underrepresented, in the speakers you invited, provided significant exposure to the perspectives of the "Other." This, along with your counter-narratives, was beneficial in a class where the students were predominately white.[11]

In spring 2007 the two EDC instructors, Virginia Walter, who was teaching the course for the first time, and I, conducted a survey of the service learning as part of our strategic plan process.[12] This plan included the following goal, with its associated evaluation indicated:

> Goal c. To devise and teach specific new ideas by which the students in our academic and professional programs can promote the values of public trust, social justice, and individual and community em-powerment.

> Indicators:
> 2. Evaluation of the service learning component in the MLIS core in order to understand whether this might be useful to extend into other aspects of IS programs.

Walter summarized the 61 responses to the survey in a memo to the faculty. There were a total of 76 students in the courses, making it an 80 percent response rate.

1. How useful was the service learning component in this course for helping you achieve its stated learning objectives? Please circle the most appropriate response.

Very useful	22	36%
Useful	30	49%
Not at all useful	4	7%
Don't know	4	7%
No answer	2	2%

2. Would you like to see service learning opportunities offered in other required courses?

Yes	19	31%
No	17	28%
Maybe	24	39%
No answer	1	2%

3. Would you like to see service learning opportunities offered in some elective courses?

Yes	25	41%
No	9	15%
Maybe	25	41%
No answer	2	3%

Many students provided comments to elucidate their responses. A few representative ones are included below to provide further explanation of the quantitative results. Students who found the service learning component to be very useful said:

> Wonderful opportunity to interact with an unfamiliar group and in a possibly uncomfortable situation. Nice to be able to start thinking about theory in practical situations.

> Learned more in service learning than I did in class.

> It made me more aware of issues covered in class and provided a chance to be an info professional in an actual work site experiencing these issues.

> I enjoyed service learning a lot. Before I started I was dreading it, but I had a lot of fun and met wonderful people and broadened my experiences.

> I loved my service learning experience and found it very rewarding. I found myself thinking about things in new ways.

The service learning portion of this core class was the best part of my UCLA experience in my first year here. It's given me confidence and honed skills that I've acquired in library science.

Service learning is integral to evaluating ethics, diversity, and change.

Very relevant to our development as IS professionals. Better than just volunteering. Great networking experience.

The service learning project worked as it was accompanied by reflection (written and scheduled into class time).

Students who found the service learning component to be not at all useful said:

I felt like the criteria for including sites on the list was not well defined, meaning that the site I worked at didn't have any idea what we were supposed to be learning. We ended up doing a task that was more "helping out" than teaching us anything about diversity or ethics.

Helpful for organization, but not necessarily for learning objectives.

The service learning would have complemented the course if I had been at a site where we interacted with community members. It didn't serve much for me to clean shelves, etc.

Three main aspects of this service learning were problematic for students. First, a few students indicated difficulty with the twenty-hour time commitment, even though two classes of the ten were substituted for service learning time. Second, because some students preferred to stay on campus, geographic location of sites was challenging. However, the most typical area that needed improvement related to the sites that were available to students for the service learning they requested. Sometimes these did not suit their interests, the contact or supervision by community partners was inefficient, or the experience was insufficiently or overly challenging. This is a challenge because there is not staff support to coordinate the sites, but as noted above the in-class opportunity through the quarter to discuss issues experienced in service learning allowed students to compare their experiences and assist each other in making their own more enriching.

Walter noted the following from reflecting upon student comments and her own experience teaching the course:

In general, students find the service learning component of IS 201 to be a valuable one. They appreciate the opportunity to get started working in an information organization before the start of their second year, and many find that the experience enhances their critical thinking about the course content. Supervising the service learning, however, is very time-consuming even without the kind of follow-up and ongoing attention to site selection that the students rightly indicate as desirable features . . . [I] found most of [the journals] to be genuinely reflective of significant learning. Students found insights and connections to course readings in the most unlikely places. Classroom discussion based on service learning was lively and thought-provoking. While the response to service learning in IS 201 was very favorable, responses about expanding service learning to other courses was mixed.

Conclusion

The experience of a core service learning class has shown that it is indeed a valuable experience. All students are required to address issues of ethics and diversity that are likely to arise in a service learning experience. Whether transformation takes place or not, students test their attitudes, knowledge, and skills in a setting they typically may not consider working in. The students learn to (a) respond to or consider in an ethical manner the challenges of the information age; (b) take on the challenges that arise when working in a multicultural community where some groups are privileged and others are oppressed, resulting in inequity of information services; (c) be open to personal, community, and professional transformation; and (d) reconsider the power relationships in the learning process in order to facilitate community engagement, organizing, building, and empowerment. Community engagement requires the redistribution of power so that all are contributors and recipients of the learning process in order that action not be without reflection and communication not be without understanding. The dismantling of hierarchy, the critical understanding of inequity in information access and representation, the ethical response to dilemmas, the recognition of privileges and biases, the openness to inquiry and critique, and the collective approach to problem solving are implicit in the critical service learning I envision and attempt to implement.

Finally, "working from within" is at the heart of the EDC course as I aim to teach it. The course enables all MLIS students at UCLA to incorporate service learning and critical pedagogy. At the end of the day, what is important is the process that creates a safe space for exploring how we can participate in information acts to change the world. We are imbued with the discourse of the majority culture in most of our information and communication channels and institutions. Thus, critical service learning that allows counter-narratives to be inserted creates a space for meaningful and real dialogue. The EDC course underscores the notion of community, action, and participatory practice that has the potential to lead to transformation in the student, the information organization, and the community served.

Appendix A
Mission and Related Statements,
UCLA Department of Information Studies

The mission statement for the Graduate School of Education and Information Studies stipulates:[13]

> GSE&IS is dedicated to inquiry, the advancement of knowledge, the improvement of professional practice, and service to the education and information professions. We develop future generations of scholars, teachers, information professionals, and institutional leaders. Our work is guided by the principles of individual responsibility and social justice, an ethic of caring, and commitment to the communities we serve.

In relation to our school, our separate departmental vision is:

> The Department of Information Studies defines, studies, and evaluates interactions among people, information, and information technology in a pluralistic society. The Department values and promotes equity, diversity, accountability, and intellectual openness.
>
> The Department integrates wide-ranging scholarly, professional, technological, and institutional perspectives in its teaching, research, and public service. Across each of these activities, the Department engages with and is driven by real world information issues and community and institutional needs. The Department also promotes the essential role played by information institutions such as libraries and archives as social, cultural, educational, and intellectual centers in our society.
>
> In particular, we examine and encourage
>
> - The design of information systems and services for individuals, communities, cultures, disciplines, and literacies;
> - The creation, preservation, documentation, and curation of information in all media and settings;
> - Access to information, in all its manifestations, that empowers and enfranchises individuals and communities in and over time; and
> - The framing of ongoing policy and institutional dialogue related to the social and intellectual implications of a global information society.

The goals for the MLIS program are:

> To educate MLIS students to become the top leaders, policy makers, and designers of information systems and services within the information professions.

To educate MLIS students with strong professional ethics and a sense of individual, institutional, social, and professional responsibility.

To educate MLIS students with the skills to become change agents within their institutions and professional communities.

To educate MLIS students who are able to work effectively in culturally diverse environments.

To educate MLIS students who are committed to their own lifelong continuing professional education.

To redesign our curriculum continuously to reflect faculty strengths and rapidly changing environmental demands.

Appendix B

Ethics, Diversity, and Change in the Information Professions: Course Requirements

Class discussion and presentation—learning within classroom community (dialogue and praxis)[14]

- readings, case studies, small group and whole class discussion, and group presentations

Service learning (application and praxis) [See appendix C for more details.]

- 20 hours

Journal (reflection)

- Each journal should include 5 entries on issues of ethics, diversity, power, and social justice that arise during your service learning experience. Each entry (approximately 2 pages) should include a brief description of the issue (what, who, where, and when), its implications for you as an information professional, and your own reflections on the issue.

- AND a conclusion with your reflection on any change or transformation (collaborative, institutional, personal, and professional) that has taken place as a result of service learning.

Final assignment (application and praxis)
For your 10-page double-spaced paper, address the following:

- Discuss the professional code of ethics/conduct (e.g., ALA, SAA, SLA, etc.) that most closely matches your own career goals. Indicate any sources of agreement and conflict between the professional ethics and your own personal ethics, and for the latter, how you might resolve the conflict(s).

- Identify an ethical information dilemma/situation, discuss how the above professional code of ethics/conduct addresses it or not, and using an ethical decision-making model, describe how you would solve this ethical issue.

Course grading: Satisfactory/Unsatisfactory

Appendix C

Guidelines for Library, Archives, or Information Service Learning

Description

Individually or in a team, IS 201 students will use their knowledge and academic and professional resources to develop and conduct a library, archives, or information service learning activity/project.[15] The individual/team will meet with project site staff, discuss and settle on the service learning to be conducted, determine how to carry out the activity/project, and implement it. The individual/team will spend 20 hours per student engaged in the service learning activity/project. During the process students will write their reflections on their service learning experience in their individual journals. Throughout the course students will discuss their service experiences in class as discussion leaders or participants. The project site contact/coordinator will provide feedback to the instructor.

Responsibilities/Activities

Students

Working individually or in teams, students will select a real-life organization for which they will develop and implement a library, archives, or information service activity/project. For teams, the members will be responsible for delegating tasks and duties among its own members. As appropriate to facilitate the communication process for teams, one student may be designated the contact person. The entire team (or individual) will meet with the class instructor or reader at least once during the quarter, and will also be responsible for orally presenting on their service learning experience in class. The service learning will not be graded, but full commitment, class presentation and participation, and a problem-solving approach are expected. Each student will:

1. After site selection and sign-up, familiarize yourself with the organization (mission, goals, organizational structure, etc.) through its literature and/or website prior to contacting the organization.
2. Communicate with the site supervisor what you would like to learn, your course requirements, your backgrounds, and your career goals.

3. Observe the work of the organization and discuss with other staff persons their roles and responsibilities, and the organization's mission.
4. Gain an understanding of the user/client community and your service learning work in relation to their information needs.
5. With the assistance of your project supervisor, track your twenty hours of service learning using the timesheet.
6. Problem solve as an individual/student team, communicate any unresolved issues with instructor or project supervisor, as appropriate.
7. Describe your experiences (ethical issues, feelings, critical incidents, insights gained, responsibilities, new skills, and accomplishments) in your journal, as appropriate.
8. As discussion leader and participant, share your service learning experiences in class.

Instructor and Readers

The instructor and readers will facilitate the students' work, providing skills, knowledge, advice, and resources as needed to complete the project. The instructor or readers will meet with each team at least once during the quarter. The instructor and readers are also available to consult with project site staff as needed.

Project Site Staff

At the first meeting with student(s) the project site contact, supervisor, and/or staff will describe the organization and its user community, learn about the students' interests and skills, discuss the potential service learning activity/project, and approve the activity/project that the student(s) will undertake. Project site staff will provide the student(s) with whatever data, space, and access to targeted activity/project clients that might be needed. They will also facilitate the students' understanding of how their work helps the diverse and/or underserved user/client community through understanding the information needs of the user/client.

Instructor or readers should be contacted with any questions. The supervisor will sign the student's service learning timesheet or e-mail the student a confirmation of his/her hours. At the completion of the service learning experience, the project site contact/coordinator will provide feedback to the teams by completing and returning to the instructor the evaluation form.

ACKNOWLEDGMENTS

I wish to thank the Students Diversity Action Group, UCLA Department of Information Studies, for their persistence and vision to push for substantive diversity content in the department. As well, I wish to thank all the EDC students for their openness in the learning process and especially Amy Guy for sharing her personal reflections from her journal.

NOTES

1. Syllabus available at www.gseis.ucla.edu/faculty/chu/220/.

2. Clara Chu, "Education for Multicultural Librarianship," in *Multiculturalism in Libraries,* ed. Rosemary Ruhig Du Mont, Lois Buttlar, and William Caynon (Westport, CT: Greenwood, 1994), 127–56.

3. Department mission and goals available at http://is.gseis.ucla.edu/about/goals .htm.

4. Learn and Serve, America's National Service-Learning Clearinghouse, www .servicelearning.org.

5. Matt Masucci and Adam Renner, "Reading the Lives of Others: The Winton Homes Library Project: A Cultural Studies Analysis of Critical Service Learning for Education," *High School Journal* 84, no. 1 (October/November 2000): 36–47.

6. Ibid.

7. These and other theories are described at www.popcultures.com/theorist.htm.

8. Syllabus available at www.gseis.ucla.edu/faculty/chu/edc/.

9. Rae Lee Siporin Library at UCLA, www.lgbt.ucla.edu/library.htm.

10. Young Adult and Children's Services at UCLA, http://polaris.gseis.ucla.edu/ yalsa/service.html.

11. Shari Lee, "A Reader's Observations of IS 201, Spring 2008," UCLA Department of Information Studies, 2008.

12. UCLA Department of Information Studies, IS Strategic Plan, 2006–07 to 2010–11.

13. Department mission and goals available at http://is.gseis.ucla.edu/about/goals .htm.

14. EDC course requirements available at www.gseis.ucla.edu/faculty/chu/edc/assign .html.

15. IS 201 Guide for Service Learning, www.gseis.ucla.edu/faculty/chu/edc/sl-guide/.

Chapter 12

Cultural Heritage Initiatives at the University of Michigan School of Information

C. Olivia Frost

"Bringing people, information, and technology together in more valuable ways" is the mission of the University of Michigan's School of Information (SI), and it is the foundation for the school's focus on societal engagement in teaching, research, and service. It is the foundation as well for a broad program of cultural heritage initiatives that are one component of an extensive network of practical engagement opportunities. The school's mission to make information and information technology valuable to human welfare results in a service ethos that is a fundamental part of the culture of the school. The importance of engagement and service-based learning is reflected in the school's requirement of a minimum of six credits in practical engagement and an opportunity to earn a maximum of fifteen credits toward completion of the forty-eight-credit-hour, ALA-accredited master of science in information degree.

Within the SI, engagement is bidirectional, and the model for engagement assumes the involvement of clients as community partners in project design, implementation, and evaluation. Likewise, both students and their community partners learn from each other, thus providing opportunities for students to work as change agents and innovators. Another guiding principle within the school is its interdisciplinary approach to information problems. This focus ensures that cultural heritage and other practical engagement projects involve students across various disciplines and specializations in the school. Students typically work in teams, with each student employing his unique disciplinary expertise to a common problem. The SI's mission, with its emphasis on maximizing the potential of information for the betterment of society, has informed the ways in which cultural heritage initiatives have taken place at Michigan. Projects have explored how digital technologies can extend the reach of cultural content, provide context for its understanding, and empower community partners to share and talk about content they have created. Cultural heritage activities at SI have provided pilot projects that illustrate this potential, and some have also helped build capacity for communities to create their own projects.

Practical engagement and service-based learning at SI include class work, directed field experiences, summer internships, and alternative spring break activities, and all of these have provided opportunities for work in cultural heritage projects.[1] In addition, there have been summer internships in South Africa and summer institutes in cultural heritage preservation. A number of credit-bearing courses have a practical engagement focus, including the Practical Engagement Workshop in Cultural Heritage Outreach.

Cultural Heritage Initiative for Community Outreach

The Cultural Heritage Initiative for Community Outreach (CHICO), largely sponsored through the W. K. Kellogg Foundation, has a mission to broaden the reach of cultural heritage and to impart socio-technical skills and knowledge needed for the dissemination of cultural heritage resources to new audiences.[2] The CHICO model places a high priority on engaging communities in a better understanding and appreciation of cultures through partnerships. Museums and other content providers offer artifacts for object-based learning. Scholars contribute specialized content expertise and recommend resources. Education specialists develop, assess, and use materials for instruction. Information specialists identify, evaluate, organize, and promote the use of web-based and other information resources. They also develop tools to capture and display content, to engage the teachers and students in dialogue, and to reach out and extend the content and resources to both local and virtual communities. Communication tools enable members of the local and virtual communities to provide reflections and engage in dialogue, as well as to contribute their own content.

The CHICO projects emphasize diverse cultural heritage content, service, and outreach to diverse communities. In addition to the design and deployment of information access tools, the projects also include the development of services that publicize, facilitate, and enrich the use of these tools. Since its inception in 1995, CHICO has developed over forty projects that have provided credit-bearing practical engagement opportunities for SI students through classes specifically devoted to cultural heritage outreach, independent study courses, and directed field experiences. The projects keep in mind the school's focus on the intersection of people, information, and technology. *People* are at the center of the projects, and the human and social aspects include end users as well as community and institutional partners, including teachers and museum professionals. *Information* has focused primarily on cultural content, broadly defined to include culture in everyday life as well as cultural artifacts residing in repositories such as museums and archives. Information also includes the placement of the cultural artifact into historical and sociological context, as well as the commentaries from users who interpret the content. *Technology* has focused on tools that extend the reach beyond the on-site setting to a global audience, and on tools that supplement and enhance the on-site experience, as well as those that enable interaction between content and user and that facilitate discourse.

Bringing Collections to a Broader Audience

A central thrust of CHICO's initial ventures in the mid-1990s was to use the then-emerging Internet technologies to make the richness of cultural heritage repositories more widely known and more widely available to those who otherwise might not be able to visit the on-site collections. CHICO has also enhanced the experience of those visiting the physical or virtual site by providing contextual information to place the resources into their cultural and historical framework. The primary audience for these sites, and for CHICO more generally, has been K–12 users and nonspecialist audiences. Key partnerships with museums and archives were instrumental in this effort. "Harlem 1900–1940: An African-American Community" was a collaboration between CHICO and the Schomburg Center for Research in Black Culture at the New York Public Library.[3] The Schomburg's mission is to collect, preserve, and provide "access to resources documenting the history and experiences of peoples of African descent throughout the world."[4] As is the case with many cultural heritage repositories, the Schomburg is able to provide only limited access to its collections, yet there is a call for access from a variety of potential audiences ranging from scholars to elementary school students. In part as a recognition of this need for broader accessibility to its collections, the Schomburg asked CHICO to provide an online virtual exhibit of one of its most popular collections, a compelling photographic portfolio depicting the Harlem Renaissance. CHICO worked with the Schomburg to develop an online presentation of the portfolio, featuring more than thirty archival photographs, accompanied by a section for educators with lesson plans and discussion guides and the addition of a time line and interactive database of artists, writers, and musicians. A similar partnership with the Schomburg resulted in the creation of a site called "The African Presence in the Americas," which chronicles the 500-year history of African people in the Americas and features a combination of online exhibits and teacher resources.[5]

In a similar partnership with a cultural repository, CHICO and other SI partners embarked on a project with the Smithsonian's National Museum of the American Indian to transform a site-specific, geographically proscribed exhibit into a broadly accessible and interactive multimedia resource. The resulting exhibit was based on content developed in partnership with members of the Alaskan Yup'ik community, including tribal elders and students, together with educators, scholars, and exhibit curators. The website brings together images of masks from museum collections around the world and the stories these masks convey; a CD-ROM features additional oral histories and audio resources. A Yup'ik artist, dancer, and scholar helped create the CD-ROM and was later invited to the annual Great Lakes Powwow in Ann Arbor with his dance troupe to be featured in the opening ceremonies. The Yup'ik resource generated response and encouragement of further collaboration with Yup'ik elders and community members. Children from Yup'ik public schools created and contributed new materials on environmental issues.

Engaging Young People

A major focus of many CHICO projects has been to engage young people in appreciation of cultural heritage. The engagement goes beyond passive involvement to active creation, reflection, and dialogue, and it encourages young people to explore cultural content available on the Web and also on-site in their own communities. By encouraging reflection and interpretation of what young people have experienced, CHICO offers opportunities for children to provide their own voices and create their own cultural expressions. Two such projects involved a CHICO collaboration with the University of Michigan Museum of Art (UMMA), local middle school children, and their teachers. In these projects, students were given the opportunity to view art they had seen in a local exhibit, create their own art inspired by what they had seen, conduct background research, and then share their creations and reflections with a broader audience.

An experimental course entitled "A Stylistic Journey" involved CHICO and UMMA in a collaborative project with middle school students and both art and technology teachers. The museum's role in the project included museum visits with on-site discussions and the viewing of original works of art illustrating artistic techniques such as Asian ink stroke and pointillism. Museum professionals also served as mentors to address students' questions in an online mentoring board. In a studio component within their school, students worked with each of the different techniques they had learned and did background research. The students published class papers and images of their original artwork in an online gallery. At the conclusion of the project, the students' families were invited to the museum to view the final website and contribute their own artwork under the children's direction. In a similar project, CHICO, UMMA, and fifth-grade students at a local school created their own guide to an exhibit of Monet's paintings. The students' guide reflected their perspectives, and the museum curators reviewed and validated the content of the site. The museum, CHICO, the school's art teacher, and a technology specialist helped the students research specific artistic resources and painting techniques in consultation with curatorial experts, write essays about the paintings, create their own works of art based on their experiences and learning, and create an online, interactive exhibit guide. A bulletin board and online quiz facilitated communication among students, educators, and the exhibit curator and welcomed responses from a larger audience.

In its activities to engage students with cultural content, CHICO adopts a broad view of cultural heritage to encompass not only works in cultural repositories such as museums, libraries, and archives but also culture as it is created by people in the community and experienced in everyday life. In these projects, students are encouraged to look within their own communities to discover art, history, and traditions. In one example, middle school students in Los Angeles were asked to think and write about the murals created by Latino artists in their neighborhoods and to reflect on public art in their community.

The resulting site shows pictures of the murals and the student reflections on them, along with information about the artists and resources for learning more about murals.[6] In another example called "Cultural Scrapbook," middle school students in Oakland, California, Ann Arbor, Michigan, and Atlanta, Georgia, were assigned to think about and talk with family members about elements of culture in their everyday lives.[7] They illustrated their thoughts with photographs they had taken and shared their impressions with students in other participating schools. The students documented activities such as Thanksgiving and Day of the Dead commemorations and shared with other children the types of foods, music, holidays, and other expressions and artifacts that make up their culture.

In the "Students on Site" project, the focus was on identifying primary resources to explore community-based teaching and learning about local history and public places.[8] The project involved a broad-based university and town partnership that included local schools, archivists, and university faculty. Together they worked to select archival materials such as maps, photographs, letters, and other primary sources documenting a historic African American neighborhood and developed a website to make the story available in an online archival resource. Children in the schools created their own stories, essays, and art to be published in the online resource. Teachers and students from third-grade and high school classes worked with archivists and other information professionals to learn how to use primary resources in their community to create their own print and web-based learning materials. The project also included the development of tutorials for teachers on how to use archival resources, a summer workshop on integrating primary resources into a curriculum, and guidance on planning an archives website. Children gathered their own primary resource material on the history in their community by conducting interviews with community members with unusual stories to tell in the "Gift of Memory" project.[9] A group of middle school students conducted video interviews with eight elders in their local community and asked them to talk about their lives. The resulting website contains stories and photographs, video clips, sound bites, and quotes from the interviewees. Visitors can also read brief histories on a few of the topics, explore links to relevant websites, and read the students' reflections on what they learned from the lives of those they interviewed.

Showcasing Performance Art at Local Cultural Events

The scope of cultural heritage in CHICO also includes performance art. CHICO students have used the power of the Web to work with community partners to showcase local cultural events featuring music, dance, and theater. The sites created have not only generated interest in the events, but provided lesson plans and learning materials that teachers could use to assist students in gaining background knowledge and appreciation for what they were about to see. In one such project, a visiting dance troupe from Senegal provided the occasion for partnering with experts from the University of Michigan's Center for Afroamerican and African Studies and the University Musical Society to develop a website providing background materials and context for the concert. A second partnership with the University Musical Society featured materials providing context for a series of plays by the Royal Shakespeare Company. In a partnership with a local theater troupe for children, CHICO students developed a site that provided background materials about three performances and the subject content they depicted: the Underground Railroad, the American immigrant experience, and American Indian folk tales.[10] The site also offers a backstage look at the productions, as well as teacher's guides, community resources, and games.

Another CHICO project focused on a local event with national significance: the annual Ann Arbor powwow gathering of American Indian dancers. For this project, CHICO worked with local scholars to provide informational material and to help K–12 audiences understand the significance of the powwow activities and their place in American Indian culture.[11] Local performances of mariachi musicians and Afro-Caribbean dancers led to the development of a salsa site and involved the collaboration of local scholars of Latin American culture. The "Salsa Stories" virtual tour includes an overview of the history and growth of salsa from the Caribbean to New York City, stories about salsa from Spanish Caribbean communities in New York City, and educational resources and a reference collection.[12] These activities reinforce CHICO's emphasis that the digital representation of the cultural artifact or activity cannot replace the actual "real-life" experience but can provide ways of enhancing that experience.

Capacity Building

Partnerships at SI have also focused on helping communities and institutions build capacity to preserve their cultural heritage and make it accessible to larger audiences. Capacity-building activities have included training in technologies used to preserve and disseminate cultural content, as well as training in planning for information work in libraries and archives. Other dimensions of capacity building include the fostering of cultural heritage awareness and the sharing of information and ideas among thought leaders and practicing professionals. As with other cultural heritage activities, the various projects in these areas are characterized by community partnerships and collaborative planning. Their focus is on engagement in building capacity for cultural heritage resource development and service, on training in technology and professional skills needed for service delivery, and on providing forums for discussion of issues and best practices.

A number of SI special projects focusing on capacity building have been undertaken during the summer terms. A signature example is an academic exchange between SI and the University of Fort Hare (UFH) in Alice, South Africa. This project, which was begun in the mid-1990s and has been led by SI Professor Margaret Hedstrom, has helped enhance the ability of the

UFH to manage, preserve, and provide access to its cultural assets. The project helped develop expertise in archives management and in the use of information technology.[13] The UFH is the oldest university in southern Africa offering higher education to nonwhites and has educated many leaders of political and national liberation movements throughout Africa. The archival collections in the university library include material from archives such as the African National Congress and the Pan African Congress. The archives hold documentation that is critical for understanding South African history but has been neglected and inaccessible. SI students in a practical engagement course, Cultural Preservation and Outreach in Emerging Democracies, participated in the early part of the Fort Hare project. Students and faculty organized and completed finding aids for archival collections, investigated digitization strategies for selected archival materials, provided basic computer training to the members of a women's craft collective, and developed e-commerce strategies for the craft collective and for promoting sales of a book of poetry from the library's collections. In 2007 SI students and faculty returned to Fort Hare for another internship, once again with the goal to help make the university's unique collections accessible for the benefit of South Africans. The SI students worked in teams on several related projects to organize and improve access to the university's rich collections of archives and records, and they developed plans for thorough archival processing of the university's records when additional resources become available.

Two SI summer institutes led by Professor Maurita Holland provided another opportunity for graduate students and faculty to build capacity through a partnership with K–12 teachers and students and community leaders in American Indian communities in Arizona and Michigan. The Cultural Heritage Preservation Institutes (CHPI) focused on widening appreciation and understanding of cultural heritage, as well as on the preservation, display, and dissemination of cultural content using digital technologies.[14] The first institute was in Arizona, for participants from the Navajo Nation community, and the second was for members of Ojibwe communities in the Upper Peninsula of Michigan. As with the Fort Hare activities, these projects also built upon a multiyear relationship, in this case, prior years of experience working with the Navajo Nation on collaborative projects. In addition to technology training, CHPI participants were immersed in cultural heritage awareness activities, including tours of local museums and sites of cultural and historic importance, and demonstrations and lectures by local artisans. The CHPI held in Michigan included one session at the SI campus in Ann Arbor that concentrated on digital technologies and a second session, held in the Upper Peninsula, that featured culturally and historically important geographic locations and their significance to the Ojibwe people. Participants used the six weeks between institute sessions to practice their skills and to gather local cultural content for the CHPI culture website. During this intersession, two communities that had been unable to attend the first institute received training by an SI graduate student. In both sessions, SI students created technology instructional materials, led discussions about how the projects fit into classroom teaching, and worked one-on-one with the participants in creating the projects. Both sessions were jointly planned by SI and cultural leaders from the community and included trips to important cultural sites led by community leaders with expertise in historical and background information. Each institute culminated in a new website describing the cultural history of the region, with images taken by the participants during the workshop and input from local communities and cultural leaders.

Two other SI capacity-building projects illustrate efforts to foster dialogue and idea sharing among cultural heritage and education professionals. A CHICO workshop for teachers and museum professionals was held to encourage partnerships between educators who were using museum resources in the classroom and museum professionals who were committed to K–12 outreach activities. While discussing common challenges and sharing best practices, the two groups studied how to encourage partnerships between cultural heritage repositories and potential new users of their content, and how to use information technologies in making these primary resources more widely available to K–12 classroom teachers and students. Outcomes of the meeting included new collaborations among the participants and venues for continued discussion and idea sharing.

Cultural heritage preservation and education involving indigenous cultures was the focus of a workshop led by SI Professor Maurita Holland in August 2001 in partnership with the National Science Foundation, the American Indian Higher Education Consortium, and the National Museum of the American Indian. "Digital Collectives in Native and Indigenous Cultures" convened information professionals and educators, digital technology researchers, representatives of cultural repositories, and funding agencies.[15] Participants included Native Alaskan, Native Hawaiian, First Nation, American Indian, Maori, Australian Aboriginal, Sami, Brazilian, and African people. Discussion centered on the needs, challenges, and opportunities in the use of information technologies in celebrating and extending indigenous cultures. Participants investigated major issues for indigenous people in creating and accessing digital resources. There was also discussion of using collaborative technology to preserve culture, stimulate knowledge creation, educate, enhance sharing, and provide new venues for research and appropriate roles for institutions of social memory. Outcomes of the meeting included several new collaborations, funding proposals, papers, and continued discussion of indigenous collections, as well as incorporation of the content into service learning experiences for students.[16]

Conclusion

An extensive set of service-based learning projects at the University of Michigan School of Information provide master's students with an opportunity to work with community partners to help in the capture, interpretation, and sharing of culture. The emphasis has been on communities whose cultures have been underrepresented in physical and online repositories and on nonspecialist audiences, particularly K–12 learners. The projects' goals are to increase access to cultural treasures and to gain greater awareness of the cultural content and its context. Students in the SI program learn practical skills in cultural heritage content development, information technology applications and management, project management, and working in teams. The students gain the reward of making a difference in the lives of community partners. The projects bring to life the school's focus on the interlinking of people, information, and technology.

NOTES

1. Available at www.si.umich.edu/outreach/pep.htm.
2. Available at www.si.umich.edu/CHICO/.
3. Available at www.si.umich.edu/CHICO/Harlem/.
4. Available at http://nypl.org/research/sc/sc.html.
5. Available at www.si.umich.edu/CHICO/Schomburg/.
6. Available at www.si.umich.edu/CHICO/Norwood/.
7. Available at www.si.umich.edu/CHICO/chico2003/.
8. Available at www.artsofcitizenship.umich.edu/sos/.
9. Available at www.si.umich.edu/CHICO/oralhistory/.
10. Available at www.si.umich.edu/CHICO/AlongtheTracks/; www.si.umich.edu/CHICO/America/; and www.si.umich.edu/CHICO/RainbowCrow/.
11. Available at www.si.umich.edu/CHICO/powwow/.
12. Available at www.si.umich.edu/CHICO/salsa/.
13. Available at www.si.umich.edu/fort-hare/grantlin.htm#um.
14. Available at www.si.umich.edu/CHPI/.
15. Available at http://si.umich.edu/pep/dc/meeting/meeting.htm.
16. The March 2002 issue of *D-Lib Magazine* focuses on issues from this conference and is available at www.dlib.org/dlib/march02/03contents.html.

Chapter 13

The Internet Public Library as Service-Based Experiential Learning

*Denise E. Agosto, Eileen G. Abels,
Lorri Mon, and Lydia Eato Harris*

> *Experiential learning is the incorporation of active, participatory learning opportunities into the course. It is sometimes called situational learning.*
>
> —Kim Hawtrey

> *Although few professionals doubt the value of experiential learning, the idea of fitting additional "real world" experiences into an already overloaded curriculum may seem impossible to achieve without jeopardizing academic excellence.*
>
> —Jane T. Walker and others

What Is Experiential Learning?

Experiential learning involves bringing real-life learning experiences into a formal program of study. In library and information science programs, experiential learning is typically obtained through internships, practica, and/or student employment in information organizations. As an online library service that combines public service with real-world learning opportunities, the Internet Public Library (IPL; www.ipl.org) is an example of one such setting for experiential learning. The three main areas in which LIS students can serve the IPL community are digital reference service, collection building and maintenance, and software and database development.

The theory behind experiential learning is based upon a Chinese proverb: "Tell me and I will forget. Show me and I may remember. Involve me and I will understand." David Kolb, a professor of organizational behavior, used this saying as the basis for developing a theory of experiential learning. His theory birthed a number of different educational movements, including Outward Bound.[1]

Kolb's model of experiential learning is designed as a four-stage learning process. The first stage is the concrete experience, during which learners gain new information. The second stage involves the cognitive process of reflection and observation, during which learners expand upon their experiences to develop abstracts ideas, theories, and principles related to the topic of study. It is in the third stage, abstract conceptualization, that learners integrate new knowledge into their existing knowledge bases. With this integration of knowledge, learners then engage in the fourth stage, active experimentation.

Kolb has his critics, even among those who laud the educational benefits of experiential learning. For example, Peggy Lo argues that the abstract conceptualization stage presents particular problems for web-based learners and educators. Because experience is subjective and dynamic, its quality cannot be verified, nor can it be quantified. When experiences have been negative, students need the educator's guidance to understand the related implications. As Lo explains, the instructor must step in "to trace back and understand [the students'] past experience, and to guide them toward a positive experience" so that they do not simply negate the experience and miss the important learning concepts.[2]

Lo proposed an alternative three-stage model based on a different conceptualization of the elements of experiential learning. Because online educators will find past experiences difficult to verify, an alternative option is to create new concrete experiences within online course contexts, thereby enabling experiential quality control. Lo suggests experiences such as case studies, games, and multimedia simulations to provide firsthand course-based learning experiences using three-dimensional virtual environments. She explains that through using "graphics, icons and symbolic images, virtual environments can facilitate a mapping between abstract knowledge and 'real' experience."[3]

In the first stage of Lo's model (concrete experience), educators create learning objectives and provide learners with concrete learning experiences. In the second stage (reflective observation), educators provide learners with facts and guidance while actively engaging them in exercises and assignments and providing opportunities for students to develop their thinking through dialogue with the instructor and other students. The third stage (active experimentation) involves applying concepts to solve problems and judging the results for relevance and usefulness.

However, Lo's approach has its own limitations for teaching LIS. Some LIS courses, such as those that focus on human information behavior and others that are theory heavy, start from the abstract and move to the concrete in opposition to the model. This does not exclude the opportunity for experiential learning, but it does require variations in the approach. In other courses, such as reference, students generally have some related past experiences, but the subjectivity and potential negativity of these experiences can limit their educational value. These experiences can still be used as learning opportunities when combined with new lessons learned from course-based experiential learning. The IPL is an ideal tool for providing these kinds of course-based, real-world learning experiences.

Students Serving the IPL Community through Reference and Collection Development

Use of the IPL in LIS courses can provide the concrete practical experiences necessary for completing Lo's three-stage learning cycle. Founded in 1995 as an LIS graduate student class project at the University of Michigan's School of Information under the direction of Joseph W. Janes, the Internet Public Library has grown into a fully realized, web-based public service organization and learning/teaching environment. It consists of two main components. The Ask a Question component is an e-mail question-answering service, with LIS students and volunteers serving as the question answerers. The IPL online collections component includes web-based exhibits and resources on special subjects as well as subject-organized and searchable, credentialed web links for adults, teens, and children.

Today the IPL is hosted by Drexel University's College of Information Science and Technology and operated jointly by three managing partners, Drexel University's College of Information Science and Technology, the University of Michigan's School of Information, and Florida State University's College of Information. Other universities, currently including the University of Illinois, Rutgers University, the University of North Carolina, and the University of Washington, are associate partners, paying an annual partnership fee and participating in IPL oversight. Still other LIS programs pay a per-student fee for IPL teaching support services, including IPL instructional materials and digital reference training and support. During the 2007–2008 academic year, eleven universities in the United States, Canada, and Germany participated in one of these ways. Two full-time employees and one part-time employee run the IPL's daily operations and provide support to students and instructors using the IPL, with additional technical assistance from the Drexel technical staff. A committee of IPL faculty fellows from the partnering universities makes policy and other administrative recommendations.

Access to the IPL's collection and Ask a Question reference service is free to the public. The IPL website receives approximately 12,000,000 hits per month, including roughly 1,500,000 unique visitors. Most of this traffic is for the online collections, which include more than 40,000 vetted resource links and a number of proprietary resources. The e-mail reference service is also popular. Ask a Question volunteers have answered over 65,000 reference questions since the service went live in 1995. Use of the reference service has increased over the years, as has the number of trained question answerers. The Ask a Question service received a total of 22,589 questions during 2007, and during the fall 2007 term alone, more than 500 LIS students were trained as reference volunteers.

Current IPL learning opportunities focus on hands-on reference and collection development activities. Additional opportunities in software and database development and maintenance are being developed for future use.

The IPL e-mail reference service has been used to train thousands of LIS students over the years. Questions come from users across the globe, with a significant portion of questioners located in developing countries that lack widespread public library access, such as the Philippines, Nigeria, and India. This is service-based experiential learning at its best. For a significant portion of patrons, the IPL is their only available public library service, and for many of the student volunteers, working for the IPL is their first experience of working for a real library service.

LIS students have also played key roles in shaping and maintaining the IPL collections. Students have created most of the IPL's online exhibits and resources, and they have evaluated and selected most of the links to exterior resources as well.

Overview of IPL Services: The Ask a Question Service

Historically, the educational focus of the IPL has been on teaching LIS students to answer e-mail reference questions. This focus on digital reference is even more important today than it was when the IPL was founded, for current and future students graduating from LIS programs will likely be employed in libraries offering not only traditional face-to-face reference services but also remote reference services using a variety of digital media. The provision of digital reference services requires knowledge and skills in guiding users to authoritative digital information sources, creating tools to assist users as they search for information, teaching users how to find information, and teaching them how to evaluate the quality of freely available information. The IPL provides service-based learning in all of these areas.

The IPL question-answering service is a web-based asynchronous system that uses a web form for requests and responses sent via e-mail to the patron. Students enrolled in reference-related courses in LIS programs have the opportunity of serving as volunteers to answer questions received from the general public.

The student learning process begins with extensive training. Students review the IPL training manual, complete a short quiz, and then complete a practice question, taken from a pool of actual reference questions received. The IPL staff review student responses to the practice questions to check the quality of the answers and the sources used and to ensure that students adhere to IPL policies and procedures.

The initial reference request forms are designed in a way to elicit information needed to provide high-quality answers in a timely fashion. Questions on the form include name, e-mail address, patron's physical location (which enables answerers to recommend sources from the patron's local public library), reply deadline, rough context and scope of the requested information, and sources already consulted. There are separate forms for adult and juvenile users. Because this is an asynchronous reference service, and because experience has shown that 80 percent of IPL users do not respond in a timely fashion to requests for clarification, student volunteers are discouraged from seeking additional information from patrons. Students must answer any questions that they claim within twenty-four hours to ensure timely service.

Through the IPL reference training, students learn how to select authoritative sources and how to prepare appropriate responses to patrons. To ensure quality and consistency among responses and to teach students best practices for remote reference, IPL answers must contain six required components: a greeting, acknowledgment of the question, the answer, source citations for at least three relevant sources, an explanation of the answerer's search strategy, and a closing. Due to its educational mission, IPL answers focus on teaching patrons how to find answers to questions, as opposed to merely providing the answers. LIS student volunteers are consequently required to provide clear descriptions of how to find the resources that they used to answer the questions.

Through the question-answering system, LIS students provide a public service while learning crucial reference skills, including

1. Knowledge of general and specialized reference sources (print and electronic)
2. The ability to recognize patrons' information needs and match these needs with the most appropriate forms of information
3. An understanding of the constraints and responsibilities that accompany digital reference service[4]

In addition to learning best reference practices, student volunteers learn to work effectively within a real-time question-answering management system. Besides question selection and response, students make notes to IPL reference administrators regarding questions and ask for help from IPL staff when necessary. The experiential learning process is extended via interaction with the individual course instructors, who review students' work and often share examples with their classes.

For student volunteers, the most gratifying part of this experience is the knowledge that they are serving real patrons with real information needs. Student volunteers greatly appreciate receiving thank-you messages from patrons, which happens approximately 10 percent of the time.

Once students have completed the basic IPL reference training and have answered a set of reference questions as part of a class assignment, there are a number of different options through which they may seek additional learning experiences related to the IPL question-answering service. In IPL workshop classes offered at the managing partner schools, students learn management skills via oversight of IPL question answerers. IPL workshop students receive additional training as reference administrators, working behind the scenes overseeing the question-answering process and assisting the IPL paid staff with the daily operations of the reference service. Reference administrators' duties include processing incoming questions, following up on improperly answered questions, helping to identify potential problems with students and other volunteers, and answering overflow questions that are not claimed within three days of the submission date.

Another role that students can play is to volunteer to answer questions that require a quick turnaround. Answering these "Quick Answer" questions requires additional training, since the responses do not include the in-depth research common to IPL answers, yet they must still meet IPL quality standards.

Overview of IPL Services: The Online Collections

In addition to reference-related experiential learning, faculty at participating universities can create assignments related to IPL collection management and development. The most common collection management projects include link checking and collection weeding, which require use of the IPL Hypatia database. Within Hypatia, students learn to edit metadata for collection maintenance. Another collection-related activity is the evaluation of online resource recommendations from IPL patrons. The resource evaluation process teaches students a number of important collection development skills. Before deciding if an item can be added to the IPL collection, students must become familiar with the IPL collection development policy.[5] Students apply evaluation criteria to each suggested resource and determine if it is appropriate for the IPL's collection. Students must also consider the relationship of the resource to other items in the collection.

In addition to links to recommended online resources, the IPL's collection contains original resources created by LIS students from the various participating universities. These include pathfinders that guide patrons to sources on given topics, Frequently Asked Reference Questions, and a variety of special collections. Some of the most popular resources created by students include the IPL Literary Criticism section, POTUS: Presidents of the United States, the Science Fair Project Resource Guide, and a special exhibit called Lighthouses: A Photographic Journey.[6] In other class assignments, students can select existing IPL resources and update them, either by removing out-of-date items or by adding new items. With all of these collection development assignments, the learning process is extended via interaction with the individual course instructors.

The IPL Serving LIS Faculty and Students through the IPL Learning Community

As part of an ongoing effort to keep the IPL services updated and responsive to faculty, student, and public user needs, Drexel University, in collaboration with Florida State University and the University of Michigan, received a 2007–2010 grant from the Institute of Museum and Library Services (IMLS) to expand the IPL into a full-featured Virtual Learning Laboratory for Digital Reference. The IPL Virtual Learning Laboratory project will (1) develop digital reference curricula and widely disseminate related learning and teaching objects; (2) design and determine the feasibility of a technological test bed for digital librarianship; and (3) develop a collaborative online learning community comprising LIS students, faculty, and working librarians to serve as a nationwide digital reference teaching and learning forum.

Under part 3 of the IMLS grant, the IPL Learning Community site (http://ipl.ci.fsu.edu) will support students, instructors, and librarians across institutions in communicating with each other, sharing files and information, and working collaboratively as a teaching and learning community on the Web. Through provision of an online collaborative space for communal interaction, students, instructors, and librarians will be able to post and read messages; ask and answer questions; create resources together; explore new information technologies; share and discuss research reports, syllabi, lesson plans, and teaching methods; and help other community members with questions and problems.

Today's online technologies can provide learners with more sophisticated collaborative educational experiences, from asynchronous e-mail and "bulletin board" threaded discussions to synchronous chat and immersive learning environments such as MOOs, MUDs, and virtual worlds. Although many libraries, museums, and institutions of higher education are launching information services in e-mail, chat, social networking websites, and virtual worlds such as Second Life and Active Worlds, not all institutions have the funding, technology, or staffing to support hands-on teaching and learning with digital technologies.[7]

The IPL Learning Community site provides a platform to integrate the exploration of technologies such as public wiki areas for cross-class, cross-institutional projects and showcases of student work, collaborative blogging, and community access to other Web 2.0 sharing tools, including a community Flickr space for photos, a YouTube video-sharing area, and Slideshare for sharing PowerPoint. Space is also built in for private collaboration among groups and for instructors to meet, share syllabi, arrange guest speakers, discuss ideas for learner activities, and access archived assignments, audio lectures, videos, and streaming media content.

Not only does the IPL Learning Community site support service-based experiential teaching and learning within the Internet Public Library, it offers another venue for community service projects through building tools and educational resources for the learning community site itself. In fall 2007 Florida State University students contributed short papers toward a learning community wiki on digital reference and Web 2.0; additionally, students created a MySpace page and a Facebook group. By late January 2008, over 100 libraries and library organizations on MySpace had "friended" the IPL's MySpace page.

Ultimately the IPL Learning Community site offers an experimental space for teaching and learning at the frontier of online education. To breach barriers of isolation for distance learners, online identity is supported with tools for creating personal presences via avatar images, customized titles, and signatures. A growing body of research suggests that a greater sense of "social presence" increases civility, trust, and mutual understanding and promotes willingness to interact with others in online learning environments.[8] Within the IPL Learning Community, anonymity is supported through a brainstorming, questioning, and feedback forum that encourages first-timers to post and emboldens learners to take greater risks in collaborative participation.[9] Other tools promoting feedback, collaboration, participation, and social presence are integrated into the learning community on a continuing basis.

Unlike the public service components of the IPL, which serve IPL patrons' needs, the IPL Learning Community serves the needs of the LIS faculty and student community. It creates a cross-class, cross-institutional, and cross-time collaboration in which successive student "generations" build upon the work of others, described by Guzdial, Rick, and Kehoe as "termlessness."[10] The boundaries of the classroom also open to collaboration with working professionals worldwide who can provide valuable feedback on student projects, creating ongoing potential for new directions in online teaching and learning. Finally, LIS faculty are served with the creation of a collaborative space for sharing class materials and other learning resources and for enabling communication with others with similar research and teaching interests.

Conclusion: The Future of the IPL as an Education and Service Organization

Thus, the Internet Public Library helps LIS faculty incorporate real-world learning experiences into their courses by connecting students to a community of real users using a real information service. Up to now the main service/learning opportunities have been in the areas of digital reference and collection maintenance, with a smaller emphasis on software and database development. The IPL is not limited to these teaching and learning areas, and part of the IPL's mission is to remain responsive to future trends in library and information services. As part of the IMLS grant to expand the IPL into a full-featured learning community, the IPL is investigating possible collaborative agreements with both the Librarians' Internet Index and with OCLC's QuestionPoint chat reference service.[11]

Regardless of the future directions it will take, the Internet Public Library will continue to evolve as the needs of the IPL user community change and as LIS faculty and students' needs change as well. As such, the IPL will continue to operate as an international forum for service-based experiential learning and as a twenty-first-century digital information service.

NOTES

The first epigraph for this chapter is from Kim Hawtrey, "Using Experiential Learning Techniques," *Journal of Economic Education* 38, no. 2 (Spring 2007): 144.

The second epigraph is from Jane T. Walker and others, "Enhancing Internships through Modules of Experiential Learning Activities," *Journal of Family and Consumer Sciences* 93, no. 4 (2001): 45.

1. David A. Kolb, *Experiential Learning: Experience as the Source of Learning and Development* (Englewood Cliffs, NJ: Prentice-Hall, 1984).

2. Peggy P. F. Lo, "Web-Based Postgraduate Course Design According to Experiential Learning," in *Proceedings of the IASTED International Conference on Web-Based Education* (Innsbruck, Austria: IASTED, 2004), 219–22.

3. Ibid.

4. Internet Public Library, 2007, www.ipl.org.

5. The collection development policy is available at www.ipl.org/div/about/colpol .html.

6. Internet Public Library, "Literary Criticism" section, www.ipl.org/div/litcrit/; "POTUS: Presidents of the United States," www.ipl.org/div/potus/; "Science Fair Project Resource Guide," www.ipl.org/div/kidspace/projectguide/; and "Lighthouses: A Photographic Journey," www.ipl.org/div/light/.

7. IPL MySpace (2007), www.myspace.com/internetpubliclibrary; SimTeach Wiki (2007), www.simteach.com/wiki/index.php?title=Main_Page; Jane Nicholson and Teresea Hopkins, "Appalachian State and Clemson Universities Partner to Research Virtual World Technology," Appalachian State University, *University News* (November 30, 2007), www.news.appstate.edu/2007/11/30/3-d-virtual/.

8. Charlotte N. Gunawardena, Ana C. Nolla, and Penne L. Wilson, "A Cross-Cultural Study of Group Process and Development in Online Conferences," *Distance Learning* 22, no. 1 (2001): 85–121; Karen L. Murphy and Lauren Cifuentes, "Using Web Tools, Collaborating, and Learning Online," *Distance Education* 22, no. 2 (2001): 285–305; and Karen L. Murphy and Mauri P. Collins, "Communication Conventions in Instructional Electronic Chats," *First Monday* 2 (November 1997), www.firstmonday.dk/issues/issue2_11/murphy/index.html.

9. Curtis Jay Bonk and Thomas H. Reynolds, "Learner-Centered Web Instruction for Higher-Order Thinking, Teamwork, and Apprenticeship," in *Web-Based Instruction,* ed. Badrul H. Khan (Englewood Cliffs, NJ: Educational Technology Publications, 1997), 168.

10. Mark Guzdial, Jochen Rick, and Colleen Kehoe, "Beyond Adoption to Invention: Teacher-Created Collaborative Activities in Higher Education," *Journal of the Learning Sciences* 10, no. 3 (2001): 265–79.

11. Librarians' Internet Index, http://lii.org; OCLC's QuestionPoint, www .questionpoint.org.

Chapter 14

A Road Map for Integrating Socially Relevant Research Projects into a Required Library and Information Science Course
From a Service Model to Community Engagement

Bharat Mehra

This chapter reflects upon the use of a "road map" to integrate socially relevant research projects in a required library and information science course that was taught during two consecutive semesters in the School of Information Sciences at the University of Tennessee. The course provided students with opportunities to apply their knowledge on information organization concepts to community engagement outcomes that make a real difference in people's lives. The learning experiences of participating students, community representatives, and an LIS faculty member while engaged in course implementations suggest a paradigmatic philosophical shift in LIS and the American academy at large. This shift is toward adopting a community engagement model that symbolizes progressive efforts to incorporate new definitions and characteristics into traditional service/outreach initiatives.

American library and information science programs and their affiliated institutions recognize a need for adopting more critical approaches to revise traditionally defined outreach and service missions that are "add-ons" to their teaching and research agendas.[1] Current developments in LIS education call for community engagement practices to accurately characterize the integration of teaching, research, and conventionalized service in ways that better capture the community essence of social equity and justice.[2] Community engagement also symbolizes a positive spirit of equality instead of perpetuating historically loaded, sociopolitically biased words such as *outreach* and/or *service* that imply imbalanced power inequities and insurmountable gaps between haves and have-nots in society.[3] Additionally, community engagement has the potential to extend LIS professions beyond a traditional conceptualization as solely information organizers and disseminators to information providers for community action involved in making community-wide social changes.[4]

Efforts incorporating socially relevant research projects in required LIS courses promote community engagement, as they allow students to build connections between core LIS competencies and skills and community development outcomes that make a real difference in people's lives.[5] LIS educators face a major challenge in reconceptualizing their required courses to integrate teaching of the profession's core functionalities with community engagement activities that partner students with local agencies to achieve meaningful community outcomes.[6] This chapter explores some answers by documenting student-community interactions while working on community-identified research projects in IS 520 Information Representation and Organization, a graduate-level LIS course required of all students in the School of Information Sciences (SIS) at the University of Tennessee.[7] This chapter reflects upon the conceptual role and praxis in developing a collaboration between the course instructor and the community liaison across the fall 2005 and spring 2006 semesters to provide 32 on-campus students—22 students in the fall semester and 10 students in the spring semester—with opportunities to apply their knowledge of information organization concepts to community technology-development outcomes. During both semesters, IS 520 students were partnered with community representatives from DiscoverET.org, a nonprofit community network and regional web portal that connects people and resources in eastern Tennessee, to develop their final class assignments on socially relevant academic research projects on topics of community significance.

This chapter identifies significant learning experiences of participating students, community members, and LIS faculty and describes course goals, assignments, stages in development, student learning, and community outcomes. The findings suggest positive gains for LIS programs that incorporate socially relevant projects in their required courses. Educational experiences in community engagement equip future LIS professionals to make stronger connections between theoretical constructs and everyday practice. Future efforts need to explore the existing and potential possibilities of integrating socially relevant research projects and community engagement activities in other required courses in other LIS programs around the country.

A Community Engagement Model to Replace Service-Based Ethics in LIS

Integrating socially relevant research projects in IS 520 is an expression of a broader philosophical point of view for adopting a community engagement model to replace service learning and service-based ethics in LIS and the American academy.[8] The phrase *community engagement* signifies not only an appropriate conceptualization and planning of socially relevant research projects in the LIS curriculum and beyond, but also recognizes the need for using the right language, vocabulary, and unbiased words to represent such efforts. Community engagement symbolizes an urgency to adopt more holistic and integrated efforts that connect teaching, research, conventional service, and student participation in collaborations of engagement with local, regional, national, and global communities to achieve socially relevant outcomes. Traditionally defined service and outreach missions in American academia do not represent this positive application. They might be perceived to symbolize a missionary zeal, reflecting imbalanced power dynamics toward disenfranchised populations. These populations on the margins of society are considered outside the realm of mainstream discourse and practices, such that their need and impoverishment requires service to uplift their downtrodden existences. Such traditional outlooks assume an active role for American academic institutions while viewing the community as passive receptors of intermediation. Thus, academic activities are expressed in terms of their unidirectional impact to improve the lot of the knowledge-deficient and information-impoverished "outside" of academia. The activeness of academic institutions in such traditional conceptualizations and the passiveness of disempowered communities are also expressed in terms of the academy making efforts to improve the conditions of those on the margins of society who are passive and helpless. They cannot do anything to improve their own lot, or contribute anything positive, in utilizing their own assets, knowledge, and experiences, toward progressive development and growth in the community. This chapter challenges such traditional views of service and outreach that might be perceived to reflect an underlying notion of imperialist dominance, colonialist agendas, and outdated morality and ethics.[9]

Instead, a community engagement interpretation of LIS students' involvement in community activities represents a more contemporary and relevant strategy in recognizing diversity and the assets and skills of the underserved populations. It takes into account the change agency and efficacy power that each individual inherits as a human being, and presents a model that is reflective and forward oriented in its efforts to build equitable partnerships involving LIS students and community members to achieve collaboratively defined community goals. Integrating socially relevant research projects in IS 520 reflects a democratic and participative ideology of community engagement that provides one example of reinterpreting the traditional notions of service and outreach. Although there are other opportunities in the LIS classroom that integrate students' efforts in community engagement such as independent study, practicum, student participation in community activities, and different forms of community-based action research projects, among others, those are beyond the scope of this chapter.[10]

What are some elements of community engagement that warrant attention in LIS teaching practices? What kinds of broad or specific questions of community engagement need to be addressed in the design and planning of LIS curricula? Table 14-1 makes a start in raising some pertinent issues, with a few sample questions and LIS assignment solutions.

Providing answers to some of these issues and seeking solutions is not an easy process. The key point is for LIS educators to consider such questions that may help them think about community engagement as an option while developing content in their required courses. Considering the realistic limitations of time and effort involved in teaching required LIS courses, it is impossible and impractical to include all the elements of community engagement as identified in table 14-1. A balanced decision based on careful consideration of course content, course scope and objectives, understanding of the community's information needs and goals, time and effort commitment, the desirability of participating in outcome-oriented efforts, and the relationship between the LIS educator and community liaison, among other factors, will help LIS professionals determine which of the various elements of community engagement they should try to integrate into their required courses, and to what degree. The following section briefly summarizes the IS 520 course description and reflects upon course activities and outcomes that were significant in integrating socially relevant research projects to achieve meaningful community outcomes.

Information Organization Concepts to Represent Community Information

For their final assignments in IS 520, LIS graduate students applied principles, standards, and tools underlying the organization of information to collect, analyze, and effectively represent community information in twelve research-based community-identified projects. This assignment constituted 40 percent of the total course grade.[11] David Massey, previous executive director of DiscoverET.org, played an instrumental role as community liaison in planning and developing the research projects for the class. His constant feedback about the community provided rich information that accurately represented community-based issues, identified potential community agencies for students to contact, presented practical implementation concerns, and explicated community-based technological realities and limitations. The success of future efforts to incorporate research-based projects in required LIS courses is highly dependent on such partnerships to facilitate information flows between LIS instructors and community liaisons, and these need to be planned accordingly.

The goal of integrating socially relevant research projects as the final assignment in IS 520 was for students to partner with DiscoverET.org and apply their knowledge of information organization concepts to develop appropriate information systems to meet specific community needs and expectations. Teams of two to four students were involved throughout the two semesters in making connections between core LIS theory, practice, and engagement with local community agencies. Students discussed, analyzed, and reinterpreted an application to a community context. Core information organization concepts included intellectual works and their manifestations, metadata standards in various environments, cataloging and authority control, metadata coding and crosswalks, digital library development, subject access and classification systems, and systems design, among others.

Course outcomes provided innovative and rich information organization solutions to community-based problems. Research projects included a comprehensive assessment/evaluation of DiscoverET.org's web-based information; organizational schemes to represent community information for surrounding counties in Tennessee; representation of community information for subject categories like youth, diversity, and international populations; analysis of web-based communication tools such as wikis and blogs for

Table 14-1. Elements of desired community engagement in LIS required courses

Elements	Sample Questions	Sample LIS Assignments
1. Critical and reflective research that trains students to question traditional LIS values, practices, ideologies, and processes[a]	What are cultural biases in the standard classification systems (e.g., LCC, DDC) and cataloging[b] and how can they be removed?	Compare the LCC and DCC with *A Women's Thesaurus*[c]
2. Recognition of traditionally identified "disenfranchised" as equals who are experts in their own ontologies, circumstances, and awareness of realities because others do not possess these experiences[d]	How can users contribute their own knowledge in digital libraries on different subjects (e.g., health, business, education, entertainment) or their use of information organization systems to equate power imbalances with "experts" in various fields?	Partner with different users to identify their conceptualization of relationships between the subject headings in the Library of Congress authority database. Are all subject headings for different topics represented in an accurate and equitable manner? What are the existing gaps of knowledge domains and subject categories between users' feedback and traditional systems? How can LIS professionals fill these missing gaps?
3. Contextualization of students' coursework in the everyday experiences of people on society's margins in ways that make a difference in their socioeconomic and sociopolitical experiences of marginalization	Are there local community agencies willing to identify their specific information needs for LIS educators who may create assignments in their courses around the community-identified information needs for students to help address?	Partner with a community agency and build a collection of digital resources on topics related to the agency's need while using CONTENTdm software for digital collections available through OCLC and gather evaluation feedback from the agency in their use of the software
4. Application of change agency and empowerment to facilitate people's own efforts for improvements in their socioeconomic and sociopolitical realities by "helping people help themselves"[e]	How can LIS professionals acknowledge and adequately represent in the design of library OPACs the vocabulary and searching mechanisms of users who are "left out" in the provision of traditional library services?	Partner with a person from an underserved or socially stigmatized group (e.g., people living with HIV/AIDS) and modify online records for works and their metadata fields (e.g., subject, keywords) using OCLC's Connexion to access WorldCat based on searching terms and natural language vocabulary of your partner for known or unknown items on topics of interest

| 5. Emphasis on social justice and social equity via action to change imbalances in distribution of resources, information, and power[f] | How can LIS students participate in efforts to develop and design online information content management systems so that local community agencies can themselves create, organize, manage, and maintain their web-based resources? | Build a database management system or design a website for a community agency to represent and organize its information; partner with a nonprofit agency to train its members in its use of Drupal content management system |

[a] Jürgen Habermas, *Justification and Application: Remarks on Discourse Ethics*, trans. Ciaran P. Cronin (Cambridge, MA: MIT Press, 1993); Charles R. McClure and Peter Hernon, eds., *Library and Information Science Research: Perspectives and Strategies for Improvement* (Norwood, NJ: Ablex, 1991).

[b] Sanford Berman, "Jackdaws Strut in Peacock Feathers: The Sham of 'Standard' Cataloging," *Librarians at Liberty* (June 1998): 1–21.

[c] Hope A. Olson, "Mapping beyond Dewey's Boundaries: Constructing Classificatory Space for Marginalized Knowledge Domains," *Library Trends 47*, no. 2 (Fall 1998): 233–54.

[d] Bharat Mehra, "Library and Information Science (LIS) and Community Development: Use of Information and Communication Technology (ICT) to Support a Social Equity Agenda," *Journal of the Community Development Society 36*, no. 1 (2005): 28–40.

[e] Bharat Mehra, Kendra S. Albright, and Kevin Rioux, "A Practical Framework for Social Justice Research in the Information Professions," in *Proceedings of the 69th Annual Meeting of the American Society for Information Science and Technology 2006: Information Realities: Shaping the Digital Future for All* (Austin, TX: American Society for Information Science and Technology, 2006).

[f] Bharat Mehra, "An Action Research (AR) Manifesto for Cyberculture Power to 'Marginalized' Cultures of Difference," in *Critical Cyberculture Studies*, edited by David Silver and Adrienne Massanari (New York: New York University Press, 2006).

meeting local community needs; assessment and design of an environmental information plan for a local air-quality forum; web-based design templates with Spanish-language translations for local community information; and an interactive relational database for volunteer recruitment in nonprofit organizations. Students were evaluated based on the criteria of creativity of research outcomes and proposed recommendations or solutions, relevance and practicality of implementation, thoroughness and examination of details, and application of the course topics to community-identified information needs.

Road Map to Organize IS 520 Research Projects: Reflection and Discussion

The use of a road map in IS 520 proved to be an effective tool for students to learn about information organization concepts while navigating their progress to achieve meaningful outcomes in their community-identified research projects. The "road map" helped students to represent, analyze, organize, and discuss community information and functioned as an outline for them to follow. Students were able to map course topics and information organization concepts in the context of their own project's information research development process. This process was identified in terms of the following stages: introduction and scope, course topic boundary setting, case study analysis, preliminary and revised design proposals, recommendations and plan of action, future considerations, documentation of individual team's process of work, and journal writing and participation. The "road map" directed student information-learning in their socially relevant research projects. It channeled their efforts and reflection to apply course topics in their community projects from start to finish while following the specific stages in the information research project development process. Table 14-2 summarizes the structural or conceptual stages of the "road map" and identifies their role in the students' information-learning process during the course.

The use of a "road map" thus helped students in IS 520 apply information organization concepts in a community context and provided a facilitation tool to integrate socially relevant research projects. The "road map" shaped student information-learning outcomes on two levels: (1) functional information-learning of course content and topics that are important in understanding the organization and representation of information; and (2) socially relevant information-learning in a community context. The "road map" helped students make connections to community context at every step in the process, from conceptualization to project completion. Table 14-3 lists selected community outcomes that were achieved in IS 520.

IS 520 is a required course in SIS, and as an instructor it was exciting to teach new students entering the profession core information organization concepts in the context of community needs while participating in socially relevant research projects. Partnering with DiscoverET.org provided students a real-life context to supplement what they learned in class. As one student wrote in the course evaluation: "The DiscoverET.org project contributed most to my learning and gave the class content a new and practical application." A key challenge in student learning was an initial struggle to relate the course content to their projects. As the semesters came to a close, students were able to develop a much clearer picture of those connections. IS 520 students' information-focused interpretations and analyses in their research projects have generated key changes in information organization mechanisms and technological and social relationships for DiscoverET.org and others. The role of the community liaison in follow-up implementations and the instructor's efforts to maintain the partnering initiative with DiscoverET.org in future courses are two significant factors that contributed to this outcome.

Table 14-2. Use of a "road map" in socially relevant research projects in IS 520 (Information Representation and Organization)

Stages	Information Learning of Course Content	Information Learning in Community Context
1. Introduction	Describes the main features of the project (e.g., expectations, scope, boundaries); establishes issues/concerns specific to the process of applying information organization concepts in the project	Recognizes scope and boundaries of the project in the context of connections between course goals and community issues
2. Course topic boundary setting in relationship to the project goals	Identifies 3–5 considerations about select course topics and how they are represented in the particular project	Draws links among specific course topics, information organization expectations in the project, and community dynamics
3. Critique of case study based on analysis of course topics	Locates and describes 3–5 web resources with information similar to the project; comparative analysis based on critique of course topics in each case study	Examines how other agencies have addressed similar community information, as in their project description
4. Design solutions/ proposed design templates	Presents design solutions based on lessons from case studies; provides web designs and analysis; presents design rationale	Makes connections between information organization designs, context, and community realities
5. Recommendations and plan of action	Identifies strategies/factors influencing implementation and operations related to information organization	Recognizes impact of community realities on information organization and design
6. Future considerations	Identifies next steps in information design solutions	Presents impact of community realities and limitations
7. Documentation report	Documents administrative modalities of work, process, and activities (e.g., role of team members, specific tasks, minutes of project meetings)	Recognizes importance of documentation and resources (e.g., time, efforts) involved in community projects and collaborative learning
8. Journal writing and participation	Identifies critical reflective learning based on participation in an information research project; understands systems design to improve information access by improved organizational methods	Develops connections between theory and practical community-based information research projects; reflects how concepts or knowledge get applied in community-based situations

Table 14-3. Community outcomes in IS 520 (Information Representation and Organization)

---

1. Comprehensive usability evaluation and user training of web-based resources on select topics, assessing their strengths, weaknesses, limitations, and strategies to expand based on limited community needs analysis

2. Application and analysis of information organization fundamentals in the context of specific research projects identified by community agencies

3. Web designs and development incorporating new and existing information materials on specific subjects of community importance

4. Collection of case studies on community networks based on overlap in mission, content, and functionalities as reflected in the research projects

5. Assessment of competitors' edge over community partners in achieving similar goals reflected in the research projects

6. Strategies for improving searching and information retrieval effectiveness of the existing systems based on updated metadata descriptions/schemes, classification options, indexing, and authority control

7. Improved interface, aesthetics, and organization of web materials based on revised menu options, hierarchical ordering, metadata coding, and relationship management of informational content

8. Better organization of community information resources and services via developing multisystem crosswalks (e.g., Spanish-language translation schema)

9. Testing and evaluation of appropriate database management systems based on consideration of time, finances, human efforts, and future maintenance

10. Use analysis of different kinds of existing and emerging community-based interactive communication and information-sharing tools (e.g., personal websites, e-mail, newsgroups, electronic discussion lists, wikis, blogs, interactive calendars)

Conclusion

This chapter calls for a paradigmatic philosophical shift in its representation of a community engagement model that reflects progressive efforts to incorporate new definitions and characteristics into traditional service and outreach initiatives. Such a position in LIS education and American academia is especially relevant in the twenty-first century because it incorporates contemporary democratic ideologies, propagates partnering relationships based on the redefinition of knowledge and its relationship to society's historical power inequities, and proposes a change that is incremental and constructive. Additionally, community engagement applies a fresh and innovative approach that integrates the three missions of the university and presents a more equitable and participative model.

Land grant academic institutions of higher learning are under tremendous pressures to show the relevance of their pursuits to the everyday lives of laypeople who support local, regional, and state colleges and universities through their taxpayer contributions. Community engagement recognizes the significance of such realities and presents a strategic approach that draws deeper connections between teaching, research, and service missions in the American academy. Community engagement helps students make stronger connections between theoretical constructs and everyday practice.[12] The entirety of experience is grounds for research where documentation of the process and analysis and interpretation of experiences in such situations creatively contributes to research outcomes and to the body of world knowledge. This enhances student learning and simultaneously addresses practical problems in contemporary society. LIS professionals can take the lead in this regard by furthering community engagement activities and discarding outdated service and outreach rhetoric that represents egocentric and imbalanced power realities.

Various LIS programs in the United States offer a combination of required and elective courses leading to the master of science degree accredited by the ALA. This chapter has examined in detail one required course in one LIS program in the country and its integration of community-based research projects to achieve socially relevant outcomes. The conceptual role and praxis in developing collaboration between the course instructor and community network liaison were instrumental toward achieving this goal. The use of a road map to direct student learning of information organization concepts in a community context also played a significant role.

In order for LIS professions to extend their role in community engagement activities, there is a need to look closely at the content of other required courses in other LIS programs. This close examination involves tracking each course for its existing and potential connections with local community-based information needs and expectations. Such links between required course content and the community's information needs can be structured in formal and informal class assignments via the use of tools such as the road map discussed in this chapter. It will lead to more practical strategies in required LIS courses to integrate students' participation in socially relevant research projects and other activities to effectively achieve desired community outcomes considered meaningful by local constituencies and stakeholders.

ACKNOWLEDGMENTS

The author wants to acknowledge the generosity of Dr. Peiling Wang, faculty member in the SIS at the University of Tennessee, for sharing her IS 520 syllabus that was modified to integrate research projects in collaboration with DiscoverET.org. The author also acknowledges the ongoing contributions of David Massey and other community representatives for their role in the partnering efforts.

NOTES

1. Robin Osborne, ed., *From Outreach to Equity: Innovative Models of Library Policy and Practice* (Chicago: American Library Association, 2004); and Frank A. Fear and Lorilee Sandmann, "Unpacking the Service Category: Reconceptualizing University Outreach for the 21st Century," *Continuing Higher Education Review* 59, no. 3 (Fall 1995): 110–22.

2. Craig Gibson, ed., *Student Engagement and Information Literacy* (Chicago: American Library Association, Association of College and Research Libraries, 2006); and Kathleen de la Peña McCook, "Reconnecting Library Education and the Mission of Community," *Library Journal* 125, no. 14 (September 1, 2000): 164–65.

3. Stephen L. Percy, Nancy L. Zimpher, and Mary J. Brukardt, eds., *Creating a New Kind of University: Institutionalizing Community-University Engagement* (Bolton, MA: Anker, 2006); and Bruce W. Speck and Sherry L. Hoppe, eds., *Service-Learning: History, Theory, and Issues* (Westport, CT: Praeger, 2004).

4. Bharat Mehra and Ramesh Srinivasan, "The Library-Community Convergence Framework for Community Action: Libraries as Catalysts of Social Change," *Libri: International Journal of Libraries and Information Services* 57, no. 3 (September 2007): 123–39; and Elfreda A. Chatman and Victoria E. M. Pendleton, "Knowledge Gap, Information-Seeking and the Poor," *Reference Librarian* 49–50 (1995): 135–45.

5. David Watson, *Managing Civic and Community Engagement* (Maidenhead, UK: Open University Press, 2007).

6. Barbara Jacoby and Associates, *Building Partnerships for Service-Learning* (San Francisco: Jossey-Bass, 2003).

7. Course syllabus at https://web.utk.edu/~bmehra/IS520Syllabus.doc.

8. Bharat Mehra, "The Cross-Cultural Learning Process of International Doctoral Students: A Case Study in Library and Information Science Education" (Ph.D. dissertation, University of Illinois at Urbana-Champaign, 2004).

9. Bharat Mehra, "Service Learning in Library and Information Science (LIS) Education: Connecting Research and Practice to Community," *InterActions: UCLA Journal of Information and Education Studies* 1, no. 1 (2004): article 3.

10. For more information, see chapter 15 in this volume, by Mehra and Sandusky.

11. Details of students' work are available online at http://web.utk.edu/~bmehra/teaching.html.

12. Mehra, "Service Learning."

Chapter 15

LIS Students as Community Partners in Elective Courses
Applying Community-Based Action Research to Meet the Needs of Underserved Populations

Bharat Mehra and Robert J. Sandusky

American library and information science education increasingly engages students in community-based experiences involving the application and use of various information and communication technologies (ICTs) to meet community needs.[1] Faculty must continue to develop new community partnerships and adapt courses to support the direct engagement of LIS students with underserved populations in the community. A significant part of course adaptation concerns creatively introducing LIS students to methods, strategies, and activities that effectively support community engagement. Community-based action research (AR) enables significant learning experiences for LIS students by connecting learning, action, and research while meeting relevant community-prioritized goals and objectives.[2] However, community-based AR may be unfamiliar to many LIS educators and practitioners. Therefore, additional LIS course examples and case studies incorporating community-based AR are needed to help LIS educators reflect upon the relevance of core functionalities in the profession to community service and thereby develop a wider and deeper range of effective LIS applications to community engagement.[3]

This chapter addresses this gap by summarizing faculty and LIS student experiences applying community-based AR in three graduate-level elective courses. The chapter describes how each course integrated learning, action, and research in different ways, tailored to each community engagement situation. The three courses that are discussed in the chapter are the following:

- IS 590 Race, Gender, and Sexuality in the Information Professions. This course was taught by Mehra as a synchronous distance education course in the School of Information Sciences (SIS) at the University of Tennessee during spring 2007. The course required student participation in community-based action projects throughout the semester in all course assignments.[4]

- LIS 590SJ Social Justice in the Information Professions. An initial version of this course developed by Ann P. Bishop formed a skeletal framework that was modified and taught by Mehra as an on-campus course in the Graduate School of Library and Information Science at the University of Illinois at Urbana-Champaign (UIUC) during fall 2004. The course required student participation in community-based research projects for a final course assignment. In addition, students were introduced to various community-based activities throughout the semester.[5]

- IS 585 Information Technologies. This course is taught by Sandusky in the SIS at the University of Tennessee. During fall 2007, IS 585 was taught as an on-campus course and incorporated student projects building or enhancing web content management systems (CMS) co-designed and co-managed by community members to meet community-defined objectives.[6]

This chapter reflects upon significant learning experiences of the students, community members, and faculty and identifies key issues, activities, and community outcomes achieved during these courses. Documenting how community-based AR has been applied in the different elective courses provides valuable lessons in how LIS educators can involve graduate students in the classroom in social justice and community-based empowerment agendas. The chapter also suggests a categorization scheme for the kinds of activities that LIS students engage in during the courses. It identifies the need to further explore potential relationships between the taxonomic core and marginal knowledge domains in the profession and applications of community-based AR.

Three Forms of Community-Based Action Research

The three elective courses discussed in this chapter have key similarities and differences in the ways they incorporate community-based AR. The similarities underlying their makeup, organization, and AR implementation in the courses emerge from a common philosophy drawing upon intersections between community engagement and service learning. There were significant differences in the implementation of community-based AR in the three courses based on the extent of community involvement with the students, the time frame of interaction, and the relevance of outcomes for the community and the students. Based on these differences, we categorize three forms of community-based AR in LIS elective courses, namely:

- Community-based action projects that focus on an ongoing engagement between partnering LIS students and community members, throughout the course duration, to improve the everyday experiences of participating members. Such course experiences develop an equal or secondary research focus for students to learn theory, but in relation to action and reflective practice.[7] Community-based action projects provide critical assessment and suggest improvements in future applications of the designed experience, based on mutual analysis of their interactions by both students and community members. There are regular interactions between the students and community representatives, and the outcomes are directly related to positive changes in the community.

- Community-based research projects that take the form of specific or final course assignments where the interaction between LIS students and community members is during a limited time of course duration to achieve information-based goals and objectives. Such course experiences incorporate a secondary focus of action to further positive change in the community's political, economic, social, cultural, and technological life. Community-based research projects identify information-oriented findings and draw implications based on students' interpretation and analysis. Outcomes are indirectly related to positive changes in the community.

- Community-based ICT development projects in which students interact with the community for the duration of a course, but where a long-term engagement with specific community-based projects is managed across multiple semesters by the faculty member. Over relatively long periods of time—months and years—the ICT system evolves in a process of continuous design.[8] Students engage in within-semester projects to review community-prioritized needs, propose design alternatives, and implement community-approved changes.

Table 15-1 summarizes key differences between the three forms of community-based AR based on selected criteria.

Each of these three forms of community-based AR projects provides the students with relevant practice that reinforces the theories, methods, and concepts they are exposed to in their LIS coursework. Although there are additional forms of activity within which students can experience community-based AR, such as independent study, practicum, participation in community activities, involvement in externally funded projects, and community-based AR in LIS required courses, among others, those are beyond the scope of discussion in this chapter. Integrating community-based action projects, research projects, and ICT development projects in LIS elective courses provide different kinds of experiences and outcomes for participating students and community members alike. All three forms are relevant based on the context

Table 15-1. Differences between three forms of community-based AR

Criteria for Comparison	Action Projects	Research Projects	ICT Development Projects
1. Extent of community involvement with the students	Deep and regular interactions	Less intense interactions for specific or final course assignments	Periodic interactions, both direct and mediated
2. Time frame of interaction	Ongoing and throughout the semester	Limited time of course duration	Long-term faculty-community relationships; shorter course-length student-community engagements
3. Relevance of outcomes for the community	Directly relevant to positive changes in the community	Indirect impact on positive community changes	ICT development typically enables other community actions
4. Relevance of outcomes for the students in learning of LIS constructs	Secondary focus of research; learning is dependent on action and reflective practice	Information-based goals and objectives are achieved	Designing ICTs/services to meet authentic community needs; ICT administration
5. Role of participants in generation of findings	Mutual cooperative analysis by students and community members	Primarily student's interpretation and analysis	Community states needs, reviews and approves design alternatives, and accepts or rejects implementation
6. Key issues	Difficult to synchronize with semester schedules and course content; rewarding in terms of directly generating positive changes in the community	Easier to plan for during the semester; wider range of application and course integration; significant role of intermediaries to operationalize student-identified outcomes to generate community impact	ICT work spans technical work, policy development, information organization, etc.; challenge of identifying correctly sized units of work; avoid overtaxing community members

of interaction because they provide unique opportunities for LIS students and community members to collaborate and partner, irrespective of the nuances of interaction. Incorporating different forms of community-based AR requires careful consideration of community goals, course content/scope and course objectives, desired outcomes, expected time and effort, willingness to devote time toward planning, role of available intermediaries, and other factors. For example, although community-based action projects are rewarding in terms of directly generating positive changes in the community, they are also more difficult to orchestrate and require greater efforts and time in planning, an ongoing relationship between participating members from academia and the community, and deeper trust levels between various members involved in the interaction.

Community-based research projects, on the other hand, are easier to plan and have a wider range of application and course integration, even though under usual circumstances they have only an indirect impact in generating positive changes in the community. However, if special circumstances permit, then the student information-focused interpretations and analysis generated during community-based research projects can become significant starting points toward greater community-wide positive impacts. Such special circumstances involve an active role for intermediaries in the situation (e.g., community representative, course instructor, community networker) who can become facilitators translating the findings from the student-developed research projects in terms of direct community-based outcomes and impacts. In addition, intermediaries can systematically channel community feedback in response to the students' research findings toward the next steps in the process of their operationalization and implementation.

The following sections summarize descriptions of the three courses under study, outline their integration of community-based AR activities, and briefly reflect upon lessons and outcomes to make connections between learning, action, and research.

Community-Based Action Projects in IS 590

IS 590 explored issues of how race, gender, and sexuality affect, and are affected by, information technologies in community-based environments, social welfare agencies, libraries, and other information-oriented settings. Six graduate students in IS 590 participated in either one of the two community-based action projects (100 percent of the total grade) that enabled them to learn from the intersections between theory, practice, and engagement with local communities/individuals: (1) the Computers for Homebound and Isolated Persons (CHIPS) program, and (2) the East Tennessee Lesbian, Gay, Bisexual, Transgender, and Questioning (LGBTQ) Youth Project. David Massey, previous executive director of DiscoverET.org, a nonprofit community network and regional web portal that connects people and resources in eastern Tennessee, was the community liaison for both the projects. The CHIPS program, initiated under the auspices of Knox County mayor Mike Ragdale's "No Senior Left Behind" initiative, trains and equips homebound persons to use technology to overcome social isolation, connect with people and resources, assert more control over their own lives, and contribute to their community. Three IS 590 students participated in the CHIPS program and were partnered with an individual client to train and equip homebound persons to use e-mail and the Internet. Participating students documented their experiences in using computers to make a difference in the lives of elderly and isolated individuals. They gathered feedback throughout the process from their CHIPS clients and developed individually tailored training materials to overcome the specific debilitating needs of the clients. Each of the three students also took a lead for one month in conducting communication and information exchanges via the CHIPS electronic discussion list to interact with the larger CHIPS community, build an ongoing relationship with other clients, spark discussions, gather feedback, let clients tell their stories, and share relevant information resources.

The East Tennessee LGBTQ Youth Project (supported in part by a technical assistance grant from the Appalachian Community Fund) comprises a small group of adults and youth who are exploring the feasibility of establishing a stand-alone nonprofit dedicated to serving the needs of LGBTQ youth in the multicounty region around Knoxville, Tennessee. Three IS 590 students participated in this project and (1) collected background literature and case study reports to build a bibliography on library and information support services for LGBTQ youth; (2) surveyed local information providers and library staff about their services for LGBTQ youth in Knox and surrounding counties to determine their awareness of, attitude toward, and policies regarding this marginalized population; (3) participated in community-based activities about issues pertinent to LGBTQ youth; and (4) conducted discussions and elicited the participation of LGBTQ youth and adults and others in information assessment strategies based on their youth experiences in child welfare programs, juvenile justice programs, and/or secondary school systems, in order to identify future directions for improvement in local information support systems for LGBTQ youth.

There were significant aspects common across the process of facilitating student-community collaborations in IS 590 for the two community-based action projects (the CHIPS program and the East Tennessee LGBTQ Youth Project). First, it was essential to integrate community activities and interaction with community activists during the formal course structure and its scheduled meeting times. Exposure to these presentations and discussion with community leaders provided students with an understanding of the community context. This was essential in their learning owing to the students' role as newcomers working on the community-based projects for the short time of course duration. Such experiences were in addition to the informal meetings and participation in community activities that each student initiated outside course time based on his unique role in the two projects. Second, both the community-based action projects involved students and community members in learning from each other during the process of discussing, analyzing, dissecting, and interpreting information technology constructions and conceptualizations of race, gender, sexual orientation, and ageism, among others, in the context of their individual situations of interaction in the two projects. Because the CHIPS program had an established process and infrastructure support already in place, IS 590 students working with homebound and isolated people found their experiences relatively easy, even though there was a greater time commitment to visit clients on a weekly basis. On the other hand, since the East Tennessee LGBTQ Youth Project was a comparatively new initiative and the topic of youth sexuality is problematic in the heart of the Bible Belt, IS 590 students working on this community-based action project found the experience difficult to navigate, especially during the initial stages. Ultimately, persistent efforts, community networking, and support from outside community agencies provided students in both projects with the specific and focused directions they needed to proceed. Students were able to report detailed analyses of issues related to the provision (or lack of provision) of information support services in the local community of Knoxville and the adjoining counties in eastern Tennessee. Based on student experiences, future plans were laid out for the organizers of the two projects to develop strategies to partner with LIS professionals, students, and others to help further recognition of nonmainstream realities and provide guidance to libraries and information support agencies to improve their services for homebound and isolated people and LGBTQ youth.

Additionally, both community-based action projects in IS 590 integrated learning, action, and research in different ways. The CHIPS program involved each participant (homebound individual and IS 590 student) to take the role of a storyteller, giving voice to their own realities in the partnership, as well as developing skills to empower each other in the process. The pilot experience helped nurture shared connections between partnering CHIP clients and LIS students, telling the story of the semester-long interaction that went beyond the traditional classroom to provide learning for all participants involved by recognizing their commonalities, providing support and sharing their strengths, and giving value to their collaborating experiences. The East Tennessee LGBTQ Project involved students in engaging with the community on issues relevant to LGBTQ youth. Students developed appropriate collections and conducted assessment and evaluation of local information support service providers—including libraries—while at the same time including LGBTQ youth and adults in important stages in the process.

Outcomes relevant to the community in both the projects included sharing of reports that documented the detailed process of storytelling during the two collaborations and identified future plans for the two community-based projects to ensure their smooth operation. Outcomes also included strategies to promote advertising and marketing to extend program outreach and development and lessons to improve project goals and promote greater tangible and intangible results. In addition, student-community member interactions resulted in improved experiences for individuals specifically involved in the interactions.

Community-Based Research Projects in LIS 590SJ

LIS 590SJ examined how issues of social justice are treated in LIS and related fields. The course provided eleven students a rich community-based context by orchestrating their participation in seven community-identified research projects through individual or group work for their final course assignment, constituting 30 percent of their total grade. Additionally, the course involved regular community-based activities with various community agencies to promote ongoing engagement between LIS students and community members on a range of topics and issues. The community-based research project provided students an opportunity to work for a portion of the semester with community members to meet their information-related needs. It gave students a chance to learn through practical work experience in information settings where social justice was actively being addressed. It also allowed students to revisit the conceptual foundations of LIS and investigate current practice related to achieving equitable, democratic, and beneficial information services for all members of society. Table 15-2 summarizes community-identified outcomes achieved in LIS 590SJ during fall 2004.

The community-based research project and community-based activities in LIS 590SJ together contributed in making the course experience relevant to both community members and students. A salient activity that proved invaluable in the course implementation and provided significant student learning about community issues was the coordination of class activities with the Information Professionals for Social Justice (IPSJ) Brown Bag Series.[9] IPSJ is a cluster of faculty, students, and staff in UIUC who share a common vision to generate consciousness, develop awareness, and focus on social justice issues in the LIS professions. Coordinating the course schedule with the IPSJ Brown Bag Series provided an avenue for students to engage with speakers from different social justice settings. Speakers shared information about various social justice–related activities, consolidated social justice efforts across the community, and identified connections for social justice work in the LIS professions. Developing ongoing community-based partnerships and collaborations with local social justice agencies and leaders since 2001 was instrumental in synchronizing the course goals and activities in resonance with the presentations and concerns of speakers for the IPSJ Brown Bag Series.

Another important community-based activity in LIS 590SJ involved student planning and orchestration of the Community Discussion Forum as part of the September Project, a "collection of people, groups, and organizations working to create a day of engagement, a day of conversation, a day of democracy" at library venues that served as "ideal hosts for community events to connect and engage neighbors across the country."[10] This assignment constituted 20 percent of the total grade. The Community Discussion Forum was synchronized with other national events planned for September 11, 2004. It involved students in planning, organizing, and partnering with community

Table 15-2. Community outcomes achieved in LIS 590SJ (Social Justice in the Information Professions)

Project Title	No. of students	Community Agency	Community Outcomes
1. Needs assessment and technology implementation plan	4	Center for Women in Transition	Information needs assessments of staff/residents via survey, interviews, and focus groups; hardware and software inventory and installations; building collection of online tools; development of training guides; development plan to identify policy changes in tech use and future directions
2. Participation in Project RiverWeb, a technical and educational framework to help create educational content	1	K–12 educators in East St. Louis, IL	Development of educational content about local history of East St. Louis for use in schools; creation of educational lesson plans
3. Computer technologies for people with disabilities	1	Persons Assuming Control of their Environment (PACE) and the Prairienet Community Network	Raising $900 plus for JAWS software . . . ; computer installation at the PACE center based on needs assessment, inventory of existing computers/software, identification of donors, and fund-raising
4. Digital collection for minority users	1	Minority users at the local branches of the academic library	Social justice collection of annotated bibliography for the library website based on needs assessment of minority users
5. Development of the LawHelpMN portal website	1	Minnesota Legal Services Coalition	Report on issues and challenges in providing online legal service information for immigrant populations
6. Collection development for Latino studies	1	Local Latino populations	Development of a virtual collection and policy
7. Web development for the Office of International Student Affairs	1	Local international populations	Web development strategic plan; usability analysis of existing resources; future recommendations for web expansion

agencies, resulting in a community-based discussion on issues of civil liberties and individual freedom in the United States. Attended by 30 to 50 community members, the event helped in

- extending the image of the library as a community place;
- developing closer and more meaningful ties between the library, community organizers, and the students;
- becoming aware of opportunities for LIS professionals in community and social justice work;
- furthering local and national dialogue on civil liberties; and
- developing and designing an advertising and exhibit space on community affairs at the local library.

LIS 590SJ students were also involved in an International Librarianship Day that helped focus attention on global development and social justice issues on a worldwide scale. The event was organized in the LIS 590SJ classroom. Supported by the Mortenson Center for International Library Programs at UIUC, it included the participation of eighteen visiting Mortenson associates from South Africa, Colombia, Vietnam, Japan, Kenya, and Uganda.[11] Additionally, having students engage in journal writing on their community-based research projects and class activities helped them develop and sharpen their reflective critical thinking skills in relation to their own community-based experiences and practices, as well as those encountered in the profession and the surrounding external environment.

Community-Based ICT Development Projects in IS 585

The IS 585 course description on the SIS website reads "evolution, trends, capabilities, and limitations of technologies applied to information capture, storage, preservation, access, and distribution." The course was traditionally structured to include a social and community informatics orientation in order to emphasize that ICTs are not neutral and that introducing or modifying existing ICTs will impact individuals and associated social and organizational relations in both predictable and unpredictable ways.[12] During fall 2007, Sandusky expanded the course to integrate activities partnering students with communities in an ICT development project, comprising 30 percent of the total grade, in addition to conventional technology-based assignments and exercises such as formal evaluation of software and hardware and a systems config-uration project. Fifteen LIS students in IS 585 learned information technologies content, including computer and network architectures, standards, and their historical evolution in the context of real-life applications using Drupal, an open source CMS. Students were provided a safe, low-risk experimental instance of Drupal to use while they learned how to configure and administer a full-featured CMS to meet specific technology-related needs of local communities.

The CMS became a vehicle for engagement with the participating community-based groups.

Two community-based ICT development projects were made available to IS 585 students, both of which emerged from Sandusky's involvement with the Latino Task Force, a coalition of eastern Tennessee community groups committed to identifying issues, developing solutions to address the issues, identifying and mentoring community leaders, and creating sustainable structures, including new organizations, to support the growing Latino population throughout eastern Tennessee. One project involved the design, implementation, and continued development of a participatory CMS for Growing Tennessee: Rural Youth Cultivate Common Ground, a project that brings youth from rural Appalachian families and seasonal and migrant agricultural workers together to learn 35-mm and digital photographic techniques and storytelling methods and to participate in intercultural engagement.[13] The other project required the design and building of a flexible website for Centro Hispano de East Tennessee, a community organization that has recently established its independent identity as a result of past Latino Task Force projects.[14] The goal of the Centro Hispano organization is to establish a community center for Hispanics in eastern Tennessee. Student activities in both projects were focused on developing the Drupal CMS to meet the needs of the partnering community organization. The work focused on either of two categories of issues. Technology-oriented issues included creating an effective user role and access control structure, a valid set of styles to support the site interface, and an effective navigational taxonomy. Organizational and policy issues included copyright and appropriate use policies as well as collection development policies.

Integrating learning, action, and research in IS 585 provided key lessons in achieving meaningful community outcomes. First, learning occurred in the context of regularly scheduled class meetings during which the Drupal CMS was introduced as a technical artifact via demonstrations, lectures, readings, and subsequent hands-on, self-directed learning. Representatives from the community organizations introduced the projects during the scheduled class meetings, and their participation provided a rich understanding of the community context for the students' work with the CMS. Sandusky directed student learning about the community organizations by developing scenarios of use from existing text documents, including e-mail exchanges with community members.[15] Design scenarios were developed as heuristic, textual representations of community participants' priorities and desired system behavior. Design scenarios are attractive expressions of system functionality when a team comprises mostly nonprogrammers/nonengineers because these scenarios can be expressed in words and do not require use or mastery of the formal requirement-gathering methodologies commonly employed by software engineers.[16]

Second, action occurred in IS 585 as the students began transforming what they had learned about the community-based organizations, their goals, and their priorities regarding ICT support of the organizations' work. The students discussed designs, debated the strengths and weaknesses of design alternatives, and generated prototypes of designs in their Drupal test instances. During the last third of the course, students presented their design ideas to the community-based organizations for feedback. At this time, students also shared reflections on their own processes, their interpretations of the organizations' needs and priorities, as well as their design prototypes with community members. They received community feedback and made final changes to their prototype designs in order to bring them closer to the vision expressed by the community-based organizations. Finally, research took place in the ICT development process as students reflected on their individual ideas and actions of community engagement, the group's activities and processes, and the interactions with the community-based organizations. In addition, the students were faced with gaps in their own knowledge and skills as information professionals and needed to conduct significant independent research to locate information to help them close those gaps.

Key issues to consider within the structure of this course and its integration of the two community-based ICT development projects include the significance of the ongoing status of relationship between the faculty member and the community-based groups, the variety of ICT backgrounds and skill sets brought to bear by participating students, and the level of attention given to the students by the community-based groups during the course of the semester.

Sandusky's efforts during the past year and a half to develop and maintain relationships with the Growing Tennessee project, the Latino Task Force, and the Centro Hispano have been essential in the integration of the two community-based ICT development projects in IS 585. Attending monthly meetings, volunteering to help with events and committees, and assisting with grant writing were some activities that helped Sandusky build collaborations and trust with the community-based groups before the two specific projects appropriate for a CMS surfaced.[17] First, the existing relationships allowed IS 585 students to become more rapidly engaged in authentic ICT issues and development than would have been possible if they had to independently establish trust relationships during the semester. Second, ongoing interactions between Sandusky and community members allowed for the organization of existing community-based materials into user scenarios that served as a starting point for the IS 585 students' understanding of the community and the community's potential uses of ICTs.

The variety of experiences and backgrounds brought to the course by IS 585 students significantly impacted the course development process and the work with specific community groups. Other LIS faculty members involved in developing such ICT development projects in their courses should be prepared to offer support to individual students or groups who might get stuck or side-tracked based on their limited experiences in either community engagement activities or in ICT design and implementation. The final key issue in planning ICT development projects in LIS elective courses is the level of attention that needs to be given to the student groups by the representatives of the community-based groups. It is possible that students may often desire a higher level of interaction or attention from the community-based group than is practical or possible owing to other obligations of community members. The faculty member should provide adequate background information to the students in order to reduce student demands on the community representatives.

Community-based ICT development projects in IS 585 during fall 2007 led to the involvement of students in future iterations of IS 585 development of CMS or other ICT capabilities for Latino and other community organizations. In addition, it is likely that IS 585 students will be called upon to extend the functionality of the Growing Tennessee and Centro Hispano sites as the needs of the community change.

Conclusion

This chapter has provided a summary of different kinds of community-based AR projects and activities that were integrated during the teaching of three LIS elective courses. Based on students' participation in various community-based activities, a select categorization scheme to represent the skills and competencies LIS students brought to the interaction with community members includes (1) community analysis and information needs assessment; (2) development of bibliographies and digital collections on topics of community relevance and collection development policies; (3) evaluation and assessment of information resources and services to best suit the community based on a detailed analysis of the context; (4) hardware and software inventory, usability testing, and implementation; (5) development of web pages and web design for local community agencies; (6) database management and web-based CMS based on community needs; and (7) computer and web training and creating appropriate training manuals.

In order to deepen and widen the range of possibilities for incorporating different kinds of community-based AR and activities in LIS courses, the first step is for each LIS program to carry out its own curriculum "asset-mapping" applications.[18] This can be achieved by identifying the strengths and potentials of including community-based AR projects and activities in each course. A curriculum "asset mapping" will involve plotting the details of course syllabi (e.g., course goals, course assignments, skills and competencies taught) and identifying intersections with existing and potential community-based AR projects and activities.

Creating such an inventory in each LIS program will develop a "lay of the land" understanding not only of the individual LIS program's curriculum scope and boundaries but also of existing and potential community-based AR. Individual LIS programs may even choose to develop and market a curriculum track focusing on community informatics or "ICTs toward community-based AR applications" based on compilation of such information.[19]

Compiling such information for all programs in a region or nation will provide a clearer picture of the larger LIS profession's scope and potential for involvement in community-based AR. Once such information is collected, it can be used in developing strategies in advertising and marketing of LIS professionals as "proactive catalysts of social change, as compared to a sometimes perceived role of bystanders."[20] These strategies will help address negative public perceptions of library professions as middle-class, white institutions of power and control that ignore the needs of minority and underserved populations.[21] Such strategies may also be used to promote greater involvement of LIS professionals in decision making and legal and political policy setting via recognition of information professionals' roles as active participants in community action and social justice.[22]

A parallel process with curriculum "asset mapping" in individual and regional LIS programs is an identification of local community-based agencies and organizations, their functionalities and services provided, and the potential of LIS students to partner with them in community-based AR. The curriculum "asset-mapping" process is based on an understanding of content, competencies, and functionalities taught to LIS students. Mapping the strengths and potentials of community-based AR will "connect the dots" between the LIS curriculum and local community agencies and their needs. This will identify the potential for LIS students to participate in efforts to further relationships between the taxonomic core and marginal knowledge domains of the profession and their integration of community-based AR projects and activities toward collaborative and democratic ideals.

ACKNOWLEDGMENTS

A word of thanks to Ann P. Bishop for sharing the syllabus of her social justice course that formed a skeletal framework for LIS 590SJ, a course reported on in this chapter.

NOTES

1. Ann Bishop and Bertram C. Bruce, "Community Informatics: Integrating Action, Research and Learning," *Bulletin of the American Society for Information Science and Technology* 31, no. 6 (August/September 2005), www.asis.org/Bulletin/Aug-05/bishopbruce.html; Randy Stoecker, "Is Community Informatics Good for Communities? Questions Confronting an Emerging Field," *Journal of Community Informatics* 1, no. 3 (2005), http://ci-journal.net/index.php/ciej/article/view/183/; and Kathleen de la Peña McCook, *A Place at the Table: Participating in Community Building* (Chicago: American Library Association, 2000).

2. Ernest T. Stringer, *Action Research* (Thousand Oaks, CA: Sage, 1999); Ann Curry, "Action Research in Action: Involving Students and Professionals," in *Proceedings of the World Library and Information Congress: 71st International Federation of Library Associations and Institutions, General Conference and Congress,* Oslo,

Norway, August 14–18, 2005, www.ifla.org/IV/ifla71/papers/046e-Curry.pdf; and Bharat Mehra, "An Action Research (AR) Manifesto for Cyberculture Power to 'Marginalized' Cultures of Difference," in *Critical Cyber-Culture Studies,* ed. David Silver and Adrienne Massanari (New York: New York University Press, 2006), 205–15.

3. Penny A. Pasque and others, *Higher Education Collaboratives for Community Engagement and Improvement* (Ann Arbor, MI: National Forum on Higher Education for the Public Good, 2005), www.thenationalforum.org/docs/pdf/wingspread_05_final_monograph.pdf.

4. Course syllabus at https://web.utk.edu/~bmehra/IS590Syllabus.rtf.

5. Course syllabus at http://leep.lis.uiuc.edu/fall04/LIS590SJ/index.html.

6. Course syllabus at http://web.utk.edu/~rsandusk/is585/.

7. Donald A. Schon, *Educating the Reflective Practitioner: Toward a New Design for Teaching and Learning in the Professions* (San Francisco: Jossey-Bass, 1996).

8. Les Gasser and others, "Understanding Continuous Design in F/OSS Projects," in *Proceedings of the 16th International Conference on Software Engineering and Its Applications (ICSSEA-03),* Paris, December 2003; Paris A. Zafiris and others, "A Practitioner's Approach to Evolving and Remodeling Large-Scale WWW Sites," in *Proceedings of the 34th Hawaii International Conference on System Sciences (HICSS),* Maui, January 3–6, 2001, http://csdl2.computer.org/comp/proceedings/hicss/2001/0981/07/09817078.pdf; and Larry Stillman and Randy Stoecker, "Structuration, ICTs, and Community Work," *Journal of Community Informatics* 1, no. 3 (2005).

9. More information is available at http://inquiry.uiuc.edu/ilabs/out.php?cilid=467.

10. More information about the September Project is available at www.theseptemberproject.org/index.htm.

11. More information about the Mortenson Center is available at www.library.uiuc.edu/mortenson/.

12. Rob Kling, "What Is Social Informatics and Why Does It Matter?" *D-Lib Magazine* 5, no. 1 (January 1999), www.dlib.org/dlib/january99/kling/01kling.html.

13. More information is available at http://glaucon.sunsite.utk.edu/growingtn/; Robert Sandusky and J. Crowe, "Growing Distributed Community Content: Designing a Participatory Content Management System for Rural Youth Photographers," in *Proceedings of the 2007 Conference on Designing User Experience,* Chicago, November 5–7, 2007.

14. More information is available at http://glaucon.sunsite.utk.edu/centro-hispano-de-east-tennessee/.

15. John M. Carroll, *Making Use: Scenario-Based Design of Human-Computer Interactions* (Cambridge, MA: MIT Press, 2000).

16. Bharat Mehra and others, "Scenarios in the Afya Project as a Participatory Action Research (PAR) Tool for Studying Information Seeking and Use across the 'Digital Divide,'" *Journal of the American Society of Information Science and Technology* 53, no. 14 (2002): 1259–66.

17. Randy Stoecker, *Research Methods for Community Change: A Project-Based Approach* (Thousand Oaks, CA: Sage, 2005).

18. John P. Kretzmann and John L. McKnight, *Building Communities from the Inside Out: A Path toward Finding and Mobilizing Community Assets* (Chicago: ACTA, 1993).

19. Bharat Mehra, "Service Learning in Library and Information Science (LIS) Education: Connecting Research and Practice to Community," *InterActions: UCLA Journal of Information and Education Studies* 1, no. 1 (2004): article 3, http://repositories.cdlib.org/gseis/interactions/vol1/iss1/art3/.

20. Bharat Mehra and Ramesh Srinivasan, "The Library-Community Convergence Framework for Community Action: Libraries as Catalysts of Social Change," *Libri: International Journal of Libraries and Information Services* 57, no. 3 (September 2007): 123–39.

21. Michael H. Harris, "The Purpose of the American Public Library: A Revisionist Interpretation of History," *Library Journal* 98, no. 16 (1973): 2509–14; and Karen M. Venturella, *Poor People and Library Services* (Jefferson, NC: McFarland, 1998).

22. McCook, *A Place at the Table*.

Chapter 16

Virtual Worlds
New Spaces for Service Learning
Joe Sanchez

I'll do what I can to help y'all. But, the game's out there, and it's play or get played. That simple.

—Omar Little, *The Wire*

When I think of service learning, the writings of Paulo Freire come to mind, particularly in regard to learning as a dialogue and the "essence of education as the practice of freedom."[1] Within this construct educators either condition their students to accept the status quo or create a space where students can creatively and critically expose realities and discover a way to transform their world. An important aspect of Freire's work is the leveling of the roles between teacher, student, and the community. Service learning is a method that is in alignment with Freire and can empower the student, teacher, and community through dialogue and reciprocal engagement. Traditionally service learning occurs in "real world" settings such as nonprofit organizations, field settings such as juvenile detention centers, or through programs like If I Can Read, I Can Do Anything.[2]

My aim in this chapter is to suggest the virtual world of Second Life (SL) as a real place or space for service learning to occur. Specifically, I will chronicle two service learning projects conducted by students enrolled in an undergraduate course I teach that incorporates Second Life. Second Life is owned by Linden Lab, has over 9,000,000 users, and is currently the most populated three-dimensional virtual world.[3] Second Life consists of users in the form of avatars, a virtual currency called Linden dollars, and objects created out of "prims" or primitive shapes such as boxes, cylinders, spheres, and prisms. Both nonprofit and for-profit organizations currently have a presence in Second Life. IBM and Cisco Systems are two of the larger corporations utilizing Second Life, while the ALA and the American Cancer Society Relay for Life are two of the more notable nonprofits with a Second Life presence. Second Life contains the following features: land, communication, groups, navigation, economy, events, and user-generated content.

A key element of service learning is the reflective process. Reflection can take many forms in a classroom such as essays, digital storytelling, and critical incident discussions.[4] In my courses students reflect by writing weekly blog entries that account for 20 percent of their course grade. In addition to reflection, student blog entries often include a fair amount of self-evaluation and become an avenue for students to make connections between text, course experiences, and prior knowledge. The challenge, especially for undergraduates, is their unfamiliarity with looking inward in regard to their own learning processes. MacGregor explains that "students have very little experience examining their academic work in any systematic way and even less experience describing it in writing."[5]

I have found the blog format to help students develop as writers. The post and comment format of blogs provides me with the ability to have an ongoing dialogue with each student and allows me to understand how each student is experiencing the course. As students learn how to write reflectively over the course of the semester, their writing becomes an "epistemic" writing experience.[6] Students learn to express how they know what they know, and in most cases they demonstrate their knowledge in the making.

In order to best tell the story about the service learning projects conducted in my courses, I am going to weave student blog entries together to form a composite narrative. By using the students' own reflections, I hope to avoid a one-sided narrative and keep within Freire's model of dialogue between learners.

Creating a Scene

Working in Virtual Worlds is an undergraduate information studies course I teach at the University of Texas at Austin. The main component of the course is a virtual team project where I ask students to form a team, find a virtual client to work with, and host an event in Second Life. Within this project students are responsible for creating a project proposal, a project management plan, and pitching their idea to a client they identify in Second Life. Students work in teams of four and divide several tasks among themselves such as marketing, accounting, outreach, and building.

When I designed the course, service learning was the farthest thing from my mind. I was hoping to create an authentic learning experience by having students work in a virtual team, but as students became invested in their projects, the majority of them incorporated a service learning component. An excerpt from a student blog explains:

> My personal belief is that everyone should give to charities, even
> if it isn't much. So, using that as a template for what a possible
> final group project could be, I started thinking of the easiest, most
> plausible, most effective projects to do that would fulfill my goal of
> charity and I came up with the idea of having a benefit concert.

Service learning in this course started with one group from my fall 2007 course who named themselves the "G3s." A member of the G3s was searching through Second Life for a possible client for her team project when she happened by a representative of a nonprofit in a space called Commonwealth Islands. Commonwealth is an area where progressive nonprofit organizations are able to place their materials, host meetings, and network. A few of the organizations with a presence there are the American Civil Liberties Union, Greenpeace, Free Tibet, and Earth First! The student described the experience in her blog:

> I met the representative of Habitat Trust at Commonwealth Island. [See figure 16-1.] She gave me a great first impression by showing me around the island and telling me about all of the nonprofits that are set up there. This nonprofit is dedicated to preserving areas that are vital to the habitat. They recently have also been helping raise money to reconstruct areas destroyed by the wildfires in California.

The G3s agreed to work with the Habitat Trust as a client for their group project. After a couple of days of brainstorming, the group decided to commit

Figure 16-1. Student meeting a representative from the Habitat Trust

to hosting a rave with live DJs at a place one of the group members found called Happy Clam. Happy Clam is a place in Second Life dedicated to sustainable living and education about global warming. One student said:

> I have never been excited about doing a group project until now. My group members and I decided this would be a good nonprofit to help out because it is small and in great need of donations. We also wanted to support their cause, and the rep is really eager to help us out. Being students has been helpful in other areas, too. Dre knew people at the Happy Clam that are letting us throw our event at their island and are helping provide us with a DJ.

After lining up their clients and arranging a place to host their event, the G3s wrote project management and group communication plans. They followed the plans and provided updates to me through instant messages in Second Life and their weekly blog post. Each week students were required to write a reflective blog post of 350 words. As the event neared, I could follow their progress by reading reports such as this:

> I have still been communicating with the representative from the nonprofit. She has been really helpful and this project has been so much easier to complete in SL than it would be in real life. It has been so easy to just sign on and talk with people who are working on the project with us.

The day of their event the students were nervous but excited. They had worked with two organizations to arrange a place to host their event; they arranged for entertainment; and they used the social networks of two organizations to market their fund-raiser. During their two-hour event the G3s raised $300 and donated all the proceeds to the Habitat Trust (see figure 16-2).

When the other students heard that the G3s had turned their project into a fund-raising event and that their virtual project was going to have a real-world impact, their groups decided to incorporate nonprofit clients into their projects. One of the groups chose to work with a group in Second Life known as Wheelies. Wheelies is a dance club and social space created for people with real disabilities. Many avatars represent their disabilities by wearing wheelchairs on their avatars (see figure 16-3). A student from the group writes:

> Wheelies is a club for disabled members of Second Life and their friends. Because many find their challenges to be part of who they are, they want them to be part of their avatar. Wheelies gives a home to the homeless of Second Life and a safe, supportive environment to those with physical and mental disabilities.

Figure 16-2. G3 fund-raiser for the Habitat Trust

Figure 16-3. Second Life residents with wheelchairs (taken from Seekersbrain's Flickr stream)

Working with Wheelies presented a unique experience for the students because the owner of the group insisted that any event or fund-raiser created be wheelchair-accessible. Students had a difficult time understanding why a physically disabled person would want to represent his avatar as disabled in a virtual place. The frustrated students kept asking, "Why would a person choose to have a disability in Second Life?" When describing the difficulty of creating a wheelchair-accessible event in Second Life, one student wrote:

> I do have one concern, which I mentioned in class. And that is having an "ADA-approved" carnival. [See figure 16-4.] I'm sure that the landscape can easily be set up to support wheelchair access, but . . . I'm just not sure about the rides. The great thing about SL is that you can defy the typical real-life conventions and laws of physics.

In the blog post the student reveals his lack of exposure to and understanding of people with physical disabilities. One way to interpret his reflection is to ask, "Why would you choose to be in a wheelchair if you don't have to be?" As the student will learn throughout his experience with the Wheelies community, some people feel their wheelchairs are a part of their embodied experience and identity, and they want them represented through their avatars.

Figure 16-4. Students hosting carnival event for Wheelies

The students working with Wheelies decided to build a carnival and host an event fund-raiser with all proceeds going to Wheelies. The students building the carnival had to ensure that avatars with wheelchairs could ride the carnival attractions and access the entire area. At first the students saw this as extra work, but as they themselves began to identify with their avatars and the Wheelies community, they began to understand the need for accessibility and even took it on as a challenge. A student posted:

> We will be partnering with Wheelies, so I do have to make things handicapped-accessible, but that should be easy enough to do. I probably just have to make one generic ramp and I can put that anywhere necessary. I guess the only way for me to find out is to test all this out, so I'll find a wheelchair for myself in SL and start trying out all the games.

By the time the night of the carnival arrived, the students were proud of themselves. They felt, regardless of the turnout, that they had given their best effort: they built a strong working relationship with their client, and they built a project that was completely accessible to avatars in wheelchairs:

> Our carnival is even entirely Wheelies friendly, even the mini-golf course! It could potentially be a huge hit for the Wheelies community, since this would probably be a first for them.

The students held a successful event and they raised nearly $100 in a two-hour period. Over the course of the event they had sixty people attend, and the event was so popular people did not want to leave. The group performed well as a team and received many accolades:

> I felt really proud during the carnival. It seemed like the Wheelies crowd was really excited and happy with the final product, and people were having a really good time. I was amazed that Fizzle, Dan, and I could put together such a successful event with people we had never seen or met.
>
> Our group worked extremely well together. I would maybe even go so far to say that the dynamics of our small three-person group was the best team I have ever worked with. Keep in mind I'm a business major, so I am CONSTANTLY working in groups that are supposed to be "efficient" and perfect . . . so this is a major accomplishment for our group.

New Spaces for Service Learning

The projects described in the previous section met three criteria for service learning. First, the projects were completed within the learning goals of the course, and course material was applied and (re)constructed through the service learning projects. Second, students provided a service for a community in need, and the community or organization reciprocated to the students by providing tools and resources to complete their project goals. Finally, the students engaged in the service learning activity were reflective practitioners throughout the project cycle. I believe the students who participated in these two projects had an authentic service learning experience. More important, though, they experienced knowledge in the making through a dialogue with the community, their client, their reflective selves, and me.[7]

Though I am proposing virtual worlds as a new place for service learning, I am not in any way suggesting that service learning through a virtual world is better than, more immersive, or even a substitute for service learning that contains placement within a community where students can use all of their senses. I am suggesting, however, that service learning can be accomplished within a virtual world, virtual learning experiences are indeed real as are the communities within the virtual world, and there are logistical advantages that virtual worlds present as avenues for service learning. One such advantage is the low cost of resources needed in order to provide assistance to a community. A student from the G3s shared her thoughts:

> First of all, we didn't spend any money putting on this event. Because products and venues aren't "disposable" in Second Life, people are much more willing to share them, and just make items copyable . . . The venue was free because someone was just cool, and didn't mind helping out students. Try finding a real-world venue to rent a building to college students for free. Hahahahaa . . . never.

Another advantage of service learning through a virtual world is the flexibility it allows for students. Students can work on their projects from anywhere with a high-speed Internet connection. They do not have to be physically located in their service learning community in order to be immersed in it. A student working on the Wheelies benefit wrote:

> Working with Polgara, the head of Wheelies and our main contact, was really great. We chatted when we were both in-world and we sent IMs if we had pressing ideas to communicate. This, like e-mail, enabled us to get things done on our own time, so the other wasn't waiting around.

I think the idea of being able to participate in a service learning project while not being "in" the community is important when considering service learning projects for distance education students. Distance education students can participate in service learning in their own communities, but what happens when they are separated by several hundred miles from other students?

Traditionally those students will not be able to participate in a team-based service learning project. Virtual world technology allows distance education students to work in geospatially distant teams on the same service learning projects while simultaneously being immersed within the same community. One member of the G3s shared this experience in his blog:

> The coolest thing about this event was I was 200 miles away from Austin at the time of the event. My family threw my grandparents a fiftieth anniversary dinner, so I went home Thursday afternoon and was still able to be "in class."

Conclusion

Students who engaged in service learning projects expressed a great deal of satisfaction and empowerment through their learning process. Students felt that they made a difference, and they played between worlds of work, fun, service, and learning.[8] Several blog posts at the end of the course shared this kind of tone and excitement:

> I have NEVER taken a class like this. Hell, I call it fun and thoughtful, and when you take a class that encompasses both of those ideas, guess what, work doesn't even seem like work, tests don't even seem like tests, and write-ups don't even seem like write-ups, because it's about a topic that interests you, and about something that is fun.

Another student expressed his excitement about his project by stating that he believes his group's work affected more than the original community they worked with. He writes that his project and the work of his fellow students became a service learning project for the entire Second Life user base:

> I think that what we are doing is something for ALL of Second Life. We are showing the public that Second Life is not just for a bunch of nerds to network socially. This is actually a viable tool that can be implemented in powerful ways to accomplish things with people who potentially could be on the opposite side of the globe, all in real time and extremely inexpensively. We are helping Second Life educators.

I will close with this final thought from a student. I find his use of the word "really" important because he is describing what many people still refer to as a "virtual" experience:

> If all of school was like this, I think more people would thoroughly enjoy attending it, and REALLY learn. When something catches

your eye and makes you think in a fun, energetic, enjoyable fashion, that makes you want to learn more.

NOTES

1. Paul Freire, *Pedagogy of the Oppressed* (New York: Seabury, 1970).

2. Mary Prentice and Rudy M. Garcia, "Service Learning: The Next Generation in Education," *Community College Journal of Research and Practice* 24, no. 1 (2000): 19–26; Nancy Hirschinger-Blank and Michael Markowitz, "An Evaluation of a Pilot Service Learning Course for Criminal Justice Undergraduate Students," *Journal of Criminal Justice Education* 17, no. 1 (April 2006): 69–86; and Loriene Roy, "Diversity in the Classroom: Incorporating Service-Learning Experiences in the Library and Information Science Curriculum," *Journal of Library Administration* 33, no. 3–4 (2001): 213.

3. Cory Ondrejka, "School of the Future: Innovation and Education in Second Life" (2007), www.academicresourcecenter.net/curriculum/pfv.aspx?ID=6820.

4. Lucy Rai, "Owning (Up to) Reflective Writing in Social Work Education," *Social Work Education* 25, no. 8 (December 2006): 785–97; Alaa Sadik, "Digital Storytelling: A Meaningful Technology-Integrated Approach for Engaged Student Learning," *Educational Technology Research and Development* 56, no. 4 (August 2006): 487–506; and Jan Fook and Gurid Aga Askeland, "Challenges of Critical Reflection: 'Nothing Ventured, Nothing Gained,'" *Social Work Education* 26, no. 5 (August 2007): 520–33.

5. Jean MacGregor, "Learning Self-Evaluation: Challenges for Students," *New Directions for Teaching and Learning* 56 (Winter 1993): 39.

6. Carl J. Waluconis, "Self-Evaluation: Settings and Uses," *New Directions for Teaching and Learning* 56 (Winter 1993): 15–33.

7. Elizabeth Ann Ellsworth, *Places of Learning: Media, Architecture, Pedagogy* (New York: RoutledgeFalmer, 2005).

8. T. L. Taylor, *Play between Worlds: Exploring Online Game Culture* (Cambridge, MA: MIT Press, 2006).

Chapter 17

Evaluation of Field-Based Experiences and Assessment of Student Learning

Gary Geisler and Elaine Yontz

One of the challenges of service learning from the instructor's perspective is the evaluation of student performance. Successful service learning may not result in accumulations of factual knowledge that can be tested. A student's attitudinal changes or growth in skills can be difficult to document and quantify. When student outcomes are difficult to measure, instructors and students may worry that evaluation will be inappropriately subjective. An "up or down" system such as satisfactory/unsatisfactory or pass/fail may be used, but this approach can minimize the chance that students will receive useful feedback on their work. Because instructors may need to evaluate student work that they are unable to observe firsthand, input from site supervisors is often relevant. This input from site supervisors can be problematic for the instructor to collect and to put into context. In short, nuanced evaluation of student performance in service learning is not easy.

An essential ingredient in meaningful evaluation is the identification of clear goals and/or learning outcomes for student learning. Goals should be documented and discussed with the student prior to the beginning of service learning experiences. For individualized service learning experiences such as an internship or fieldwork, the student's participation in the identification and negotiation of the goals may be appropriate. Because the site for the service learning must be one in which the learning goals can be achieved, the goals should be confirmed in advance, then used to help locate and assign sites. Goals must be clearly communicated to site supervisors. A midterm check with student and site supervisor, based on the goals, can be helpful in keeping a service learning project on track.

Monitoring Student Progress with Blogs

Although a midterm check can keep the instructor generally aware of project progress, recent developments in information technology provide opportunities to more effectively monitor a service learning project and to improve the experience for both student and instructor. Among the Web 2.0, or social software, tools increasingly being integrated into libraries and classroom instruction is the web log, more commonly referred to as a blog. A blog is a web-based journal or diary where entries are easily added and displayed in reverse chronological order. A blog entry is typically text based but can also include links, images, and other media. From an educational standpoint, integrating blogs into the classroom can be useful in engaging student interest, facilitating collaboration, and encouraging less outgoing students to share their thoughts and ideas. These potential benefits also make blogs a tool instructors should consider asking service learning students to use to document and reflect upon their experience.

Asking a student to establish and maintain a blog as part of the service learning experience is a reasonably simple requirement. There is a broad range of free, easy-to-use blogging software available from providers such as Blogger, TypePad, and WordPress. Most of the popular blogging software operates directly from the provider's server, requiring only that the student register for a free account to begin using it. The student can then use a simple form interface in a web browser to add entries to the blog. Important from the instructor perspective, the popular blogging services typically enable subscription to a blog through web syndication, such as an Atom or RSS feed, an XML-based format that distributes updates to a website. This means that once the student has established a blog for her service learning experience and passed on the URL to the instructor, the instructor can subscribe to the blog and see when the student has added or updated blog entries using a feed aggregator or reader, such as a dedicated feed reader like NetNewsWire or Google Reader, or in an e-mail client or web browser that supports RSS or Atom feed subscriptions, such as Apple's Safari.

Blogs are now prevalent enough that most students regularly read blogs and many already keep a blog themselves. For students without blogging experience, the requirement to keep a blog can be seen as an opportunity to learn and use a tool they know about but have not had a good reason to use previously. There may be situations where the student is not comfortable discussing his service experience in a public forum, or it is not appropriate to do so for other reasons, but there are a range of options for mitigating these concerns, as one can always post blog entries anonymously. The more popular blogging services provide more formal privacy options, including restricting visibility to only specified users. In our experience, service learning students have been quite receptive to the idea of maintaining a blog.

As a tool for documenting and reflecting upon the service learning experience, the blog provides several benefits for both student and instructor. For the student, simply setting up and using the blog software can be a useful technical skill to learn. More important, the blog encourages more frequent and timely documentation by the student by providing a convenient vehicle to jot down ideas and issues at the time they happen. The student does not have to keep track of a document on her personal computer—which might not be available at the service learning location—to record an event or idea; she simply goes to the URL of her blog and adds a new entry. For the instructor, the blog provides a convenient and immediate way to give general encouragement, provide specific advice, and ask pedagogical questions. By following student progress on a more regular basis, the instructor is better able to suggest that the student explore different alternatives, apply previous coursework to a particular problem or project objective, and more generally guide the student toward connecting the service work being done to initial learning outcomes that might gradually be forgotten after the student becomes involved in the day-to-day work. Even if the instructor does nothing more than read the student's blog entries, this small time investment is likely to give the instructor a much clearer idea of how the student is progressing than relying on one or two progress meetings during the project period.

At the beginning, the instructor and student should discuss whether it would be appropriate to share the blog with the site supervisor. In some cases, this could be very beneficial in enabling the site supervisor to monitor the student's work and contribute his own thoughts and ideas. In other situations, it might be more appropriate to not share the blog with the site supervisor and other employees of the service learning site so that the student and instructor can discuss issues and concerns more freely.

A blog is a free and relatively easy way to encourage student reflection and improve instructor understanding of what the student has accomplished. Although it should not be seen as a primary product for evaluating the student, a blog can strengthen the learning experience by providing a way for the student to keep in mind learning outcomes and goals over the course of the project as she increasingly focuses on the day-to-day work. It can also make evaluation easier by giving the instructor a low-effort way to monitor student progress and engagement and thus have a basis for more informed grading.

Grading Rubric

Fitzgerald has designed a service learning project that includes a grading rubric.[1] The project is a basic cataloging course for emerging school library media specialists. Service learning sites are found by canvassing alumni who manage school library media centers. A list of available sites with descriptions of work needed at each site is then assembled. The assignment includes specific instructions to the students for choosing a site from the prepared list, identifying skills necessary to complete the selected project, preparing for the site visits, and reflecting on the value of the experience afterward. This is designed to be a group project. The material submitted by the students for evaluation includes evidence of their preparation for the project, attendance notes signed by the site supervisor, an artifact that illustrates something that the students completed, a written reflection from each individual student, and one completed rubric form per group. Options for the artifacts include photographs, completed catalog records, and written statements from site supervisors. As shown in figure 17-1, the rubric includes room for each student's self-rating of each component. When such an approach is used, the students have a clear explanation in advance of what specific elements will be evaluated and what outcomes are expected. Another advantage of this form is that space and directions are included for students' self-evaluations.

Input from Site Supervisors

Input from site supervisors is essential to the meaningful evaluation of student performance in many service learning situations. As McCook points out, this input can be gathered in various ways, including an in-person meeting, a telephone conversation, or an e-mail message. McCook recommends that site supervisors be asked to comment on the student's "initiative, ability to apply principles to practice, interaction with library users, interaction with staff, capacity to work independently, and flexibility."[2] O'Neill suggests inviting the site supervisor to comment on "positive qualities or reservations."[3]

Site supervisors' feedback on student performance can be documented through the use of checklists. O'Neill's checklist of reference desk skills, which asks the rater to choose "satisfactory" or "needs work" for each item, offers a model that can be adapted for coaching the student toward better performance and for evaluating the student's learning. San Jose State University's Site Supervisor Evaluation form combines open-ended questions about achievement of learning outcomes, strengths, and areas for improvement with Likert-scale ratings of professionalism, ability to work with others, and employability.[4]

Blogging can also be considered as a mechanism for providing convenient communication between the site supervisor and the instructor. As discussed above, many blogging sites offer privacy options that can be set to restrict viewing of posts to specific individuals. It is possible to set up the service learning project blog so that the instructor and the site supervisor can have a dialogue that does not include the student. A three-way discussion among student, site supervisor, and instructor would also be possible. Such an approach is another way to elicit student self-evaluation. This might offer a useful substitute for in-person meetings when distance or competing commitments make a site visit by the instructor impractical.

How to fairly incorporate the site supervisor's comments into the determination of a student's grade deserves careful thought. The instructor's expectations in regard to site supervisor feedback should be discussed with potential site supervisors before students are assigned and must be documented in descriptions of the service learning project. Likewise, if the site supervisor's input can affect the grade, this must be clearly stated in writing and should be pointed out to the student at the outset. The instructor should consider the site supervisor's comments carefully, taking care that the student not be inappropriately penalized for input that may be affected by bias or inattention on the part of the site supervisor. The site supervisor's input can be compared

	6380 Service Project Rubric Include one rubric for group. If necessary, indicate individual contributions.		
Component	**Self-review: each group member should be represented here**	**Instructor's review**
All components present and complete: ☐ preregistration of project ☐ evidence that required skills were studied or practiced prior to visit ☐ host-signed notes from visit ☐ artifact ☐ reflection: includes preparation; account; what you learned; relevance of this to your goals; what you still need to know; link to American Association of School Libraries competencies ☐ rubric with self-assessment 60 percent, or 15 points. Deduct proportionately.		
Individual progress toward competence: project provides ample evidence of learning. Each group member made an effort to gain the necessary prerequisite skills. 5 points		
Service activities made a genuine contribution to the host media program. Reflection should address this explicitly. Choose one: ☐ no ☐ unlikely ☐ probably ☐ definitely 4 points		
Mechanics: ☐ should be clean enough for efficient communication (not distracting to the evaluator) ☐ format specs are followed 1 point		
Total		

Figure 17-1. Example of service project grading rubric

to information submitted by the student and to the instructor's perceptions to help to ensure that a balanced picture emerges. San Jose State University requires a student who has completed an internship to evaluate the site.[5] Such an evaluation might make the instructor aware of any potential issues with the site supervisor's evaluation of the student and can provide useful information when considering whether or not to use that site in the future.

Conclusion

The evaluation of student performance in service learning raises issues that are often absent from the evaluation processes in traditional coursework. Effective evaluation of service learning is helped immensely when goals for student learning are clear, documented, taken into consideration during site selection, and communicated fully to all parties before the student begins. After a project is under way, a mechanism for encouraging ongoing student reflection and project status reporting, such as a blog, can help student and instructor communicate about progress on a regular basis. Input from site supervisors, when thoughtfully incorporated, can make the evaluation of the student's work much more meaningful. Mechanisms for collecting and considering students' reflections should be incorporated. Student products are most useful when the student is required to provide information and reflections in a spontaneous and timely fashion. Careful attention to the products and processes used for evaluation can increase the satisfaction of the student, the site supervisor, and the instructor.

NOTES

1. Mary Ann Fitzgerald, "EDIT 6380 Service Project" (2008), http://it.coe.uga .edu/%7Emfitzger/6380/service-project.html.

2. Kathleen de la Peña McCook, "Guidelines for Supervised Fieldwork" (2004), www.cas.usf.edu/lis/mccook/fwGuidelines.htm.

3. Nancy O'Neill, "Internships in a Public Library Reference Department," in *Public Library Internships: Advice from the Field*, ed. Cindy Mediavilla (Lanham, MD: Scarecrow, 2006).

4. San Jose State University, School of Library and Information Science, LIBR 294 Professional Experience: Internships, "Site Supervisor Evaluation," http://slisweb .sjsu.edu/classes/294/forms/294supevalofstu.php.

5. San Jose State University, School of Library and Information Science, LIBR 294 Professional Experience: Internships, "Student Evaluation of Site," http://slisweb .sjsu.edu/classes/294/forms/294studentsiteeval.php.

Chapter 18

Practicum and Internship Experiences in LIS Education
A Perspective from ALA Emerging Leaders

Molly Krichten, Sarah Stohr, and Stefanie Warlick

As part of the American Library Association's 2008 Emerging Leaders Program—an initiative designed to get participants on the fast track toward ALA and professional leadership—our group of five members was asked to look at the possibilities of creating a searchable, ALA-hosted, web-based database of capstone/fieldwork/practicum listings that library and information science students across the country could use to connect to relevant opportunities. When we came together as a group at our first Emerging Leaders meeting, we instantly realized the potential benefits that such a database could provide. Each of us had participated in a practicum or fieldwork experience and recognized its importance to our own education.

A database of fieldwork and practicum or internship opportunities (which we will refer to as "practical experiences" for our purposes) would connect students with relevant, timely information and provide them with the chance to discover prospective opportunities that they otherwise might not have known about. Our group was especially excited about the possibility of connecting students completing their degrees online and in locations far removed from their LIS programs with opportunities that are local to the students and that they might not have found if they were only able to use information made available by their programs. For instance, a student living in Portland, Oregon, who is completing her degree online through the University of Wisconsin would be more easily able to locate opportunities in Oregon with such a database.

Our vision for a successful database hinged upon the willingness of LIS programs to share their practicum and fieldwork information. At the institutions from which group members graduated, students discovered practical experience opportunities through a number of methods: on-campus bulletin boards, electronic discussion lists, password-protected websites, or a designated faculty or staff member at the institution. After our initial meeting, it became clear to us that in order to create a viable database we would need buy-in from LIS programs. Our first order of business, then, was to contact programs across the country to discern whether they would be interested in making their locally hosted information available to the ALA.

We began by surveying a group of LIS programs to explore how institutions would feel about sharing their information. Only a small number of schools responded to our request. Of those that did respond, it was clear that there was interest in centralizing information but also concern for how to best keep the information up-to-date and accurate. Many agreed that perhaps a centralized list of links to the practicum information made available by various institutions would be a good route to take because it would help ensure that the information being made available would be timely and reliable. For one responding school, however, it was important to keep the information proprietary so that they could continue to personally match students with opportunities.

With the underwhelming response from LIS programs, we decided that we wanted to turn to present LIS students and recent graduates to determine if the need for this type of database was present and to assess the value of practical experience opportunities in LIS education. Perhaps if we could learn more about students' experiences with practical opportunities and demonstrate that there was student support for a centralized tool, institutions might be more willing to contribute their information. We created a survey using SurveyMonkey, basing the questions on the information we had gathered from the LIS programs we had contacted initially.

Survey Findings: Who We Surveyed

We decided to turn first to our Emerging Leaders colleagues, men and women who are recent graduates of library science programs who could share their experiences of finding practicum and internship opportunities during their studies. The survey was sent to the 2007 and 2008 Emerging Leaders cohorts. This group was selected because of ease of communication, likelihood of survey participation, likelihood of contemporary LIS education experience, and because the ALA had selected these individuals as outstanding in the library science field. Of the over 200 people to receive the survey, we gathered responses from 94, almost all of whom had graduated from an LIS program in 2001 or later.

Although the survey audience was limited to a narrow and arguably biased subset of LIS graduates, the responsiveness of the Emerging Leaders cohorts offered interesting feedback and surprisingly broad perspectives. Public librarians represented 42 percent of the respondents, and academic librarians represented another 42 percent. The remaining survey participants were employed by school or special libraries or were currently unemployed. A total of 35 schools, or over half of the 57 ALA-accredited master's programs in the United States and Canada, were represented by at least one survey respondent.

Survey Findings: LIS Programs and Their Involvement in Practical Experience Placements

Based on our survey, 52 percent of these Emerging Leaders were not required to participate in an internship or practicum to complete their degrees.

Furthermore, 50 percent of respondents reported that their LIS programs had no formal matching process to connect students with practical experience even when the experience was required. When asked how participants arranged for the practical experience, 56 percent of those who completed an internship or practicum cited a personal or professional connection. Only 24 percent of survey participants who completed a practicum or internship did so through a school representative's referral or coordination.

Despite the surprising lack of requirement, about 60 percent—or 56 survey respondents—participated in at least one practical experience opportunity during their LIS education. Of the Emerging Leaders who did not participate in a practicum or internship, 24 reported it was because they had other relevant work experience, 7 asserted that it was because their educational institution did not emphasize such opportunities, and 6 cited other reasons.

Survey Findings: The Value of Practical Experience to LIS Students

Before examining what Emerging Leaders thought about a centralized database, we wanted to ascertain if the cohorts thought that practical experience opportunities were valuable. The response to these questions was overwhelmingly positive.

Approximately 89 percent of the respondents indicated that they enjoyed their practical experience, with nearly that many (83 percent) reporting that they developed useful skills or acquired useful knowledge as a result of engaging in fieldwork. Around half (56 percent) of the LIS graduates felt that the practicum actually helped them locate a paid position. Most telling were their responses to the last question: nearly all (94 percent) of those who participated in an internship or practicum recommended that other LIS students do the same. (See table 18-1.)

To further assess the value of practical experience to LIS students, we asked survey participants to explain why they participated in service learning. Specifically, we asked the respondents to assess to what extent their practical experience opportunity helped them to acquire skills, network, gain insight, and gain confidence. Table 18-2 shows that, although students equated service learning with a number of positive gains, nearly all of the respondents (96 percent) felt they gained confidence from their practical experience.

Survey Findings: Thoughts about a Database of Opportunities

A clear majority of the survey participants responded that a centralized ALA-hosted database of practical experience opportunities would be a helpful resource for LIS students. Survey respondents were very vocal about the types of features that would be important if such a database were created. Responses included

> Accurate information. Vigilance in maintaining an updated list of opportunities two and three years down the line.

Table 18-1. Emerging Leaders' perceptions of the value of service learning

	Strongly Agree	Agree	Neutral	Disagree	Strongly Disagree
I enjoyed my internship/ practicum.	64.8% 35	24.1% 13	9.3% 5	1.9% 1	0.0% 0
The skills/ knowledge that I developed during my internship/ practicum proved useful in my paid professional work.	48.1% 26	35.2% 19	11.1% 6	5.6% 3	0.0% 0
Participating in an internship/ practicum helped me secure a paid professional position (either in the same institution or elsewhere).	37.7% 20	18.9% 10	22.6% 12	17.0% 9	3.8% 2
I would recommend participation in an internship or practicum to current LIS students.	70.4% 38	24.1% 13	3.7% 2	0.0% 0	1.9% 1

Information about whether or not the internship is "accepted" for credit by library schools.

Very up-to-date material. Very detailed information as to what the internship entails and contact information for individuals who have worked at said internship and are willing to discuss what it was like.

Students should be able to look for internships based on geographical location. It would also be helpful to list paid and unpaid internships separately.

Information such as location, qualifications, pay, time commitment, etc.

The ability to search by location and timeliness of posted opportunities were two important features that were suggested by many of the survey

Table 18-2. Why Emerging Leaders participated in service learning

	To a Great Extent	To Some Extent	Very Little	Not at All
Acquire or hone professional skills	61.1% 33	29.6% 16	9.3% 5	0.0% 0
Network with professionals in the field	44.4% 24	38.9% 21	16.7% 9	0.0% 0
Gain insight into the politics and culture of the institution and/or field	55.6% 30	31.5% 17	11.1% 6	1.9% 1
Make contacts to be used as references for job applications	53.7% 29	31.5% 17	11.1% 6	3.7% 2
Boost confidence in professional abilities	57.4% 31	38.9% 21	3.7% 2	0.0% 0

respondents. Detailed information about the type of library, job responsibilities, and compensation was also desired by numerous respondents.

Conclusion

The responses and feedback collected through this exploration of practical experiences available to LIS students provided some useful data that can be used to continue to examine the issue of creating a centralized database of practicum and internship opportunities. Other than some brief descriptive language to frame the focus of the inquiries to the individual programs or within the survey, no clear or concise definition of practical experience opportunities was offered to survey participants. It appears that this ambiguity allowed for a wider variety of responses and, therefore, some insight as to what activities individuals consider practical experience during their LIS training. Examples of practical experiences include credit and noncredit, paid and unpaid, and library setting and nontraditional opportunities.

Aggregated survey responses offered insight into the ways in which practical experiences enhance the education of LIS students, lead to professional opportunities, and offer a general benefit to students. Responses indicated that there is value in practical experience. It is important to note that although a large number of LIS programs do not require that students engage in practical experiences, students seem to recognize the importance of such opportunities and therefore pursue them on their own accord. The most noted benefits found within survey results included networking with professionals, identifying reference contacts for job applications, exposure to institutional culture and politics, and, finally, increased confidence when entering the profession. These benefits represent skills and experiences that can often be difficult to simulate within the classroom.

In addition to serving as a learning tool for LIS students, the survey respondents reported that many of their practical experiences led to future professional opportunities; in other words, these experiences aided in obtaining employment. Overwhelmingly, respondents would recommend practical experiences to future students. That said, a number of participants reported that practical experiences were unnecessary due to employment or exposure to library settings prior to or during the completion of their LIS programs. In other words, while the majority reported value in pursuing practical experiences, there is a contingent of LIS students who find additional practical experience opportunities, whether required or not, of little consequence to their own ability to secure a professional position.

There appears to be a perception that practical experience is an important part of the LIS student education. This importance is evidenced by the commitment of many programs to connect students with opportunities and reports from a subset of recent graduates affirming so. As LIS programs continue to develop and strive to offer the best education to future library professionals, it will be important to maintain an emphasis on practical experiences. Considerations for the future may include a change to requiring that all ALA-accredited programs include practical experiences within the curriculum. Encouraging LIS programs to share practical experience opportunities in a centralized database may also offer benefits to the greater LIS community, as the survey results suggest.

With the value that students place on practical experience and the interest LIS programs have in serving the needs of their students, it is clear that continuing to think about the ways in which students can be connected with opportunities is critical. The LIS programs from which we graduated and the programs contacted for our project each had different ways of connecting students with opportunities. Although there may be no perfect method, rethinking the way in which information about practical experiences is offered, advertised, listed, and distributed—whether locally or nationally—may result in better and more consistent opportunities for LIS students across the country.

Bibliography

This bibliography cites most references included in individual chapters, as well as selected additional readings on service learning.

Acuña, Rodolfo F. *U.S. Latino Issues*. Westport, CT: Greenwood, 2003.

American Association for Adult and Continuing Education. www.aaace.org.

American Association of School Librarians and Association for Educational Communications and Technology. *Information Power: Building Partnerships for Learning*. Chicago: American Library Association, 1998.

American Library Association. Office for Accreditation. "Standards for Accreditation of Master's Programs in Library and Information Studies." 2008. www.ala.org/ala/educationcareers/education/accreditedprograms/standards/standards_2008.pdf.

Anderson, Debra K., and Barbara M. Harris. "Teaching Social Welfare Policy: A Comparison of Two-Part Pedagogical Approaches." *Journal of Social Work Education* 41, no. 3 (Fall 2005): 511–26.

Assembly of Alaska Native Educators. *Guidelines for Respecting Cultural Knowledge*. Anchorage, AK, 2000. www.ankn.uaf.edu/publications/knowledge.html.

Bajjaly, Stephen T. "Contemporary Recruitment in Traditional Libraries." *Journal of Library and Information Science Education* 46, no. 1 (Winter 2005): 53–58.

Ball, Mary Alice. "Practicums and Service Learning in LIS Education." *Journal of Education for Library and Information Science* 49, no. 1 (Winter 2008): 70–82.

Ball, Mary Alice, and Katherine Schilling. "Service Learning, Technology, and LIS Education." *Journal of Library and Information Science Education* 47, no. 4 (Fall 2006): 277–90.

Banks, Julie, and Ben H. Lents. "A Practicum: Views of Two Supervising Librarians." *Journal of Education for Library and Information Science* 33 (Summer 1992): 241–47.

Becker, Nancy J. "Service Learning in the Curriculum: Preparing LIS Students for the Next Millennium." *Journal of Education for Library and Information Science* 41, no. 4 (Fall 2000): 285–93.

Bell, Fiona. "Service-Learning in LIS Education: The Case of the University of Natal's Inadi Initiative." *South African Journal of Librarianship and Information Science* 73, no. 2 (2007): 147–55.

Bell, Rebecca, Andrew Furco, Mary Sue Ammon, Parisa Muller, and V. Sorgen. *Institutionalizing Service-Learning in Higher Education: Findings from a Study of the Western Region Campus Compact Consortium.* Bellingham, WA: Western Region Campus Compact Consortium, 2000.

Benson, Lee, Ira Harkavy, and John Puckett. *Dewey's Dream: Universities and Democracies in the Age of Education Reform; Civil Society, Public Schools, and Democratic Citizenship.* Philadelphia: Temple University Press, 2007.

Berman, Sanford. "Jackdaws Strut in Peacock Feathers: The Sham of 'Standard' Cataloging." *Librarians at Liberty* (June 1998): 1–21.

Berry, John N., III. "The Practice Prerequisite." *Library Journal* 130, no. 15 (September 15, 2005): 8.

Bishop, Ann, and Bertram C. Bruce. "Community Informatics: Integrating Action, Research and Learning." *Bulletin of the American Society for Information Science and Technology* 31, no. 6 (August/September 2005): 6–10.

Bolton, Charles Knowles. "The Librarian's Duty as a Citizen." *Library Journal* 21, no. 5 (May 1896): 219.

Bonk, Curtis Jay, and Thomas H. Reynolds. "Learner-Centered Web Instruction for Higher-Order Thinking, Teamwork, and Apprenticeship." In *Web-Based Instruction,* edited by Badrul H. Khan. Englewood Cliffs, NJ: Educational Technology Publications, 1997.

Botello, Keri S. "Library School Internship Programs: How UCLA Does It." In *Public Library Internships: Advice from the Field,* edited by Cindy Mediavilla. Lanham, MD: Scarecrow, 2006.

Boyer, Ernest L. "The Scholarship of Engagement." *Journal of Public Service and Outreach* 1, no. 1 (Spring 1996): 11–20.

Boyle-Baise, Marilynne. *Multicultural Service Learning: Educating Teachers in Diverse Communities.* New York: Teachers College Press, 2002.

Boyte, Harry Chatten. "A Different Kind of Politics: John Dewey and the Meaning of Citizenship in the 21st Century." *Good Society* 12, no. 2 (2003): 1–15.

Bringle, Robert G., Richard Games, and Edward A. Malloy. *Colleges and Universities as Citizens.* Boston: Allyn and Bacon, 1999.

Bringle, Robert G., and Julie A. Hatcher. "A Service-Learning Curriculum for Faculty." *Michigan Journal of Community Service-Learning* (Fall 1995): 112–22.

Brundin, Robert E. "The Place of the Practicum in Teaching Reference Interview Techniques." *Reference Librarian* 11, no. 25–26 (1989): 449–64.

Bundy, Mary Lee. *The Devil Has a Ph.D.* College Park, MD: Urban Information Interpreters, [1974?].

Bundy, Mary Lee, and Richard Moses. *A New Approach to Educational Preparation for Public Library Service: An Experimental Program in Library Education to Work with a Specialized Clientele; Interim Report, Project no. 7-1139.* Washington, DC: U.S.

Department of Health, Education, and Welfare, Office of Education, Bureau of Research, March 1969.

Bundy, Mary Lee, and Paul Wasserman. "A Departure in Library Education." *Journal of Education for Librarianship* 8, no. 2 (Fall 1967): 124–32.

Burek Pierce, Jennifer. "Library Students Making a Difference." *American Libraries* 36, no. 7 (August 2005): 83.

Buschman, John E., and Gloria J. Leckie, eds. *The Library as Place: History, Community, and Culture.* Westport, CT: Libraries Unlimited, 2007.

Butin, Dan W. "Focusing Our Aim: Strengthening Faculty Commitment to Community Engagement." *Change* 39, no. 6 (November/December 2007): 34–37.

Cajete, Gregory. *Look to the Mountain: An Ecology of Indigenous Education.* Skyland, NC: Kivaki, 1994.

Campus Compact. "Campus Compact Annual Membership Survey, 2006." 2007. www.compact.org/about/statistics/2006/.

Carroll, John M. *Making Use: Scenario-Based Design of Human-Computer Interactions.* Cambridge, MA: MIT Press, 2000.

Chatman, Elfreda A. "The Impoverished Life-World of Outsiders." *Journal of the American Society for Information Science* 47, no. 3 (March 1996): 193–206.

Chatman, Elfreda A., and Victoria E. M. Pendleton. "Knowledge Gap, Information-Seeking and the Poor." *Reference Librarian* 49–50 (1995): 135–45.

Chu, Clara M. "Aprendizaje Socio-Crítico en Servicio: Educación Para la Participación Estudiantil en los Estudios de la Información" [Critical Service Learning: Student Participation in Information Studies Education]. In *La Participación en las Administraciones Públicas: ¿Cooperación o Enfrentamiento?* edited by Antonio Colomer Viadel. Valencia, Spain: Editorial UPV, 2006.

———. "Education for Multicultural Librarianship." In *Multiculturalism in Libraries,* edited by Rosemary Ruhig Du Mont, Lois Buttlar, and William Caynon. Westport, CT: Greenwood, 1994.

———. "Ethics, Diversity, and Change: A Core MLIS Course Engaging Students and Community." Paper presented at the annual meeting of the American Association of Library and Information Science Education, Philadelphia, January 8–11, 2008.

———. IS 289 Ethics, Diversity and Change in the Information Professions. N.d. www.gseis.ucla.edu/faculty/chu/edc/.

Chun, Malcolm Naea. *Pono: The Way of Living.* Honolulu: University of Hawaii, Curriculum Research and Development Group, 2006.

Claggett, Laura, Jan Chindlund, Cathy Friedman, Maureen Malinowski, Krista Pospisil, Bonnie Tilton Sebby, Megan Sweeney, Prudence Dalrymple, and Elisa Topper. "Library Practicum 101." *Information Outlook* 6, no. 9 (September 2002): 36–38, 40–42.

Clapp, Elsie Ripley. *Community Schools in Action.* New York: Viking, 1939.

Clark, Sheila, and Erica MacCreaigh. *Library Services to the Incarcerated: Applying the Public Library Model in Correctional Facility Libraries.* Westport, CT: Libraries Unlimited, 2006.

Coleman, J. Gordon. "The Role of the Practicum in Library Schools." *Journal of Education for Library and Information Science* 30 (Summer 1989): 19–27.

Colson, John C. "The Agony of Outreach: Some Reconsiderations Based on the High John Project." *Library Journal* 98, no. 17 (October 1, 1973): 2817–20.

Connors, Kara, and Sarena D. Seifer. "Reflection in Higher Education Service-Learning." 2005. www.servicelearning.org/resources/fact_sheets/he_facts/he_reflection/index.php.

Cuban, Sondra, and Elisabeth Hayes. "Perspectives of Five Library and Information Studies Students Involved in Service Learning at a Community-Based Literacy Program." *Journal of Education for Library and Information Science* 42, no. 2 (Spring 2001): 86–95.

Curry, Ann. "Action Research in Action: Involving Students and Professionals." In *Proceedings of the World Library and Information Congress: 71st International Federation of Library Associations and Institutions, General Conference and Congress (Libraries—A Voyage of Discovery),* Oslo, Norway, August 14–18, 2005. www.ifla.org/IV/ifla71/papers/046e-Curry.pdf.

Cveljo, Katherine. "Internationalizing LIS Degree Programs: Internationalizing Library and Information Science Degree Programs—Benefits and Challenges for Special Librarians." Paper presented at the Mid-Missouri Chapter meeting of the Special Library Association, Columbia, MO, April 25, 1996. www.sla.org/content/SLA/professional/businesscase/acteng/cveljo.cfm?style=text.

Damasco, Ione T., and Melanie J. McGurr. "A Survey of Cataloger Perspectives on Practicum Experiences." *Cataloging and Classification Quarterly* 45, no. 4 (2008): 43–64.

Danielson, Charlotte. *Enhancing Professional Practice: A Framework for Teaching.* 2nd edition. Alexandria, VA: Association for Supervision and Curriculum Development, 2007.

Day, Peter, and Douglas Schuler, eds. *Community Practice in the Network Society: Local Action/Global Interaction.* London: Routledge, 2004.

Dewey, John. "The School as Social Center." *Elementary School Teacher* 3, no. 2 (October 1902): 73–86.

Dewey, Melvil. "School of Library Economy at Columbia College." *Library Journal* 9, no. 7 (July 1894): 118.

Driscoll, Amy, and Ernest A. Lynton. *Making Outreach Visible: A Guide to Documenting Professional Service and Outreach.* Washington, DC: American Association for Higher Education, 1999.

Dryfoos, Joy G., Jane Quinn, and Carol Barkin, eds. *Community Schools in Action: Lessons from a Decade of Practice.* New York: Oxford University Press, 2005.

Dutcher, Gale A., Melvin Spann, and Cynthia Gaines. "Addressing Health Disparities and Environmental Justice: The National Library of Medicine's Environmental Health Information Outreach Program." *Journal of the Medical Library Association* 95, no. 3 (July 2007): 330–36.

Ellsworth, Elizabeth Ann. *Places of Learning: Media, Architechture, Pedagogy.* New York: RoutledgeFalmer, 2005.

Elmborg, James K. "Critical Information Literacy: Implications for Instructional Practice." *Journal of Academic Librarianship* 32, no. 2 (March 2006): 192–99.

Elmborg, James K., Heather Leighton, Holly Huffman, Jane Bradbury, Tim Bryant, Denise Britigan, Connie Ghinazzi, Stacy Light, Sarah Andrews, and Chris Miller. "Service Learning in the Library and Information Science Curriculum: The Perspectives and Experiences of One Multimedia/User Education Class." *Research Strategies* 18, no. 4 (Winter 2001): 265–81.

Estabrook, Leigh S. "Distance Education at the University of Illinois." In *Benchmarks in Distance Education: The LIS Experience*, edited by Daniel D. Barron. Westport, CT: Libraries Unlimited, 2003.

Eyler, Janet S. "What Do We Most Need to Know about the Impact of Service-Learning on Student Learning?" Special issue. *Michigan Journal of Community Service Learning* (Fall 2000): 11–17.

Eyler, Janet S., and Dwight E. Giles. *Where's the Learning in Service-Learning?* San Francisco: Jossey-Bass, 1999.

Fallis, Don, and Martin Fricke. "Not by Library School Alone." *Library Journal* 124, no. 17 (October 15, 1999): 44–45.

Fear, Frank A., and Lorilee Sandmann. "Unpacking the Service Category: Reconceptualizing University Outreach for the 21st Century." *Continuing Higher Education Review* 59, no. 3 (Fall 1995): 110–22.

Felten, Peter, Leigh Z. Gilchrist, and Alexa Darby. "Emotion and Learning: Feeling Our Way toward a New Theory of Reflection in Service-Learning." *Michigan Journal of Community Service Learning* 12, no. 2 (Spring 2006): 38–46.

Ferguson, Carroy Ugene. "A New Paradigm of Learning for Urban Adult Learners: Challenges for Educators and Policymakers Regarding Education and Community Service." *Journal of Pedagogy, Pluralism and Practice* 1, no. 1 (Spring 1997): article 4. www.lesley.edu/journals/jppp/1/jp3ii4.html.

Fine, Michelle. "Working the Hyphens: Reinventing Self and Other in Qualitative Research." In *The Landscape of Qualitative Research: Theories and Issues*, edited by Norman K. Denzin and Yvonna S. Lincoln. Thousand Oaks, CA: Sage, 1998.

Fisher, Bradley J., and Marvin S. Finkelstein. "The Gerontology Practicum as Service-Learning." *Educational Gerontology* 25, no. 5 (July/August 1999): 393–409.

Fiske, Edward B. *Learning in Deed: The Power of Service-Learning for American Schools*. Battle Creek, MI: W. K. Kellogg Foundation, 2001. www.learningindeed.org.

Fitzgerald, Mary Ann. "EDIT 6380 Service Project." 2008. http://it.coe.uga .edu/%7Emfitzger/6380/service-project.html.

Fook, Jan, and Gurid Aga Askeland. "Challenges of Critical Reflection: 'Nothing Ventured, Nothing Gained.'" *Social Work Education* 26, no. 5 (August 2007): 520–33.

Frey, Timothy. "Determining the Impact of Online Practicum Facilitation for Inservice Teachers." *Journal of Technology and Teacher Education* 16, no. 2 (2008): 181–201.

Furco, Andrew. "Advancing Service-Learning at Research Universities." In *Developing and Implementing Service-Learning Programs*, edited by Mark Canada and Bruce W. Speck, 67–78. San Francisco: Jossey-Bass, 2001.

———. "Service Learning: A Balanced Approach to Experiential Education." In *Expanding Boundaries: Service and Learning*. Washington, DC: Corporation for National Service, 1996.

Garrett, LeAnn. "Dewey, Dale, and Bruner: Educational Philosophy, Experiential Learning, and Library School Cataloging Instruction at the School of Library and Information Studies, University of Hawaii." *Journal of Education for Library and Information Science* 38 (Spring 1997): 129–36.

Gasser, Les, Walt Scacchi, Gabriel Ripoche, and Bryan Penne. "Understanding Continuous Design in F/OSS Projects." In *Proceedings of the 16th International Conference on Software Engineering and Its Applications (ICSSEA-03)*, Paris, December 2003.

Gibson, Craig, ed. *Student Engagement and Information Literacy*. Chicago: American Library Association, Association of College and Research Libraries, 2006.

Giroux, Henry A. *The University in Chains: Confronting the Military-Industrial-Academic Complex*. Boulder, CO: Paradigm, 2007.

Godwin, Donald R. "Will They Heed the Call to Service? A Different Look at the Service-Learning Question." *Educational Horizons* 81, no. 1 (Fall 2002): 16–17.

Gracia, Jorge J. E. *Hispanic/Latino Identity: A Philosophical Perspective*. Malden, MA: Blackwell, 2000.

Greene, Maxine. "Teaching as Possibility: A Light in Dark Times." *Journal of Pedagogy, Pluralism and Practice* 1, no. 1 (Spring 1997): article 2. www.lesley .edu/journals/jppp/1/jp3ii1.html.

Greer, Roger. *Anatomy of a Small Public Library: A Study of Current and Projected Needs of a Suburban Community and New Town with a Proposed Plan for Library Development*. ERIC document ED115286. Syracuse, NY: School of Information Studies, 1974.

Gunawardena, Charlotte N., Ana C. Nolla, and Penne L. Wilson. "A Cross-Cultural Study of Group Process and Development in Online Conferences." *Distance Learning* 22, no. 1 (2001): 85–121.

Guzdial, Mark, Jochen Rick, and Colleen Kehoe. "Beyond Adoption to Invention: Teacher-Created Collaborative Activities in Higher Education." *Journal of the Learning Sciences* 10, no. 3 (2001): 265–79.

Habermas, Jürgen. *Justification and Application: Remarks on Discourse Ethics*. Translated by Ciaran P. Cronin. Cambridge, MA: MIT Press, 1993.

Harger, Elaine, and Kathleen de la Peña McCook. "PLG—Presenté! Report from the United States Social Forum." *Progressive Librarian* 30 (Winter 2007/08): 79–102.

Harkavy, Ira. "Service-Learning and the Development of Democratic Universities, Democratic Schools, and Democratic Good Societies in the 21st Century." In *New Perspectives in Service-Learning: Research to Advance the Field*, edited by Marshall Welch and Shelley H. Billig. Greenwich, CT: Information Age, 2004.

Harris, Michael H. "The Purpose of the American Public Library: A Revisionist Interpretation of History." *Library Journal* 98, no. 16 (1973): 2509–14.

Hawkins, David. "Messing About in Science." *Science and Children* 2, no. 5 (1965): 5–9.

Hawtrey, Kim. "Using Experiential Learning Techniques." *Journal of Economic Education* 38, no. 2 (Spring 2007): 143–52.

Hickman, Larry A. *John Dewey's Pragmatic Technology*. Bloomington: Indiana University Press, 1990.

Hirschinger-Blank, Nancy, and Michael Markowitz. "An Evaluation of a Pilot Service Learning Course for Criminal Justice Undergraduate Students." *Journal of Criminal Justice Education* 17, no. 1 (April 2006): 69–86.

Hoffman, Martin L. "Developmental Synthesis of Affect and Cognition and Its Implications for Altruistic Motivation." *Developmental Psychology* 11, no. 5 (1975): 607–22.

Hutchins, Robert Maynard. *The Higher Learning in America*. New Haven, CT: Yale University Press, 1936.

Internet Public Library. www.ipl.org.

Jacoby, Barbara, and Associates. *Building Partnerships for Service-Learning*. San Francisco: Jossey-Bass, 2003.

John Dewey Project on Progressive Education. "A Brief Overview of Progressive Education." 2002. www.uvm.edu/~dewey/articles/proged.html.

Jones, Plummer Alston, Jr. *Still Struggling for Equality: American Public Library Services with Minorities*. Westport, CT: Libraries Unlimited, 2004.

Josey, E. J. "Meeting the Challenge: Educating for Universal Library and Information Service." In *Translating an International Education to a National Environment: Papers Presented at the International Doctoral Student Conference, Sponsored by the Doctoral Guild at the University of Pittsburgh, School of Library and Information Science, September 23–25, 1988,* edited by Julie I. Tallman and Joseph B. Ojiambo, 1–12. Metuchen, NJ: Scarecrow, 1990.

Kazmer, Michelle M. "Community-Embedded Learning." *Library Quarterly* 75, no. 2 (2005): 190–212.

Kellogg Commission on the Future of State and Land-Grant Universities. "Renewing the Covenant: Learning, Discovery, and Engagement in a New Age and Different World." 2000. www.nasulgc.org/NetCommunity/Page .aspx?pid=305&srcid=751.

Kibler, John M. "Latino Voices in Children's Literature: Instructional Approaches for Developing Cultural Understanding in the Classroom." In *Children of La Frontera: Binational Efforts to Serve Mexican Migrant and Immigrant Students,* edited by Judith LeBlanc Flores. Charleston, WV: ERIC, 1996.

King, Martin Luther, Jr. "Beyond Vietnam." 1967. www.mlkonline.net/vietnam.html.

Kling, Rob. "What Is Social Informatics and Why Does It Matter?" *D-Lib Magazine* 5, no. 1 (January 1999). www.dlib.org/dlib/january99/kling/01kling.html.

Kochhar, Rakesh, Roberto Suro, and Sonya Tafoya. "The New Latino South: The Context and Consequences of Rapid Population Growth." Pew Hispanic Center. 2005. http://pewhispanic.org/reports/report.php?ReportID=50.

Kolb, David A. *Experiential Learning: Experience as the Source of Learning and Development*. Englewood Cliffs, NJ: Prentice-Hall, 1984.

Kretzmann, John P., and John L. McKnight. *Building Communities from the Inside Out: A Path toward Finding and Mobilizing Community Assets.* Chicago: ACTA, 1993.

Kusow, Abdi M. "Beyond Indigenous Authenticity: Reflections on the Insider/ Outsider Debate in Immigration Research." *Symbolic Interaction* 26, no. 4 (Fall 2003): 591–99.

Larsen, Ronald L. "Groups of Leading Colleges Launch Major Effort to Put the Information Field on the Map." *News from the iWorld,* August 21, 2007.

Learn and Serve, America's National Service-Learning Clearinghouse. 2008. www .servicelearning.org.

Lemieux, Catherine M., and Priscilla D. Allen. "Service Learning in Social Work Education: The State of Knowledge, Pedagogical Practicalities, and Practice Conundrums." *Journal of Social Work Education* 43, no. 2 (Spring/Summer 2007): 309–25.

Leonard, Barbara G., and Donna Z. Pontau. "Sculpting Future Librarians through Structured Practicums: The Role of Academic Librarians." *Journal of Academic Librarianship* 17, no. 1 (March 1991): 26–30.

"Libraries and Information in World Social Forum Context." Special Issue. *Information for Social Change* 24 (Winter 2006–2007). http://libr.org/isc/toc.html.

Libraries for the Future. www.lff.org.

Lo, Peggy P. F. "Web-Based Postgraduate Course Design According to Experiential Learning." In *Proceedings of the IASTED International Conference on Web-Based Education.* Innsbruck, Austria: IASTED, 2004.

Lowe, Martyn, and Toni Samek. "Editorial: Libraries and Information Workers in Conflict Situations." *Information for Social Change Journal* 25 (Summer 2007). http://libr.org/isc/toc.html.

Lyders, Josetta, and Patricia Jane Wilson. "A National Survey: Field Experience in Library Education." *School Library Journal* 37 (January 1991): 31–35.

MacGregor, Jean. "Learning Self-Evaluation: Challenges for Students." *New Directions for Teaching and Learning* 56 (Winter 1993): 35–46.

Mardis, Marcia A. "From One-to-One to One-to-Many: A Study of the Practicum in the Transition from Teacher to School Library Media Specialist." *Journal of Education for Library and Information Science* 48, no. 3 (Summer 2007): 218–35.

Mark, Amy E. "Libraries without Walls: An Internship at Oshkosh Correctional Institution Library." *Behavioral and Social Science Librarian* 23, no. 2 (2005): 97–111.

Masucci, Matt, and Adam Renner. "Reading the Lives of Others: The Winton Homes Library Project—A Cultural Studies Analysis of Critical Service Learning for Education." *High School Journal* 84, no. 1 (October/November 2000): 36–47.

McClam, Tricia, Joel F. Diambra, Bobbie Burton, Angie Fuss, and Daniel L. Fudge. "An Analysis of a Service-Learning Project: Students' Expectations, Concerns, and Reflections." *Journal of Experiential Education* 30, no. 3 (March 2008): 236–49.

McClure, Charles R., and Peter Hernon, eds. *Library and Information Science Research: Perspectives and Strategies for Improvement.* Norwood, NJ: Ablex, 1991.

McCook, Kathleen de la Peña. "Guidelines for Supervised Fieldwork." 2004. www.cas
    .usf.edu/lis/mccook/fwGuidelines.htm.

———. "Librarians as Advocates for the Human Rights of Immigrants." *Progressive
    Librarian* 29 (Summer 2007): 51–55.

———. *A Place at the Table: Participating in Community Building.* Chicago: American
    Library Association, 2000.

———. "Reconnecting Library Education and the Mission of Community." *Library
    Journal* 125, no. 14 (September 1, 2000): 164–65.

———. "There Is Power in a Union—Union Activism 2006 Timeline." *Progressive
    Librarian* 28 (Winter 2006/2007): 101–4.

———. "Ya es Hora Ciudadania." *REFORMA Newsletter* 25 (Spring/Summer 2007):
    9–10.

McCook, Kathleen de la Peña, and Katharine J. Phenix. "Public Libraries
    and Human Rights." *Public Library Quarterly* 25, no. 1–2 (2006):
    57–73.

McLuhan, Marshall. *Understanding Media.* London: Routledge, 2006.

Mediavilla, Cindy. "FILLing in the Public-Librarian Ranks." *American Libraries* 34,
    no. 6 (June/July 2003): 61–62.

Mehra, Bharat. "An Action Research (AR) Manifesto for Cyberculture Power to
    'Marginalized' Cultures of Difference." In *Critical Cyberculture Studies,* edited by
    David Silver and Adrienne Massanari. New York: New York University Press,
    2006.

———. "The Cross-Cultural Learning Process of International Doctoral Students: A
    Case Study in Library and Information Science Education." Ph.D. dissertation.
    University of Illinois at Urbana-Champaign, 2004.

———. "Library and Information Science (LIS) and Community Development:
    Use of Information and Communication Technology (ICT) to Support a Social
    Equity Agenda." *Journal of the Community Development Society* 36, no. 1 (2005):
    28–40.

———. "Service Learning in Library and Information Science (LIS) Education:
    Connecting Research and Practice to Community." *InterActions: UCLA Journal of
    Information and Education Studies* 1, no. 1 (2004): article 3.

Mehra, Bharat, Kendra S. Albright, and Kevin Rioux. "A Practical Framework for
    Social Justice Research in the Information Professions." In *Proceedings of the 69th
    Annual Meeting of the American Society for Information Science and Technology 2006:
    Information Realities; Shaping the Digital Future for All.* Austin, TX: American
    Society for Information Science and Technology, 2006.

Mehra, Bharat, and Ann Bishop. "Cross-Cultural Perspectives of International
    Doctoral Students: Two-Way Learning in Library and Information Science
    Education." *International Journal of Progressive Education* 3, no. 1 (2007): 44–64.

Mehra, Bharat, Ann Bishop, I. Bazzell, and C. Smith. "Scenarios in the Afya Project
    as a Participatory Action Research (PAR) Tool for Studying Information Seeking
    and Use across the 'Digital Divide.'" *Journal of the American Society of Information
    Science and Technology* 53, no. 14 (2002): 1259–66.

Mehra, Bharat, and Ramesh Srinivasan. "The Library-Community Convergence Framework for Community Action: Libraries as Catalysts of Social Change." *Libri: International Journal of Libraries and Information Services* 57, no. 3 (September 2007): 123–39.

Merriam, Sharan B., Juanita Johnson-Bailey, Ming-Yeh Lee, Youngwha Kee, Gabo Ntseane, and Mazanah Muhamad. "Power and Positionality: Negotiating Insider/Outsider Status within and across Cultures." *International Journal of Lifelong Education* 20, no. 5 (September/October 2001): 405–16.

Miranda-Murillo, Diana. "New Immigrants Center at the Austin Public Library." *Texas Library Journal* 82, no. 4 (Winter 2006): 144–47.

Mitchell, Tania D. "Critical Service-Learning as Social Justice Education: A Case Study of the Citizen Scholars Program." *Equity and Excellence in Education* 40, no. 2 (April 2007): 101–12.

Murphy, Karen L., and Lauren Cifuentes. "Using Web Tools, Collaborating, and Learning Online." *Distance Education* 22, no. 2 (2001): 285–305.

Murphy, Karen L., and Mauri P. Collins. "Communication Conventions in Instructional Electronic Chats." *First Monday* 2 (November 1997). www .firstmonday.dk/issues/issue2_11/murphy/index.html.

Nazarova, Muzhgan. "Service Learning and Career Development: A Case Study in Library and Information Science." Ph.D. dissertation. University of Illinois at Urbana-Champaign, 2007.

Nicholson, Jane, and Teresea Hopkins. "Appalachian State and Clemson Universities Partner to Research Virtual World Technology." Appalachian State University, *University News* (November 30, 2007). www.news.appstate.edu/2007/11/30/3-d-virtual/.

Northern Arizona University. "Institutional Review Board for the Protection of Human Subjects: The Informed Consent Procedure." 2008. www.research .nau.edu/vpr/IRB/icdprocess.htm#D.

Northern Kentucky University. Office of the Associate Provost for Outreach. "Public Engagement Terminology." www.nku.edu/~nkuope/definitions .html.

Oberg, Dianne, and Toni Samek. "Humble Empowerment: The LIS Practicum." *PNLA Quarterly* 63, no. 3 (Spring 1999): 20–22.

Oboler, Suzanne. *Ethnic Labels, Latino Lives: Identity and the Politics of (Re)presentation in the United States.* Minneapolis: University of Minnesota Press, 1995.

———. "The Politics of Labeling: Latino/a Cultural Identities of Self and Others." In *Transnational Latina/o Communities: Politics, Processes, and Cultures,* edited by Carlos G. Vélez-Ibàñez and Anna Sampio. Lanham, MD: Rowman and Littlefield, 2002.

O'Connor, John S. "Civic Engagement in Higher Education." *Change* 38, no. 5 (September/October 2006): 52–58.

Olson, Hope A. "Mapping beyond Dewey's Boundaries: Constructing Classificatory Space for Marginalized Knowledge Domains." *Library Trends* 47, no. 2 (Fall 1998): 233–54.

O'Meara, KerryAnne. "Graduate Education and Civic Engagement." NERCHE Brief. 2007. www.nerche.org/briefs/briefs.htm.

Ondrejka, Cory. "School of the Future: Innovation and Education in Second Life." 2007. www.academicresourcecenter.net/curriculum/pfv.aspx?ID=6820.

O'Neill, Nancy. "Internships in a Public Library Reference Department." In *Public Library Internships: Advice from the Field,* edited by Cindy Mediavilla. Lanham, MD: Scarecrow, 2006.

Osborne, Robin, ed. *From Outreach to Equity: Innovative Models of Library Policy and Practice.* Chicago: American Library Association, Office for Literacy and Outreach Services, 2004.

Pasque, Penny A., Ryan E. Smerek, Brighid Dwyer, Nick Bowman, and Bruce L. Mallory. *Higher Education Collaboratives for Community Engagement and Improvement.* Ann Arbor, MI: National Forum on Higher Education for the Public Good, 2005. www.thenationalforum.org/docs/pdf/wingspread_05_final_monograph.pdf.

Percy, Stephen L., Nancy L. Zimpher, and Mary J. Brukardt, eds. *Creating a New Kind of University: Institutionalizing Community-University Engagement.* Bolton, MA: Anker, 2006.

Peterson, Lorna. "Using a Homeless Shelter as a Library Education Learning Laboratory: Incorporating Service-Learning in a Graduate-Level Information Sources and Services in the Social Sciences Course." *Reference and User Services Quarterly* 42, no. 4 (Summer 2003): 307–10.

Pew Hispanic Center. "Statistical Portrait of Hispanics in the United States, 2006." 2008. http://pewhispanic.org/factsheets/factsheet.php?FactsheetID=35.

Phenix, Katharine J., and Kathleen de la Peña McCook. "Human Rights and Librarians." *Reference and User Services Quarterly* 45, no. 1 (Fall 2005): 23–26.

Portes, Alejandro, and Dag MacLeod. "What Shall I Call Myself? Hispanic Identity Formation in the Second Generation." *Ethnic and Racial Studies* 19, no. 3 (1996): 523–47.

Prentice, Mary. "Social Justice through Service Learning: Community Colleges as Ground Zero." *Equity and Excellence in Education* 40, no. 3 (August 2007): 266–73.

Prentice, Mary, and Rudy M. Garcia. "Service Learning: The Next Generation in Education." *Community College Journal of Research and Practice* 24, no. 1 (January 2000): 19–26.

Rai, Lucy. "Owning (Up to) Reflective Writing in Social Work Education." *Social Work Education* 25, no. 8 (December 2006): 785–97.

Ramos, Jorge. *The Latino Wave: How Hispanics Will Elect the Next American President.* New York: Rayo HarperCollins, 2004.

Reardon, Kenneth M. "Participatory Action Research as Service Learning." *New Directions for Teaching and Learning* 73 (1998): 57–64.

Rex, Leslie A. "Higher Education Has Done Well, We Can Do More: A Report from the Wingspread Access, Equity and Social Justice Committee." In *Taking*

Responsibility: A Call for Higher Education's Engagement in a Society of Complex Global Challenges, edited by Penny A. Pasque, Lori A. Hendricks, and Nicholas A. Bowman. Ann Arbor, MI: National Forum on Higher Education for the Public Good, 2006.

Rhodes, Naomi J., and Judith M. Davis. "Using Service Learning to Get Positive Reactions in the Library." *Computers in Libraries* 21, no. 1 (January 2001): 32–35.

Ricoeur, Paul. *Oneself as Another.* Chicago: University of Chicago Press, 1992.

Rothman, Michael, Elisha Anderson, and Julia Schaffer, eds. *Service Matters: Engaging Higher Education in the Renewal of America's Communities and American Democracy.* Providence, RI: Campus Compact, 1998.

Rouverol, Alicia J. "Collaborative Oral History in a Correctional Setting: Promise and Pitfalls." *Oral History Review* 30, no. 1 (Winter/Spring 2003): 61–85.

Roy, Loriene. "Building Tribal Community Support for Technology Access." *Electronic Library* 24, no. 4 (2006): 517–29.

———. "Diversity in the Classroom: Incorporating Service-Learning Experiences in the Library and Information Science Curriculum." *Journal of Library Administration* 33, no. 3–4 (2001): 213–28.

———. "Supporting LIS Education Through Practice." 2007. www.ala.org/ala/hrdr/abouthrdr/hrdrliaisoncomm/committeeoned/EdForum2007Roy-SRA.pdf.

Roy, Loriene, and Peter Larsen. "Oksale: An Indigenous Approach to Creating a Virtual Library of Education Resources." *D-Lib Magazine* 8, no. 3 (March 2002). www.dlib.org/dlib/march02/roy/03roy.html.

Ryan, Greg, Susan Toohey, and Chris Hughes. "The Purpose, Value, and Structure of the Practicum in Higher Education: A Literature Review." *Higher Education* 31, no. 3 (April 1996): 355–77.

Sadik, Alaa. "Digital Storytelling: A Meaningful Technology-Integrated Approach for Engaged Student Learning." *Educational Technology Research and Development* 56, no. 4 (August 2008): 487–506.

Samek, Toni. *Librarianship and Human Rights: A Twenty-first Century Guide.* Oxford, UK: Chandos, 2007.

Samek, Toni, and Dianne Oberg. "A New Model for Field-Based Learning in Today's LIS Education at the University of Alberta." *Feliciter* 44, no. 5 (May 1998): 34–37.

San Jose State University. School of Library and Information Science. LIBR 294 Professional Experience: Internships. "Site Supervisor Evaluation." http://slisweb.sjsu.edu/classes/294/forms/294supevalofstu.php.

———. LIBR 294 Professional Experience: Internships. "Student Evaluation of Site." http://slisweb.sjsu.edu/classes/294/forms/294studentsiteeval.php.

———. "Statement of Core Competencies." http://slisweb.sjsu.edu/slis/competencies.htm.

Schomberg, Steven F., and James A. Farmer Jr. "The Evolving Concept of Public Service and Implications for Rewarding Faculty." *Continuing Higher Education Review* 58, no. 3 (Fall 1994): 122–40.

Schon, Donald A. *Educating the Reflective Practitioner: Toward a New Design for Teaching and Learning in the Professions.* San Francisco: Jossey-Bass, 1996.

Shannon, Donna. "The Education and Competencies of School Library Media Specialists: A Review of the Literature." *School Library Media Research* 5 (2002). www.ala.org/ala/aasl/aaslpubsandjournals/slmrb/slmrcontents/volume52002/shannon.cfm.

————. "Preparation of School Library Media Specialists in the United States." *School Library Media Research* 7 (2004). www.ala.org/ala/aasl/aaslpubsandjournals/slmrb/slmrcontents/volume72004/shannon.cfm.

Shapiro, Joseph P. "Do-Gooding: When It Gets Complicated." *U.S. News and World Report* 114, no. 3 (January 25, 1993): 66.

Shay, Suellen. "Assessment at the Boundaries: Service Learning as Case Study." *British Educational Research Journal* 34, no. 4 (August 2008): 525–40.

Shea, Alison. "It's Pracademic." *AALL Spectrum* 12, no. 3 (December 2007): 20–23.

Shopes, Linda. "Commentary: Sharing Authority." *Oral History Review* 30, no. 1 (Winter/Spring 2003): 103–10.

Silver, Isabel Dale. "The LIS Practicum: An Internship with Academic Credit." In *Public Library Internships: Advice from the Field,* edited by Cindy Mediavilla. Lanham, MD: Scarecrow, 2006.

Sitter, Clara L. "Learning by Serving." *Knowledge Quest* 34, no. 5 (May/June 2006): 23–26.

Smith, Linda Tuhiwai. *Decolonizing Methodologies: Research and Indigenous Peoples.* London and New York: Zed Books; Dunedin, NZ: University of Otago Press, 1999.

Smith, M. Cecil. "Does Service Learning Promote Adult Development? Theoretical Perspectives and Directions for Research." *New Directions for Adult and Continuing Education* 118 (Summer 2008): 5–15.

Speck, Bruce W., and Sherry L. Hoppe, eds. *Service-Learning: History, Theory, and Issues.* Westport, CT: Praeger, 2004.

Stephens, Michael. *Web 2.0 and Libraries: Best Practices for Social Software.* Library Technology Reports 42, no. 4. Chicago: ALA TechSource, 2006.

Stillman, Larry, and Randy Stoecker. "Structuration, ICTs, and Community Work." *Journal of Community Informatics* 1, no. 3 (2005): 83–102.

Stoecker, Randy. "Is Community Informatics Good for Communities? Questions Confronting an Emerging Field." *Journal of Community Informatics* 1, no. 3 (2005): 13–26.

————. *Research Methods for Community Change: A Project-Based Approach.* Thousand Oaks, CA: Sage, 2005.

Stringer, Ernest T. *Action Research.* Thousand Oaks, CA: Sage, 1999.

Sweeney, Irene. "Learning by Doing: Engaged Service and the MLS." *American Libraries* 33, no. 2 (February 2002): 44–46.

Tauroa, Hiwi, and Pat Tauroa. *Te Marae: A Guide to Customs and Protocol.* Auckland, NZ: Reed, 1986.

Taylor, T. L. *Play between Worlds: Exploring Online Game Culture*. Cambridge, MA: MIT Press, 2006.

Toi, Miho, and C. Daniel Batson. "More Evidence That Empathy Is a Source of Altruistic Motivation." *Journal of Personality and Social Psychology* 43, no. 2 (August 1982): 281–92.

UC Books to Prisoners. 2008. www.books2prisoners.org.

United States Social Forum. "Another World Is Possible. Another U.S. Is Necessary." Atlanta, GA, June 27–July 1, 2007. www.ussf2007.org.

University of Illinois and São Tomé e Príncipe Partnership blog. 2008. http:// saotomeproject.wordpress.com.

University of Illinois at Urbana-Champaign. "Community Informatics Initiative." 2008. www.cii.uiuc.edu.

———. "The East St. Louis Action Research Project." 2008. www.eslarp.uiuc .edu.

———. Board of Trustees. Office of the Chancellor. "Welcome to the Chancellor's Office." 2004. www.oc.uiuc.edu/welcome/index.html.

———. Graduate School of Library and Information Science. "Prairienet Community Network." 2008. www.prairienet.org.

———. Graduate School of Library and Information Science. Progressive Librarians Guild. "GSLIS Chapter." 2008. www.lis.uiuc.edu/plg/.

University of South Carolina. Consortium for Latino Immigration Studies. "The Economic and Social Implications of the Growing Latino Population in South Carolina." 2007. www.sph.sc.edu/cli/documents/CMAReport0809.pdf.

———. "Latinos in South Carolina—Fast Facts." 2007. www.sph.sc.edu/cli/ SCdatafacts.htm.

University of Texas at Austin. School of Information. "Capstone Information." 2001–2008. www.ischool.utexas.edu/programs/capstone/.

Urban Libraries Council. www.urbanlibraries.org.

U.S. Census Bureau. "Minority Population Tops 100 Million." 2007. www.census.gov/ Press-Release/www/releases/archives/population/010048.html.

———. "Young, Diverse, Urban: Hispanic Population Reaches All-Time High of 38.8 Million, New Census Bureau Estimates Show." 2005. http://209.85.215.104/ search?q=cache:tsOHQiHVaw8J:www.census.gov/Press-Release/www/releases/ archives/population/011193.html+Young,+diverse,+urban:+Hispanic&hl=en&ct= clnk&cd=7&gl=us.

U.S. National Institutes of Health. Office of Extramural Research. "Protecting Human Research Participants." 2008. http://phrp.nihtraining.com/users/login.php.

Vansickle, Sharon. "Educating Preservice Media Specialists: Developing School Leaders." *School Libraries Worldwide* 6, no. 2 (July 2000): 1–20.

Venturella, Karen M. *Poor People and Library Services*. Jefferson, NC: McFarland, 1998.

Vickers, Margaret, Catherine Harris, and Florence McCarthy. "University-Community Engagement: Exploring Service-Learning Options within the Practicum." *Asia-Pacific Journal of Teacher Education* 32, no. 2 (July 2004): 129–41.

Walker, Jane T., Carolyn S. Turner, Sarah M. Shoffner, and Fay Y. Gibson. "Enhancing Internships through Modules of Experiential Learning Activities." *Journal of Family and Consumer Sciences* 93, no. 4 (2001): 45–46.

Walker, Thomas D. "Learning on the Job: The Value of Internships and Practica." *Mississippi Libraries* 64, no. 3 (Fall 2000): 83–84.

Wallace, Virginia. "Supervising the High School Library Media Center Internship." *Book Report* 18, no. 2 (September/October 1998): 28–30.

Waluconis, Carl J. "Self-Evaluation: Settings and Uses." *New Directions for Teaching and Learning* 56 (Winter 1993): 15–33.

Waterman, Alan S., ed. *Service-Learning: Applications from the Research.* Mahwah, NJ: Lawrence Erlbaum Associates, 1997.

Watson, David. 2007. *Managing Civic and Community Engagement.* Maidenhead, UK: Open University Press, 2007.

Weibel, Kathleen. "The Evolution of Library Outreach 1960–75 and Its Effect on Reader Services: Some Considerations." Occasional Papers, no. 156. Champaign: University of Illinois, Graduate School of Library and Information Science, 1982.

Witbodi, S. L. "Service Learning in the Library and Information Studies Curriculum at the University of the Western Cape: An Exploratory Study." *Mousaion* 22, no. 1 (2004): 89–102.

Wolske, Martin. LIS 451 Introduction to Networked Information Systems. 2008. http://courseweb.lis.uiuc.edu/lis/2008su/lis451al1/syllabusLIS451SU08.xhtml.

Yontz, Elaine. "Be Outstanding in Your Fieldwork." *American Libraries* 39, no. 6 (June/July 2008): 56–59.

Yontz, Elaine, and Kathleen de la Peña McCook. "Service-Learning in LIS Education." *Journal of Library and Information Science Education* 44, no. 1 (Winter 2003): 58–68.

Zafiris, Paris A., Nektarios P. Georgantis, George E. Kalamaras, Sotiris P. Christodoulous, and Theodore S. Papatheodorou. "A Practitioner's Approach to Evolving and Remodeling Large-Scale WWW Sites." In *Proceedings of the 34th Hawaii International Conference on System Sciences (HICSS),* Maui, January 3–6, 2001. http://csdl2.computer.org/comp/proceedings/hicss/2001/0981/07/09817078.pdf.

Zlotkowski, Edward. "Mapping New Terrain: Service-Learning across the Disciplines." *Change* 33, no. 1 (January/February 2001): 25–33.

Author Biographies

Eileen G. Abels is master's program director and associate professor in the College of Information Science and Technology at Drexel University. Prior to joining the faculty at Drexel in 2007, she spent more than fifteen years at the College of Information Studies at the University of Maryland. Her research focuses on digital reference education, remote reference services, and automated question-answering services. She is working with colleagues at Drexel, the University of Michigan, and Florida State University to transform the Internet Public Library into a virtual learning laboratory.

Denise E. Agosto is an associate professor in the College of Information Science and Technology at Drexel University. Her research and teaching interests include youth information behavior, gender and information behavior, public libraries, and multicultural issues in youth library services. She has published more than fifty articles, book chapters, and scholarly reviews in these areas, and she has completed a number of related funded research projects as well.

Sara Albert graduated from the School of Information at the University of Texas at Austin in 2005. She has worked as an adjunct reference librarian for Austin Community College and as assistant to the 2006–2007 president-elect of the American Library Association. She now lives in the Portland, Oregon, area and plans to continue her career as a librarian.

Ann Bishop is an associate professor in the Graduate School of Library and Information Science at the University of Illinois at Urbana-Champaign.

Bertram C. Bruce is a professor in Library and Information Science, Curriculum and Instruction, with appointments in Bioengineering, the Center for Writing Studies, and the Center for East Asian and Pacific Studies at the University of Illinois at Urbana-Champaign. His background in computer science reflects a continuing interest in the promise and perils that information and communication technologies offer for understanding, representing, and transforming our lived experiences. His explorations of the nature of knowledge, democratic participation, community, technology, and literacy are discussed in recent books, including *Libr@ries: Changing Information Space and Practice* (2006, with Cushla Kapitzke) and *Literacy in the Information Age: Inquiries into Meaning Making with New Technologies* (2003). He is involved in the projects of the Community Informatics Initiative (which he and Ann Bishop cofounded) and in the development of computer systems to support collaboration and community action, such as Quill, the Inquiry Page, and Community Inquiry Labs.

Gilok Choi is a recent Ph.D. graduate from the School of Information at the University of Texas at Austin. Her interests include human computer interaction, user interface design, usability studies and methodologies, technical implementation of multimedia and web applications, and digital libraries. Her research agenda concerns system development and interface design based on an understanding of users' needs and abilities.

Clara M. Chu is an associate professor at the UCLA Department of Information Studies. She specializes in the social construction of information systems, institutions, and access in order to understand the usage of and barriers to information in multicultural communities. As a Peruvian-born, Chinese Canadian American, her transnational and ethnic minority experiences give her a distinctive and critical lens with which to examine information issues and to inform professional practice. She is a leading voice on multicultural library and information issues. Chu has led initiatives to diversify the LIS curriculum and student body at both the master's and doctoral levels.

C. Olivia Frost is a professor at the University of Michigan School of Information, where she has also served as associate dean and interim dean. Her research and service activities build on a background in cataloging and classification and focus on the potential for digital technologies to broaden access to multimedia information resources. Frost has been active in promoting cultural heritage outreach in virtual and real-world environments. She founded and directed the Cultural Heritage Initiative for Community Outreach, a community outreach initiative in which Michigan School of Information students work with museums, libraries, and area schools to broaden the reach of multicultural heritage materials, and develop partnerships with communities to capture and disseminate their cultural heritage using information and collaboration technology.

Gary Geisler is an assistant professor in the School of Information at the University of Texas at Austin. His research focuses on digital multimedia, digital libraries, and interaction design and includes projects funded by the National Science Foundation, the National Institutes of Health, and the Institute of Museum and Library Services. He teaches graduate courses in research methods, database design and development, digital libraries, and digital media collection development.

Lydia Eato Harris is an assistant professor in the School of Communication, Information and Library Studies at Rutgers, State University of New Jersey, and is completing her doctorate at the Information School of the University of Washington in Seattle. Her research interests include information services and sources in all media, distance education, librarians as users, activity theory, and information behavior in context.

Sunny Jeong is a doctoral student in the Graduate School of Library and Information Science at the University of Illinois at Urbana-Champaign.

Johan Koren is an associate professor and coordinator for the Library Media Program at Murray State University in Kentucky, where he is responsible for an online post-master's program. He has worked as an elementary teacher and a regional librarian in Norway and taught library studies at universities and colleges in the United States and Norway. His library degrees are from the University of Michigan in Ann Arbor.

Molly Krichten is associate director of the Guthrie Memorial Library, the public library in Hanover, Pennsylvania. She holds an MLS degree from the University of Pittsburgh. She was a participant in the American Library Association's 2008 Emerging Leaders program, during which she and four other librarians researched the value and incidence of internship experience among library and information science graduates. She is an active member of the Young Adult Library Services Association.

Beth Larkee is currently the information technology librarian at Hollins University in Roanoke, Virginia. In addition to maintaining the library's systems and electronic resources, she is interested in the role of technology in service learning projects and distance education. She earned both her MS and a certificate of advanced studies from the Graduate School of Library and Information Science at the University of Illinois at Urbana-Champaign. While a student, she worked on service learning projects in both Illinois and West Africa for two and a half years.

Kathleen de la Peña McCook is distinguished university professor at the University of South Florida in Tampa. Her background in human rights includes analysis of gender and ethnic issues in the delivery of library services. She also monitors union activity on the blog *Union Librarian*. Among her recent publications is *Introduction to Public Librarianship* (2004). She received the Beta Phi Mu Award for distinguished service to education for librarianship in 2003 and the Latino Librarian of the Year award in 2002 from REFORMA.

Bharat Mehra is an assistant professor at the School of Information Sciences of the University of Tennessee. His work involves representing diversity and intercultural issues in social justice and social equity efforts to meet the needs of minority and underserved populations. Mehra is currently partnering with local and regional sexual minorities, international students, African American women graduate students, and others in initiatives that apply participatory action research and community-building strategies to equate perceived power imbalances and social inequities in the eastern Tennessee region.

Lorri Mon is an assistant professor in the College of Information at Florida State University. Her research focuses on information services and question-and-answer interactions via different information technologies and settings including digital libraries, e-government, virtual worlds, and Web 2.0. She received the ASIS&T SIG-USE Elfreda A. Chatman Research Award in 2007.

Rae-Anne Montague is assistant dean for student affairs at the Graduate School of Library and Information Science at the University of Illinois at Urbana-Champaign. Her research interests include multimodal education, learning technologies, and diversity. She is currently principal investigator for the Institute of Museum and Library Services' Laura Bush 21st Century Librarian grant-funded program, the LIS Access Midwest Program.

Jamie Campbell Naidoo is an assistant professor at the University of Alabama's School of Library and Information Studies, where he researches and teaches in the areas of intercultural and international youth literature and library services to diverse populations. His primary research emphasis is on literacy and library services for Latino children. He is the codirector and cofounder of the Annual Celebration of Latino Children's Literature Conference, initiated in April 2008. He also established ¡Imagínense Libros! a virtual evaluation collection of Latino children's and young adult literature launched in fall 2008.

Lorna Peterson is an associate professor in library and information studies at the University at Buffalo, State University of New York. She has been on the faculty at Buffalo since 1990. Previous to her faculty appointment there, she was a reference librarian and cataloger at Wright State University in Dayton, Ohio, and Ohio University in Athens, Ohio. At Iowa State University she earned tenure and promotion to associate librarian. Her research areas are race and multicultural issues in librarianship and critical issues in library education.

Joe Sanchez is a Ph.D. candidate in the School of Information at the University of Texas at Austin. He is interested in the study of virtual worlds, particularly the areas of socio-technical systems, communities of practice, and the user experience. He has been using the virtual world of Second Life in his teaching since fall 2006. Professionally, Sanchez has worked as an instructional technologist and faculty development specialist. His work in Second Life has been featured in *USA Today, Texas Technology Magazine,* and the *Chronicle of Higher Education.*

Robert J. Sandusky is clinical associate professor and assistant university librarian for information technology at the University of Illinois at Chicago, where he manages public and staff computing infrastructure and digital library services. Previously he was an assistant professor and faculty coordinator for the undergraduate minor in information studies and technology at the School of Information Sciences at the University of Tennessee, Knoxville. His research centers on the investigation of the information practices employed by distributed and virtual communities as they collaborate to achieve their goals. He has performed research in multiple domains, including open source software engineering, digital libraries, and the management of distributed infrastructure.

A. Arro Smith is the technical services manager at the San Marcos Public Library. He has been a librarian in San Marcos, Texas, since 1990. He is currently pursuing a Ph.D. at the School of Information at the University of Texas at Austin. His research focuses on developing practical tools and methods for collection development, bibliographic control and classification, and oral history. He is currently the project director for Capturing Our Stories, an oral history program for retired and retiring librarians.

Sarah Stohr is a distance services librarian at the University of New Mexico and also completed a post-MSLS residency program there. She received her graduate degree at the University of Kentucky, where she focused her studies on library services to Latinos and underrepresented populations. Stohr was named a 2008 ALA Emerging Leader.

Stefanie Warlick is currently the health and human services librarian at James Madison University in Harrisonburg, Virginia. She holds an MLIS degree from the University of North Carolina at Chapel Hill. Warlick recently completed the ALA's 2008 Emerging Leaders program. In addition to her membership and service in the American Library Association, Warlick is an active member of the Mid-Atlantic Chapter of the Medical Library Association.

Martin Wolske is a senior research scientist for community informatics at the Graduate School of Library and Information Science at the University of Illinois at Urbana-Champaign. His research interests center around the effective application of technologies for community building in economically distressed communities. Wolske has presented at a number of conferences on service learning in LIS education. He holds a Ph.D. in behavioral neuroscience from Rutgers, State University of New Jersey.

Elaine Yontz is a professor in the Master of Library and Information Science Program at Valdosta State University, Georgia. She has published on service learning in the *Journal of Education for Library and Information Science* and *American Libraries*. She was a faculty member in the University of South Florida's School of Library and Information Science and a catalog librarian at the University of Florida in Gainesville. Her participation in the American Library Association has included serving as a member of the Presidential Task Force on Supporting LIS Education Through Practice, chair of the Association for Library Resources and Technical Services Council of Regional Groups, and president of the New Members Round Table.

Index